EXPANDED EDITION
TWILIGHT OF THE GREAT TRAINS

FRED W. FRAILEY

Indiana University Press
Bloomington and Indianapolis

For Catherine Patricia Bennett

JACKET: *Southern Railway's* Southern Crescent *pauses beside the colonial-styled station in Alexandria, Virginia, in 1971. Having ruthlessly pruned its other passenger trains during the prior five years, Southern could afford to operate a glamorous train. (Mike Schafer)*

TITLE PAGE: *Dawn greets a late-running* City of San Francisco, *as it charges upward from Wells, Nevada, toward the summit of the Pequops, in 1965. On the front of this 20-plus car train are four big Alco PA-2 and three General Motors F units. (Richard Steinheimer)*

Railroads Past and Present
George M. Smerk, editor

Book design: Fred W. Frailey
Jacket design: Kristi Ludwig

This book is a publication of

Indiana University Press
601 North Morton Street
Bloomington, Indiana 47404-3797 USA

www.iupress.indiana.edu

Telephone orders	800-842-6796
Fax orders	812-855-7931
Orders by e-mail	iuporder@indiana.edu

First edition published 1998
© 1998, 2010 by Fred W. Frailey
All rights reserved

This book is printed on acid-free paper.

Manufactured in China

The first edition was catalogued by the Library of Congress as follows:

Frailey, Fred W.
Twilight of the Great Trains / Fred W. Frailey. — 1st ed.
p. cm   Includes index
ISBN: 0-89024-178-3

1. Railroads—Passenger traffic—Economic aspects—United States.
2. Railroads—Passenger cars. I. Title.

HE2583.F73 1998   385'.262'0973
                                                  QB197-41037

ISBN 978-0-253-35477-8 (cl)

1 2 3 4 5   15 14 13 12 11 10

CONTENTS

THE VIEW FROM 1960

Back then you could still pretend that passenger trains had a future.
It was a hopeful interlude that ended too soon.

◀ *Relay, Maryland, was where the American passenger train began. You're standing astride Baltimore & Ohio's Old Main Line Subdivision, where on May 24, 1830, a team of horses pulled the first regularly scheduled passenger train on a 13-mile, 90-minute run between Baltimore and Ellicott's Mills. On this day some 135 years later, the* Capitol Limited *is making somewhat better time toward the nation's capital on the Washington Subdivision. Two decades earlier, a gothic hotel stood at this junction, hard against the Thomas Viaduct that crosses the Patapsco River. But now Relay is just a sleepy neighborhood on the far south side of Baltimore. (Herbert H. Harwood, Jr.)*

At the dawn of the seventh decade of the twentieth century, a transportation icon that had served the public well since the presidency of Andrew Jackson stood in a precarious way. I'm speaking of the passenger train, of course, and it was beginning to totter. In 1944, near the end of World War II, 74 percent of intercity travel by public transport was by rail. By 1949 the rail share had fallen to 48 percent, and by 1960, to 29 percent.

Most people wouldn't have known this. Those who still wanted to travel by train retained plenty of choices. The hemorrhaging occurred on the margin, the all-Pullman trains of railroads such as New York Central and Santa Fe adding coaches, while marginal trains serving the least purpose disappeared altogether. All of the better trains had been reequipped with new cars and locomotives since the war, and they remained in service. But now the wear and tear was showing.

So without doubt, the 1960s would test the commitment of Americans to passenger trains, not to mention the willingness of railroad management to offer a service that people wanted to patronize. The popular notion was that railroads didn't give a damn. Railroad presidents stood somewhere between cemetery lot salesmen and carnival pitchmen in public esteem, and the common wisdom was that passenger trains weren't doing well because their owners didn't want them to. Why, with a little bit of enthusiasm and some buckets of paint (not to mention charm schools for on-board employees), the passenger problem would heal itself. This, at least, was the popular opinion uttered by editorial writers.

Twilight of the Great Trains examines that premise. You'll see how 11 railroad systems withstood or welcomed, fought or embraced the inevitable decline of their passenger services. No two railroads reacted quite the same way. Heroes and villains abound on the pages that follow. You will be looking over their shoulders—second-guessing them, even. And maybe in reading this your assumptions about what was killing the intercity passenger train will be tested. That, at least, was the case during the sixties with perhaps the nation's best known railfan, an introverted and introspective magazine editor named David P. Morgan.

Education of an editor

Morgan, the slender, chain-smoking son of a southern Presbyterian preacher, was possessed of rare analytical abilities, which he displayed every month in the "Railroad News & Editorial Comment" section of *Trains*, the magazine he edited for 34 years. To read his periodic editorials on passenger trains from the late 1950s to the early 1970s is revealing. In November 1958, he took on Canadian National president Donald Gordon for his "total lack of faith in the passenger train." Speaking before a committee of Parliament, Gordon had said every railroad in the U.S. was "begging" to get out of the passenger business, that not a single CN train was paying its keep and that his railroad wouldn't buy another passenger car "if we can possibly avoid it." Wrote Morgan: "Far be it from *Trains* to imply that Canadian National's passenger business today is an unmitigated blessing or that such an astute mind in higher finances as Mr. Gordon's is fabricating poppycock out of thin air. We do insist, however, that he may turn a retreat into a disorderly, costly rout. And before the battle is even decided."

The next month his ire at a critique of passenger trains spilled over into a three-page essay. The occasion was the prediction, by Interstate Commerce Commission hearing examiner Howard Hosmer, that if current trends continued, the Pullman car would be history by 1965 and the intercity passenger train kaput by 1970. Hosmer had been told by the ICC to study the passenger train deficit and to suggest ways to reduce or eliminate those losses. But Hosmer more or less punted when it came to constructive suggestions, and Morgan steamed: "The Hosmer report does a distinct disservice to the industry and its public when it itemizes ills and shuns remedies. . . . An investigation charged with finding ways to reduce or eliminate the deficit should offer something better for the money than the implication that euthanasia is the only antidote to cancer."

Okay, Morgan must have thought to himself then, if that rascal Hosmer won't focus his thoughts, then maybe I will. The result, four months later, was probably the most pungent and incisive—not to mention exhaustive—look at the passenger problem ever written under deadline. At 38 pages, "Who Shot the Passenger Train?" consumed the entire feature section of the April 1959 *Trains*. Morgan was not at all ready to give up. He called travel of up to 500 miles "uniquely subject to rail exploitation" and said even very long-distance trains could survive as "cruiseliners." He pleaded with rail management to awaken from its bureaucratic stupor and revive the marketing prowess that once gave the world a *Twentieth Century Limited* and a *Phoebe Snow*. Prophetically, he urged that passenger service be run as a business separate from freight service—a suggestion that Congress would adopt more than 11 years later, when it created Amtrak. So yes, Dave Morgan remained an optimist that the passenger train could be revived.

Now flash ahead five years. In 1964, when Paul Reistrup took over the passenger department of Baltimore & Ohio, with orders from the top to manage that business to eliminate the avoidable losses ($3.3 million), Morgan was more guarded as to whether anyone could pull it off: "For a season on B&O the varnish will be neither the abused orphan it is so frequently elsewhere in the East nor the window dressing it represents so often in the West. It will be on its own, accorded at long last an opportunity to prove whether or not intelligently operated and merchandised coach and sleeping cars are indeed economic passenger vehicles." Again, in February 1965, he berated railroads for their defeatism and demanded they "come to grips" with the problems of passenger trains. "As a starter," Morgan wrote, "could we expect an end to senseless service duplication, a common acceptance of credit cards and reduced off-peak fares, and a willingness to smile in public if not in private?"

But then it's as if a switch were thrown in David Morgan's mind. In the seven years since Canadian National's boss had written off passenger service before Parliament, the railroad had undergone an epiphany. Now CN was slashing fares, sprucing up trains, buying diners and Pullmans and dome cars from less stalwart U.S. passenger carriers. Was Morgan pleased? You would have wondered, reading his reaction to these events. Far from praising CN, he demanded that the railroad open its books and reveal how much money it was pouring down the drain making these nice things happen.

That was December of 1965. By January of 1967 the editor of *Trains* felt defeated. He had come to accept the ICC's 1914-era formula of fully allocated costs as gospel—this the accounting that socked passenger trains with part of the chairman's salary and that of dispatchers and maintenance workers who would all remain employed if there were no passenger trains, and the accounting that the ICC itself had long since quit giving even lip service to. That fully allocated loss came to $421 million in 1965. Wrote Morgan: "If there is no profit incentive in carrying people on trains, then rail passenger carriage has ceased to be a business and we question the morality of seeking to further impose its deficits upon the industry."

▶ *What better symbol of glamor and luxury on the rails in 1960 than the streamlined observation car at speed? This is the tavern-lounge-observation on the rear of Illinois Central's* City of Miami, *as the train accelerates toward 100 miles per hour south of Champaign, Illinois, in late 1959. (J. Parker Lamb)*

In other words, he was saying, it's all but over. And soon enough—the end of that very year, in fact—the overnight loss of mail revenues that had bolstered passenger revenues throughout the 1960s caused the passenger network in this nation to begin imploding. Between 1966 and 1968, passenger miles fell by a third, sleeping car revenues by almost half and mail and express revenues by nearly two thirds. Far from being a ninny, Howard Hosmer was close to becoming a prophet.

In praise of the almighty buck

I devote so many words to the thinking of David Morgan because, more than most of us, he was able to put aside emotions and look at the passenger train as it was rather than as we wished it were. Passenger service was a business, and it was failing. When two-car trains appear in place of what had been 12-car and 22-car trains, there's no denying they fulfill no economic purpose and possibly not even a social one.

So in looking back at that momentus decade, the 1960s, *Twilight of the Great Trains* tries to portray not only the trains of 11 railroad systems but the environment in which they toiled. Who were the railroad executives who stood behind them or sought their demise? How did they react to events then? You'd expect from this the same story told 11 times. Not so. For every Benjamin Biaggini or Louis Menk or William Brosnan or Donald Russell who lamented the burden of passenger trains their railroads bore, there was a Thomas Rice or John Reed or William Deramus or Harry Murphy who said this was no burden at all, or at least one worth carrying.

Those among these people who were still alive were all eager to talk. Others speak to us from the memos and notes they wrote contemporaneously. And from all this begins to emerge a rather remarkable fact: The passenger bears and bulls—the men who had given up and those who kept the faith—

all reacted to the numbers in front of them. To state it another way, very few railroads willingly operated passenger trains as a charity. They either made money (or convinced themselves they did, which amounts to the same thing) or tried to get out of the business of carrying people. The converse was true as well. I've rarely found the railroad president who tried to rid his railroad of a passenger train that was profitable by his way of reckoning.

And what numbers were they looking at? The government had established two methods of cost analysis: directly related costs (such as crews, fuel, maintenance, passenger stations and other identifi-

▲ Its convulsive liquidation lay 16 years in Rock Island Lines' future when the Twin Star Rocket *out of Minneapolis strode across the Santa Fe and Burlington lines in Saginaw, just north of Fort Worth, on Independence Day, 1963. This* Rocket *could still sparkle: a brace of head-end cars, two coaches, a diner and two sleepers. Who would have thought that unsteady, pipe-driven Tower 29 would outlast the train and the railroad itself? (Fred W. Frailey)*

able expenses) and indirect costs that were borne in common with freight trains and were apportioned between both types of trains. Economists and consultants argued that indirect costs, which would include depreciation, track and signal maintenance, dispatching and the cost of supervision (including, in theory, a bit of the railroad president's pay) be thrown into the pot. Maybe they were right—I've always been of two minds.

But the interesting thing is that virtually all railroads kept a private set of passenger ledgers by which they judged the operation, and invariably they included only direct, solely related costs. So by their own actions railroad executives didn't believe in a cost structure that dinged passenger trains for some of every signal maintainer's health insurance, as if a railroad would extinguish its signals if one train no longer ran. In making decisions, railroad executives utterly ignored fully allocated costs.

Instead, they based their decisions to keep or get rid of a train on solely related costs. Even such public foes of passenger trains as Southern Pacific's Donald Russell and Southern's Bill Brosnan had underlings compile profit-and-loss reports based on costs directly attributable to passenger trains— and acted on the basis of those numbers. In 1960, when the fully allocated loss of all U.S. passenger trains was $485 million, the loss based on solely related expenses was a mere $10 million and would turn into a $17 million profit in 1961. At the dawn of the 1960s there was reason for some people to believe passenger trains could be with us forever.

No train an island unto itself

Railroaders have an expression for the cars on a train and the order in which they are arranged— the *consist* (with accent on the first syllable). These you will find spread throughout the book in the form of diagrams. They are normal train makeups at one point in time and in almost every instance are drawn from documents issued by the railroad

Bright spot: Penn Central's Metroliners, *new in 1969, marked the start of the Northeast Corridor's overdue rebirth. (William D. Middleton)*

operating departments. I don't think there's one among you who won't be impressed by the girth of Union Pacific's *City* streamliners, at the way Katy made its *Texas Special* and Missouri Pacific its *Texas Eagle* spread their wings across the namesake state, or at how a *Champion* could be one train leaving New York City or Richmond, but four or five as the cars and their people were distributed across North Carolina, Georgia, Alabama and Florida. Even Penn Central could make the successor to the *Twentieth Century Limited* touch virtually

every major line of the old New York Central. And look at those mail trains—what Santa Fe did with the *Fast Mail Express* and companion trains 3 and 4. For that matter, marvel at the volume of mail and express virtually all the trains carried. Therein lies the reason that the pre-Amtrak passenger train lasted as long as it did. Mail and express haulage was a wholesale enterprise for which railroads were paid retail rates. This revenue was the cushion upon which the whole passenger operation rested; without mail you couldn't maintain a passenger train network, as was proven once when the postmaster general pulled the cars off passenger trains as a matter of policy beginning in 1967, and proven again by Amtrak when it bent schedules every which way in the 1990s to get mail revenue needed to stay afloat.

Who shot or what killed the passenger train as we knew it? You can't name one cause to the exclusion of all others. But it may be useful to answer the rhetorical question this way: The passenger train was wounded by competition, technology, unfair treatment by government and management indifference or ineptness and labor's refusal to change, and then put out of its misery by the postal service. Without that last shove, the process would have played itself out for maybe another decade. You'll read on these pages how individual railroads sought, most valiantly, to stem the inevitable ending. But that sometime this end would come—that passenger trains would be bought and paid for by government subsidy or disappear entirely—became an inescapable conclusion as the sixties wore on. I should have realized as much a lot earlier than I did. I just didn't want to. And neither, it turns out, did a lot of railroaders.

WHAT PASSENGER PROBLEM?

By Kansas City Southern's way of thinking, it didn't have a problem.
Lucky for its customers.

◄ *Louisiana dayride: At the required 25 miles per hour, an airborne train 9, bound from Shreveport to New Orleans in June, 1960, ascends the two-mile-long bridge lifting it over the Mississippi River and into Baton Rouge. Just 20 years earlier, trains were still ferried across the Big Muddy. All but the E unit on the point originated the night before in Kansas City as No. 15. Behind the two coaches is one of the four tavern-observation cars recently bought from New York Central by a KCS management expert at bargain-hunting. (J. Parker Lamb)*

What you're about to read runs counter to just about everything in this book. Against all probabilities, Kansas City Southern:

❒ Maintained its two-trains-each-way policy of the late 1950s right into the jaws of the passenger drought of the late 1960s.

❒ Did so in a territory mostly devoid of the one element believed most essential to profitable passenger service: people. Between Kansas City and Shreveport—561 miles, down the entire main stem of the railroad—lay just three towns with populations exceeding 10,000.

❒ Logged precisely as many passenger miles—that's one passenger carried one mile—in 1966 as it did a decade earlier, and did so running fewer passenger trains.

❒ Bought, in 1965, the last new intercity passenger coaches (except for Penn Central's *Metroliner* cars) purchased before Amtrak.

❒ Proved its affinity with the traveling public by adorning its all-stops local train with lightweight observation cars, by providing hot food at modest prices on all trains and by holding fares ultra-low.

❒ Did all this under the stewardship of a man reviled from Missouri to Texas for his supposed public-be-damned attitude.

Running north to south in an industry oriented east to west, KCS stubbornly went its own way. In essense, the railroad spent money as if the next depression were just around the corner, and made its dollars by counting all the pennies. In the passenger era, economy meant cherry-picking used cars and locomotives from passenger-weary railroads willing to sell good assets at junk prices, making equipment as maintenance-free as possible, publishing schedules that left time for giving priority to the railroad's mile-and-a-half-long freights at meeting points, spurning defeatist gestures on passenger trains when its own books indicated they covered their costs, cutting fares to the bone and fitting service to the needs of a clientele that neither desired nor could afford the fancy extras—but giving them some nice extras anyway. This customer-friendly formula worked so well for so long that Kansas City Southern, unawares, walked right off the cliff with those passenger trains late in 1967.

Ambitious plans go awry

For the first 15 years after World War II, KCS and its wholly owned Dallas–New Orleans subsidiary, Louisiana & Arkansas, saw the passenger business run true to form—euphoria buttressed by new equipment in the late 1940s, disillusionment when ridership and revenues fell in the late 1950s and then cutbacks in service. In that sense, it differed little from neighbors Katy and Frisco.

Kansas City Southern's flagship was the *Southern Belle*, a Kansas City–New Orleans streamliner begun in 1940 on a 21½-hour schedule over the 870-mile route—quite a feat for a railroad running on light rail and atop chat ballast. A reequipped *Belle* debuted in 1949 on a schedule tightened to 18 hours, or a brisk 48 miles per hour overall. A Port Arthur section of the train began then, too. On the schedule of the old *Belle* was added a new Kansas City–New Orleans train, nameless 9 and 10. The *Flying Crow*, trains 15 and 16, made the local stops between Kansas City and Port Arthur, with a section running to New Orleans. In the early 1950s the *Belle* ceased to run to Port Arthur, and the *Flying Crow* lost its New Orleans arm.

There matters rested until disillusionment in 1958—costs too high, revenues too low. Trains 9 and 10 were dropped north of Shreveport that year, trains 15 and 16 became nameless. A Shreveport–Hope, Ark., local lasted until 1962.

Definitely unorthodox

The closing years of the 1950s became Kansas City Southern's opportunity to hack away at frequencies, amenities and maintenance. Virtually every other railroad in the region did. But rather than gut its remaining passenger trains, KCS began to improve them. The process began in 1956 with delivery of five more coaches from ACF to augment the 15 lightweights already on hand. Then in 1959—the year after it cut train frequency—KCS bought 10 new lightweight baggage cars from Pull-

On a sticky summer evening in 1960, a classy E6 awaits the southbound Southern Belle *at Shreveport, for the run to New Orleans. (J. Parker Lamb)*

man-Standard for handling storage mail. And from New York Central that year, for $25,250 apiece, came four tavern-observation cars built by Budd in 1948. In due course these cars went through the shops in Pittsburg, Kan., and emerged as lunch counter-lounge-observations.

Unusual enough that KCS spent money to improve its car fleet so late in the game. The railroad went further by improving creature comforts on remaining trains, too, while rescheduling them to heighten their appeal to both the public and the trains' biggest customer, the U.S. Postal Service:

❏ Trains 1 and 2, the *Southern Belle*, had run on a 4 p.m.-to-10 a.m. cycle between Kansas City and New Orleans. Now it assumed the timings of trains 9 and 10—the pre-1949 *Southern Belle* schedule.

This put it overnight between Shreveport and New Orleans and in daylight north of Shreveport. It continued to display the best of everything—the newest coaches, a 36-seat full-service diner and a 14-roomette 4-bedroom sleeper. The rescheduling allowed the *Belle* to carry storage mail cars formerly handled on 9 and 10.

❏ Trains 15 and 16 were the mirror image of the *Belle* north of Shreveport, operating overnight. But in utter contradiction to railroad orthodoxy of that era, KCS supplemented the single coach on this train with both a 14-4 sleeper and a lunch counter-lounge-observation, of NYC heritage. South of Shreveport, trains 9 and 10 continued to run to New Orleans, taking a coach and the observation from Kansas City off train 15 and 16. A separate lunch counter-lounge-observation (the 1940-era *Good Cheer* and *Hospitality*) rotated on trains 15 and 16 between Shreveport and Port Arthur.

❏ KCS went to Pullman-Standard in 1965 for 10 new 72-seat coaches. The new cars reeked of efficiency—high capacity, linoleum floors, formica walls, tinted windows (but no shades) and vinyl seat covers. By 1965, in fact, virtually all KCS passenger-carrying cars were post-War War II light-

▶ *You're looking south from the fireman's side of unit 20, an E7, on No. 15 as No. 2, the northward* Southern Belle, *comes up the main line with a heavy train, on July 18, 1966, at Wickes, Arkansas, north of Texarkana. Unit 30 was one of eight red-and-yellow freight Fs equipped with steam boilers. (Louis A. Marre)*

weights. There was even talk that the railroad would buy Katy's sleeper-lounge-observation *Stephen F. Austin*, but this never came about.

Secrets of success

Kansas City Southern possessed no bag of magic tricks, beyond its legendary ability to squeeze a penny until the copper ran liquid. It was blessed by one accident of development: no real rail competition north of Shreveport and no potent highway competition anywhere its passenger trains ran. Roads south of Kansas City through the small towns the railroad served were circuitous all the way to Louisiana. Lo and behold, if you ran clean trains (it did) with low fares (they were) and reasonably priced menus (yes, again), you could attract a loyal clientele even at that late date, and KCS did.

Had the railroad bisected the flatlands instead of the mountains, visited the larger cities of the region (and hence come against better roads) or run east-to-west with the current of transportation, things might have ended badly for its passenger trains much sooner. The lack of highway competition really paid off in mail revenue. Truckers simply couldn't match KCS schedules through the Ozarks. Mail and express accounted for 40 percent of passenger train revenues in 1957, but almost 50 percent eight years later—in effect propping up the whole service, as it did for many railroads.

All night with an old *Crow*

No. 15 had a visitor out of Kansas City on February 28, 1963: E. L. (Tommy) Thompson, a veteran Baltimore & Ohio passenger man on a busman's holiday. Three decades later, his 12 single-spaced typewritten pages of notes survive to describe a typical trip to New Orleans in that relaxed era.

His train that night, behind a single E unit, is five head-end cars, the sleeper, a coach, the lunch counter-lounge-observation and (tacked to the rear) a car of storage mail to be uncoupled in Joplin,

Missouri. Just 38 miles out of Union Station, No. 15 goes into the siding at Cleveland, Mo., to clear a 213-car northbound freight (No. 42)—an 18-minute delay. Waiting for opposing freights becomes the rule. At Noel (3:43 a.m.) there's a brief halt for No. 82, and again at Heavener, Oklahoma (7:20 a.m.), for the next edition of No. 42. The train crawls into Blanchard, Louisiana (12:27 p.m.), just north of Shreveport, as the next No. 82 clears. South of Shreveport, No. 9 sits while a 119-car No. 42 (the third so far) winds through the 36-car siding at Coushatta (2:30 p.m.).

From 10:15 p.m. one night until 8:03 p.m. the next, Thompson sits awake and alert in the rear of the observation car, acting as Boswell to this old *Crow.* By and large, he has a great time:

❏ In virtually any town of any size, KCS passenger trains come and go the hard way. Joplin's "union station" is set off from the main line, causing passenger trains to open a switch to enter the depot track, stop again to close it, stop a third time to open the switch at the other end and a fourth time to close it—an eight-minute hit, Thompson figures. Texarkana Union Station is a pull-in, back-out operation for KCS—another nine minutes shot just getting in and out. Alexandria, La., is reached by a stub track that costs four minutes backing in and pulling out.

Shreveport puts them all to shame. No. 15 pulls past the wye at Dalzell Street and backs into the railroad's stub-end downtown depot. That's the easy part. Leaving with the New Orleans connection, three-car No. 9 with its E unit pulls forward briefly to Wilson Street, backs past the depot and down a couple of city streets; stops to line and then reline switches at Franklin Street Junction; continues backing around one leg of the wye at Commerce Street Junction; pulls forward across another leg of that wye; stops twice to line and reline switches at Silver Lake Junction and heads down the Red River delta—2.2 miles in 18 minutes! (Harold K. Vollrath,

◀ *The sparsity of people in Kansas City Southern's service area is demonstrated in these Southern Belle scenes. At Howe, Oklahoma (population 392), just north of Heavener, train 2 barrels over Rock Island's Memphis–Tucumcari line beside the new prefabricated station on December 30, 1962. (Louis A. Marre)*

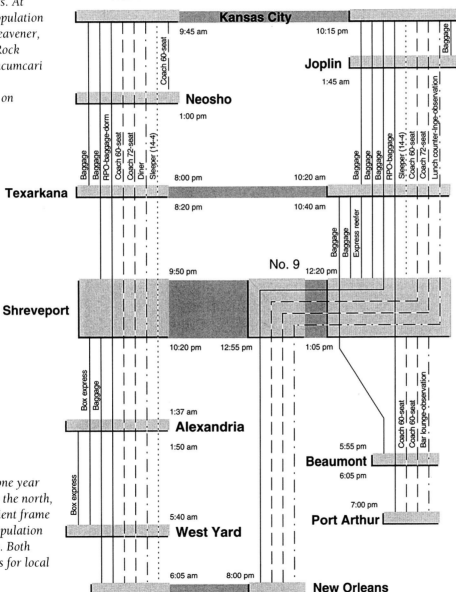

Summer 1965

Southern Belle No. 1 **Kansas City** (Flying Crow) No. 15

◀ *Almost precisely one year later and 16 miles to the north, No. 1 passes the ancient frame depot at Panama (population 937) with seven cars. Both towns were flag stops for local trains 15 and 16. (Louis A. Marre)*

a labor relations officer, was once presented with a 30-minute contractual time claim by No. 9's crew for "turning" the train on the Commerce Street Junction wye. "I beat 'em on that," says Vollrath, "by pointing out that they used only two legs of the wye, and to turn a train you need all three.")

❏ Meal service in the Kansas City–New Orleans obs is as spartan as the decor, but cheap. "Not a bad menu," writes Tommy. Continental breakfast is 60 cents, bacon and eggs with toast $1.15, coffee 15 cents. "There wasn't much choice for 'dinner': Hamburger steak, chef's salad, bread and butter and beverage was $1.35; ham steak and the rest was $1.50. I had the hamburger, and it wasn't bad." A cook and waiter do it all.

❏ Ride quality varies between okay and awful; speed limits are observed if engineers feel so inclined: "This [south of Siloam Springs, Okla.] KCS used to advertise 'Route of the Flying Crow—Straight as the Arrow Flies.' Oh brother, there is nothing straight about this line as we whip back and forth around curves. . . . Track [south of Shreveport] leaves much to be desired. Several bad kinks in curves, and most grade crossings on curves aren't true . . . . We have 58 mph speed limit [from Shreveport] to Baton Rouge. But it's obvious that engineers don't pay much attention to it, although seldom getting up to any more than 70 mph."

No. 15 leaves Kansas City on time that trip and is 43 minutes late just north of Texarkana after taking siding for the northbound *Southern Belle*. Yet despite perhaps 90 minutes of combined delays en route, Tommy's train stops in New Orleans just eight minutes late, and our man trudges to the Lafayette Hotel five blocks away, observing that "nobody had to rock me to sleep."

The hands on the throttle

And so Kansas City Southern ambled through the 1960s, seemingly oblivious to the havoc being wreaked on the passenger train everywhere else

◄ *Train 1, the* Southern Belle, *has pulled into Texarkana Union Station on a warm, quiet June night in 1969. The essense of civility, the Belle will play out its days in fewer than five months. (David W. Salter)*

but on its home turf. Based on solely related costs, passenger train losses as reported to the Interstate Commerce Commission consistently ran $2 million to $3 million a year. Was management asleep?

Not at all. Kansas City Southern was personified by William Neal Deramus Jr., who joined the railroad early in this century, became president in 1940 and took pride in knowing virtually every employee of the combined enterprise. At heart, he was extremely frugal. But Deramus gladly spent money to make money. Those six new coaches in 1956, the four NYC observations in 1959 (refurbished for another $95,150) and the 10 new mail storage cars that same year came on his watch. ICC formula or no ICC formula, by KCS bookkeeping its passenger trains earned their costs, or darn close to their costs, into the early 1960s—no other explanation is remotely plausible.

Deramus, disabled by a stroke in 1961 (he died

▶ *One of Louis A. Marre's favorite photo locations was the KCS crossing of the Arkansas River at Redland, Oklahoma, not far from his home in Fort Smith, Arkansas. On May 6, 1966, he found a seven-car southbound Belle, only 15 minutes or so from its next stop in Sallisaw. The classic truss span was later replaced by a deck.*

December 2, 1965), was succeeded by his son, William N. Deramus III. The younger Deramus was even more of a skinflint, and his reputation was tarnished by highhanded treatment of employees and passengers when he ran the Katy (see page 75), which teetered on bankruptcy. We're left to wonder why those black trains with red and yellow stripes continued to run, oblivious to all else happening around them. Says Vollrath: "Whether Deramus kept the trains going out of loyalty to his dad, I have serious doubts. The thing he talked about was whether they made money—that was what he cared about." Claims Thomas Carter, who succeeded Deramus as KCS president: "They covered their costs, so long as they carried the mail."

Requiems for lightweights

Kansas City Southern's seldom-remarked streamliners got overdue recognition in the November 1967 issue of *Trains*—a delightful 10-page narrative by Louis A. Marre. "We have no intention of getting out of the passenger business," Deramus III had written in the public timetable. And it was possible to read that article and believe his vow.

By the end of November, however, another letter from Deramus greeted passengers: "We deeply regret. . ." it began. On December 4, 1967, Kansas City Southern told the ICC it had every intention of quitting the passenger business after all. The reason was all too familiar. The postal service had informed KCS that it would end RPO and storage

◀ *No. 15 speeds through Fisher, Louisiana, south of Leesville on the line to Port Arthur, Texas, in a cloud of dust in July 1965, with a 1940-era tavern-obs on the end of the five-car train. (John B. Charles)*

coaches and a lunch counter-lounge-observation.

The last *Southern Belle* arrived in Kansas City and New Orleans on November 3, 1969. Wrote Deramus III to shareholders: "We eliminated once and for all what has been a significant drag on earnings in the past." *Significant drag on earnings?* Such an ungracious sendoff! I'll leave it to Louis Marre to deliver the proper benediction: "A crow had to carry its own provisions over the territory of those trains—it was a sparse market. But the Deramuses milked it for all it was worth, and came closer to breaking even than anyone in the industry. They were bargain hunters, picking up some real deals which kept them going. And it all went very nicely until the postal service sabatoged them. I know of no other passenger operation remotely like it." Thank you, Louis, and amen.

▲ *At Pittsburg, on a wet late autumn Kansas day in 1969, No. 1, the* Southern Belle, *has changed engines and accelerates toward the Ozarks.* (Joe McMillan)

▶ *In the twilight of its passenger era, KCS gave locomotives a clean, all-white look. No. 1 prepares to leave Kansas City in July 1969.* (Joe McMillan)

mail contracts, taking away more than $800,000 in revenue and some $650,000 in profits that had sustained the trains. Railway Express Agency adopted a new regional hub system that excluded KCS trains—another $330,000 in lost revenue.

The ICC gave the railroad half what it wanted. Trains 15 and 16 and their New Orleans connections, 9 and 10, made their last runs the following April. This left just the *Southern Belle*, which the ICC ordered continued. Class acts they remained, too, during that interim—from the front back, two baggage cars, a sleeper, two of the Class-of-'65

ALL HAIL THE "CITY OF EVERYWHERE"

Union Pacific's one-train-does-all streamliner—it got longer and longer
as the railroad retreated to a single core train.

◄ *Gosh, could UP put on a show! For the Golden Spike centennial in 1969, the railroad hosts a 20-car special originating in New York City, and puts its 4-8-4 8444 on the front of another special from Omaha. Both descended upon Ogden and Salt Lake City for celebrations that briefly brought everyday life in Utah to a halt. On May 10, the centennial day of the driving of the golden spike that joined a continent at Promontory Point, the* City of Los Angeles–City of St. Louis *rushes east toward Ogden, stars and stripes aflutter. At magic moments like this, the* City *streamliners seemed immortal.*
(Victor Hand)

The obituary of Union Pacific's *City* trains, were you to write it, might read like this: They were born as the three-car, bubble-shaped, aluminum-sided *City of Salina* on New Year's Day, 1935. They lived precisely 36 years and four months, until May Day, 1971. At their zenith they numbered seven, including the all-coach *Challenger* and the short-lived *City of Las Vegas*. Their fatal illness began in 1967, when UP's passenger revenue nosedived from a plateau of $23 million (3.8 percent of the railroad's revenue) the previous year. Into the 1990s, they were survived by Amtrak's *California Zephyr*, *Pioneer* and *Desert Wind*.

This is the story of that autumnal decline—the final years of some of America's most famous name trains. First of all, a bow to Union Pacific, if you please. If ever a family of streamliners grew old gracefully, it was the *City* fleet. As mail contracts lapsed and passengers faded away in the years leading to Amtrak, Union Pacific improvised solutions. Ultimately, the railroad squeezed virtually its entire passenger service into a single core train of gargantuan length that by combinations and split-offs

visited every city of note on its 9,700-mile system, and did so in style.

You'll comprehend the scope of this massive contraction by looking at the schematic drawings that begin when you turn the page. Let's start in mid-1967, when the *City* network was in its final season of full bloom. You could travel in style by roomette from Chicago to Los Angeles back then for all of $55.75, and a sirloin steak dinner aboard the dome diner of First 103 was yours for $4.75. Your choice of streamliners:

❏ First 103-104, Chicago to Los Angeles: Sleeping cars of the combined *City of Los Angeles* and *City of San Francisco*.

❏ Second 103-104, Chicago to Los Angeles: Coaches of the combined *City of Los Angeles* and *City of San Francisco*.

❏ No. 101-102, Ogden, Utah, to Oakland: *City of San Francisco*, via Southern Pacific.

❏ No. 111-112 and 105-106, Chicago to Portland: Combined *City of Denver–City of Portland*.

❏ No. 9-10, St. Louis to Ogden: *City of St. Louis*, via Norfolk & Western east of Kansas City.

Dateline: Ogden   Summer 1967

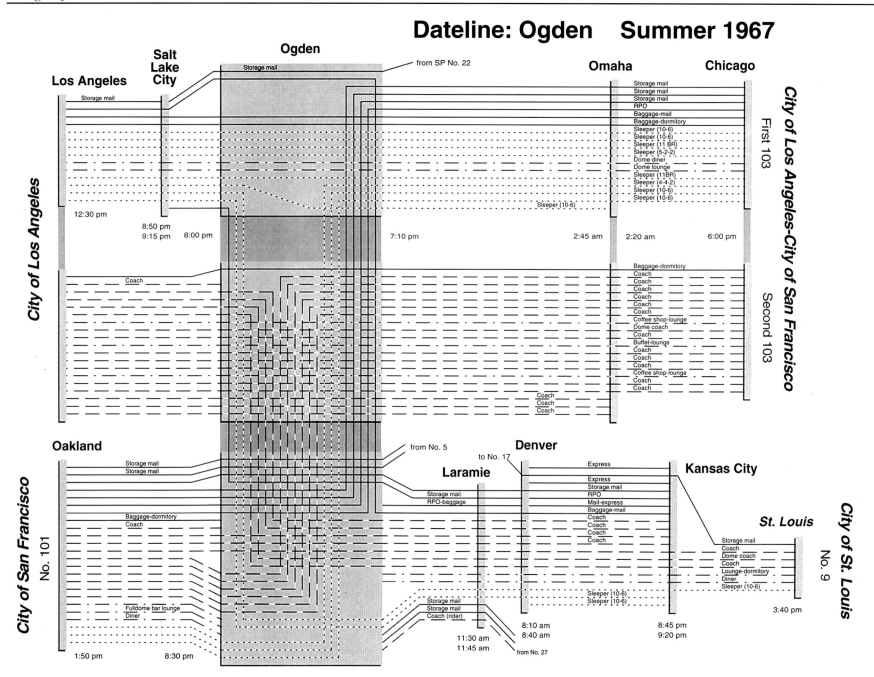

Salt Lake City

Ogden

from SP No. 22

Omaha

Chicago

Los Angeles

Storage mail

Storage mail

City of Los Angeles–City of San Francisco

First 103

Storage mail
Storage mail
Storage mail
RPO
Baggage-mail
Baggage-dormitory
Sleeper (10-6)
Sleeper (10-6)
Sleeper (11 BR)
Sleeper (5-2-2)
Dome diner
Dome lounge
Sleeper (11BR)
Sleeper (4-4-2)
Sleeper (10-6)
Sleeper (10-6)

Sleeper (10-6)

City of Los Angeles

12:30 pm

8:50 pm
9:15 pm   8:00 pm

7:10 pm

2:45 am   2:20 am   6:00 pm

Coach

Baggage-dormitory
Coach
Coach
Coach
Coach
Coach
Coffee shop-lounge
Dome coach
Coach
Buffet-lounge
Coach
Coach
Coach
Coffee shop-lounge
Coach
Coach

Second 103

Coach
Coach
Coach

Oakland

from No. 5

Denver

to No. 17

Express

Kansas City

City of San Francisco

No. 101

Storage mail
Storage mail

Laramie

Express
Storage mail
RPO
Mail-express
Baggage-mail
Coach
Coach
Coach
Coach

Storage mail
RPO-baggage

Baggage-dormitory
Coach

Storage mail
Coach
Dome coach
Coach
Lounge-dormitory
Diner
Sleeper (10-6)

St. Louis

City of St. Louis

No. 9

Sleeper (10-6)
Sleeper (10-6)

Fulldome bar lounge
Diner

Storage mail
Storage mail
Coach (rider)

8:10 am
8:40 am

8:45 pm
9:20 pm

3:40 pm

1:50 pm   8:30 pm

11:30 am
11:45 am

from No. 27

Train time on the desert

All roads led to Ogden. First 103 was Union Pacific's jewel—one of just three all-sleeper trains in the U.S. that summer (the others being Pennsylvania's *Broadway Limited* and Illinois Central's *Panama Limited*). On its block came Second 103, which west of Omaha blossomed to a 20-car train including no fewer than 16 coaches. And No. 9, the *City of St. Louis*, brought as many as 19 cars.

The three trains converged on 10-track Ogden Union Railway & Depot (jointly owned by UP and SP) within a 20-minute period. OUR&D's task each evening was to take this 55-car onslaught and assemble No. 101 from all three arriving trains *and* divide the rest of No. 9 among First and Second 103 and the storage tracks *and* deal simultaneously with No. 6, UP's eastbound Los Angeles–Omaha mail train, and SP's connecting mail train from Oakland, which required considerable switching of their lengthy strings of head-end equipment, too. Oh yes: Do all this, please, in an hour, and don't delay the northbound *Butte Special*. That constituted the evening rush. Each morning the folks in Ogden did essentially the same thing, except that the *City* trains were heading east and the two sizable mail trains were going west.

Bad enough that these cars had to be shuffled like a deck of canasta cards. Ogden's track layout compounded the challenge. First, the depot wasn't a run-through affair, except for Oakland-bound trains. Chicago–Los Angeles passenger trains entered via a wye near Riverdale Yard on the east edge of town, and had to be pulled back to UP's main track by an OUR&D switcher (or, conversely, be pulled into the depot). Second, only a single track emerged from the westbound (geographically north) end of the depot—meaning that just one switcher at a time could shuffle cars on that side of the terminal with any degree of efficiency.

What a spectacle it must have been. I showed the diagram on the opposite page to Roland Bills,

then superintendent of Ogden Union Railway & Depot. "You know," he replied, "we didn't think there was anything we couldn't do in those days. We had a big terminal here, and this was routine switching—no big problem, really. That summer, we'd use two switchers at each end of the station, but the two on the north [west] end had to take turns on the single lead. While we did this, No. 101's engines would wait on the water track north of the depot."

No big problem? Just for fun, figure out how

▲ *Fronted by a dirty and chipped E8, the eastbound* City of Los Angeles *awaits its departure from Ogden Union Railway & Depot on April 11, 1970. A UP switcher assigned to OUR&D stands at parade rest. In an hour or so No. 104 will be climbing Echo Canyon below the snow-mantled peaks of the Wasatch Mountains. (Steve Patterson)*

◀ *In the autumn of 1969, train 104 works its way up Sherman Hill at Dale Junction, Wyoming, behind more than 11,000 horse-power—then, an enormous amount. But then this was an enormous train, the "City of Everywhere" that was the combination of all Union Pacific City streamliners. (John C. Lucas)*

▲ *In the summer of 1968, the modest-sized* City of San Fran-cisco–City of St. Louis *makes its way west, also at Dale Junction. The business car on the rear gives this train a classic appearance, but it's obvious this train doesn't have critical mass. (John C. Lucas)*

you would have done it. Bills insists it was all a matter of "making a few cuts and shoves." We know better.

Uncle Pete's wide-ranging fleet

These, of course, weren't the only passenger trains crossing the Overland Route. The combined *City of Portland–City of Denver*, trains 111-112 east of Denver and 105-106 to the west, operated independently of other *City* trains, leaving Chicago three hours ahead of No. 103, swooping into Denver, backtracking toward Laramie and setting off for Portland. The *Las Vegas Holiday Special* (the old *City of Las Vegas*) ran daily that summer, too, until its final trip that July.

Then there were UP's real money makers. Out of Omaha for Los Angeles late each morning, No. 5, the "Overland Mail" (the train was nameless, but this is the name it went by), was a monster—usually 20 cars (and sometimes as many as 40) of mail and express collected primarily from Burlington's Chicago–Omaha *Fast Mail*. Two coaches rode near the front for passengers, another coach at the rear for the flagman. It honored 15 regular and flag stops, observed any of 42 conditional stops and still made Cheyenne in 10 hours—51 miles per hour.

At Cheyenne the Overland Mail exchanged mail cars with its Kansas City counterpart, No. 17, the *Portland Rose*. The *Rose* displayed more of a passenger orientation, passing Cheyenne with both a buffet-lounge and a sleeper, plus three coaches.

The Overland Mail in 1966 booked revenues of $11 million-plus—more than any other Union Pacific train—and earned almost $6 million after its out-of-pocket costs. Between them, the Overland Mail and *Portland Rose* accounted for 60 percent of UP's mail and express revenue.

A second mail train left Omaha at 11:40 p.m. for Laramie. No. 27's pedigree traced to November 13, 1887, as the *Overland Flyer*, which later became the all-Pullman *Overland Limited*. But evolution over the decades left a nameless train that trudged west through the night and into the next morning, distributing mail and express cars to such Nebraska towns as Columbus, Grand Island and North Platte, and acting as conduit for transcontinental mail that piled up at Omaha after No. 5's departure the previous morning. Its length into Laramie varied from a single coach to as many as nine cars. Whatever reached Laramie went on the rear of the *City of St. Louis* to Ogden.

Two other UP trains stand largely forgotten after all these years. The overnight *Butte Special* between Salt Lake City and Butte via Ogden, Pocatello and Idaho Falls, swelled to 16 cars (including two sleepers and a lounge) in mid 1967. By 1970 it was of even more humble stripe. Food preparation occurred on a hotplate installed in

what had been one upper-lower section of the lone sleeping car, and the car's porter doubled as cook. For a while this makeshift arrangement served up steak dinners.

Closer to my heart was the nameless local I took to calling the "Kansas Prairie Dog." Train 69 left Kansas City Union Station at last call—11 p.m. It worked its way slowly west to Salina, 187 miles, and then became mixed train 369 before finally succumbing, at daybreak, 115 miles beyond at Ellis, a tiny western Kansas village. Less than two hours later, eastbound No. 370 (No. 70 east of Salina) began collecting milk cans, mailbags, caskets, company mail and whatnot, including a few patient passengers, on its way back to Kansas City. I rode the Prairie Dog while in college, and found it user-friendly—relaxed, unpretentious and semi-prosperous, just like small-town Kansas

through which this train made its humble living.

So UP as late as mid 1967 could boast of a passenger service with both girth and heft. But it could not prevail. Ridership declined that summer. In the autumn almost all the mail business was removed by the postal authorities, and in an instant, half of the revenue supporting these trains vanished. The time came to retrench.

Cheyenne—the new pivot point

"The higherups would come in and say, 'We're gonna cut this and this and this,'" relates Morris Andreasen, then UP's assistant superintendent of transportation. "So we'd sit down and see what we could lose and still keep a good operation. All the officers wanted passenger service run well. If it weren't, you'd be in trouble."

By late summer of 1967, the higher-ups wanted to cut costs, fast. In the early 1960s the *City of St. Louis*, for instance, cleared $1 million a year above its direct costs. But the loss of mail revenue threw every first-class train into the red. As usual since 1960, the *City of Los Angeles* and *City of San Francisco* reverted to a single section at the end of summer. But the combined *City of Portland* and *City of Denver* underwent a rerouting. The primary train bypassed Denver, continuing straight west to Cheyenne; a stub *City of Denver* left North Platte with five cars for its namesake city via the former route through Julesburg and Sterling, Colo. For Pacific Northwest travelers who formerly had taken the *City of Portland* out of Denver, two coaches and a sleeper transferred from the *City of St. Louis* to the *City of Portland* at Cheyenne.

The true significance of the schedule and consist changes in late 1967 was the integration all the *City* trains, using Cheyenne as the hub. The Cheyenne Shuffle included the *City of Portland*, which had run independently of the other *City* trains. At Cheyenne, UP's yard engines could perform the canasta-deck shuffling at lower cost than was pos-

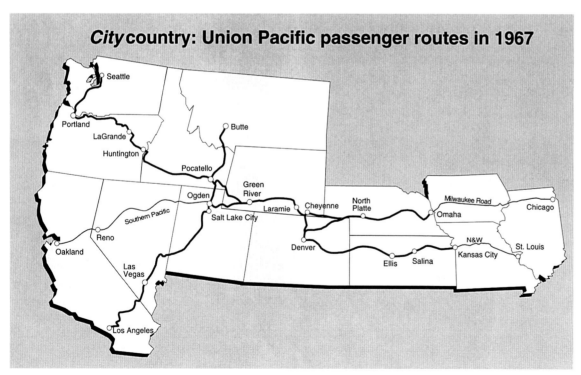

City country: Union Pacific passenger routes in 1967

▶ *A 10-car Overland Mail has topped the hills just east of Cheyenne and accelerates through tiny Archer, Wyoming, en route to Omaha, in 1961. (R. H. Kindig; A. J. Wolff collection)*

sible in Ogden. The entire *City* fleet standing side by side on the Cheyenne station tracks must have made a sight to see. Even the Oakland and Los Angeles cars separated in Cheyenne, the Oakland cars going west to Ogden as No. 9, which carried the name *City of St. Louis–City of San Francisco* west of Cheyenne. For awhile, No. 103 and No. 104 didn't even visit Ogden Union Railway & Depot; if you wanted to board the *City of Los Angeles*, you had to catch it at the Riverdale yard office.

Toward the all-in-one train

From late 1967 on, Union Pacific ran its passenger service like an army general managing an orderly retreat in the face of a superior foe. UP's foe was inadequate revenue—initially, in 1967, the collapse of head-end business, then the slow, debilitating decline of passenger volume aboard the *City* trains.

▶ *A lengthy Overland Mail has topped the hills just east of Cheyenne and accelerates through tiny Archer, Wyoming, en route to Omaha, in 1961. (R. H. Kindig; A. J. Wolff collection)*

▼ *Business car in tow, the westbound* City of Portland *glides down Sherman Hill at Dale Junction, Wyoming, in June 1969. Veering to the left is the Harriman Cutoff—a low-grade crossing of the Laramie Range built in the early 1950s. Two years earlier this train would run 18 cars past here. Now, within three months, it will be merged with all the other City streamliners. (John C. Lucas)*

▲ *Minutes behind the* City of Portland *that same warm June morning comes No. 103, the 19-car, superpowered* City of Los Angeles–City of San Francisco–City of Kansas City, *resplendent with three dome cars, including the soon-to-be-removed dome diner—an expensive-to-maintain luxury that UP decided it could no longer justify in regular service.* (John C. Lucas)

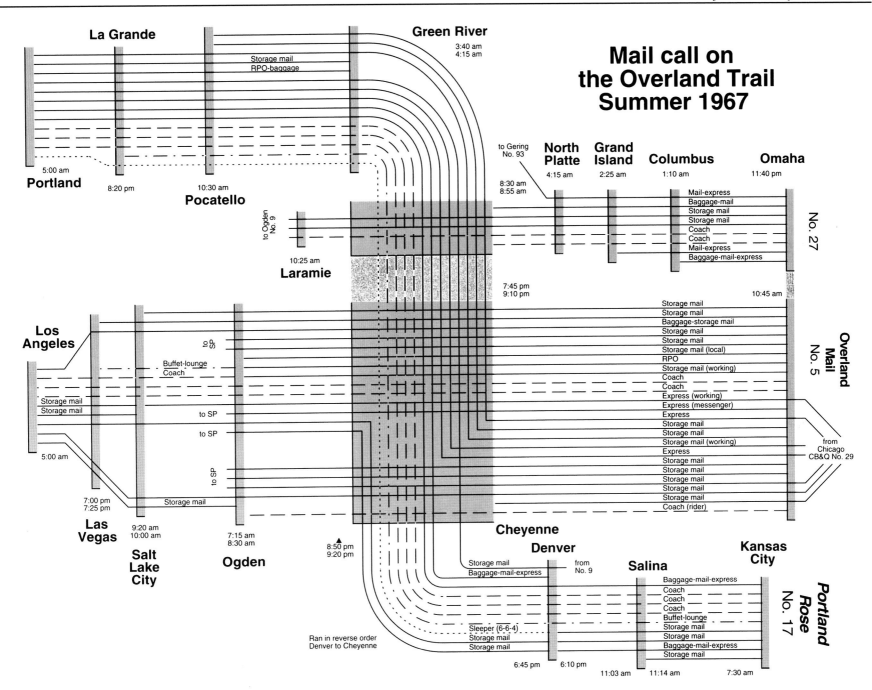

Mail call on the Overland Trail Summer 1967

La Grande

Green River
3:40 am
4:15 am

Storage mail
RPO-baggage

Portland
5:00 am

8:20 pm

10:30 am

Pocatello

to Gering No. 93

to Ogden No. 9

8:30 am
8:55 am

North Platte
4:15 am

Grand Island
2:25 am

Columbus
1:10 am

Omaha
11:40 pm

Mail-express
Baggage-mail
Storage mail
Storage mail
Coach
Coach
Mail-express
Baggage-mail-express

No. 27

10:25 am

Laramie

7:45 pm
9:10 pm

10:45 am

Los Angeles

to SP

Buffet-lounge
Coach

Storage mail
Storage mail

to SP

to SP

to SP

5:00 am

Storage mail

7:00 pm
7:25 pm

Storage mail
Storage mail
Baggage-storage mail
Storage mail
Storage mail
Storage mail (local)
RPO
Storage mail (working)
Coach
Coach
Express (working)
Express (messenger)
Express
Storage mail
Storage mail
Storage mail (working)
Express
Storage mail
Storage mail
Storage mail
Storage mail
Storage mail
Coach (rider)

Overland Mail No. 5

from Chicago CB&Q No. 29

Las Vegas
9:20 am
10:00 am

Salt Lake City

Ogden
7:15 am
8:30 am

8:50 pm
9:20 pm

Cheyenne

Denver

Storage mail
Baggage-mail-express

from No. 9

Salina

Baggage-mail-express
Coach
Coach
Coach
Buffet-lounge
Storage mail
Storage mail
Baggage-mail-express
Storage mail

Kansas City

Portland Rose No. 17

Sleeper (6-6-4)
Storage mail
Storage mail

Ran in reverse order
Denver to Cheyenne

6:45 pm

6:10 pm

11:03 am

11:14 am

7:30 am

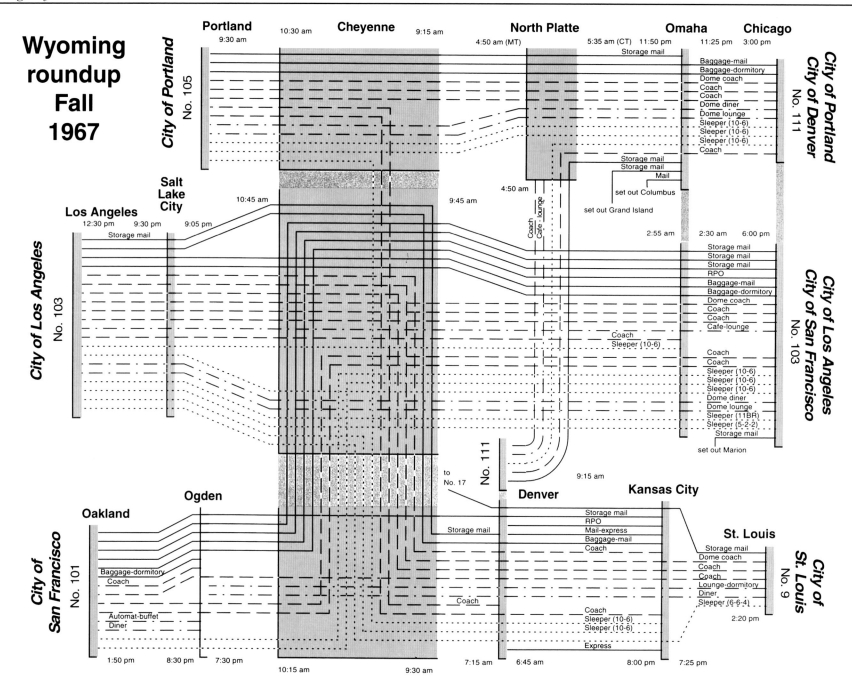

Wyoming roundup Fall 1967

Portland 9:30 am — 10:30 am — Cheyenne — 9:15 am — North Platte 4:50 am (MT) — 5:35 am (CT) — 11:50 pm Omaha — 11:25 pm — 3:00 pm Chicago

Storage mail
Baggage-mail
Baggage-dormitory
Dome coach
Coach
Coach
Dome diner
Dome lounge
Sleeper (10-6)
Sleeper (10-6)
Sleeper (10-6)
Coach

Storage mail
Storage mail
Mail
set out Columbus
set out Grand Island

City of Portland No. 105

City of Portland / City of Denver No. 111

Salt Lake City

10:45 am — 9:45 am

Los Angeles 12:30 pm — 9:30 pm — 9:05 pm

4:50 am

Coach
Cafe - lounge

2:55 am — 2:30 am — 6:00 pm

Storage mail
Storage mail
Storage mail
Storage mail
RPO
Baggage-mail
Baggage-dormitory
Dome coach
Coach
Coach
Cafe-lounge

Coach
Sleeper (10-6)

Coach
Coach
Sleeper (10-6)
Sleeper (10-6)
Sleeper (10-6)
Dome diner
Dome lounge
Sleeper (11BR)
Sleeper (5-2-2)
Storage mail
set out Marion

City of Los Angeles No. 103

City of Los Angeles / City of San Francisco No. 103

No. 111

to No. 17

9:15 am

Denver — Kansas City

Ogden

Oakland

Storage mail
RPO
Mail-express
Baggage-mail
Coach

Storage mail

Coach

Coach
Sleeper (10-6)
Sleeper (10-6)

Express

Baggage-dormitory
Coach

Automat-buffet
Diner

St. Louis

Storage mail
Dome coach
Coach
Coach
Lounge-dormitory
Diner
Sleeper (6-6-4)

2:20 pm

City of San Francisco No. 101

City of St. Louis No. 9

1:50 pm — 8:30 pm — 7:30 pm

10:15 am — 9:30 am

7:15 am — 6:45 am — 8:00 pm — 7:25 pm

Gradually over the next two years, the service segued into a one-train-does-all affair.

Dome diners left the *City of Portland* in 1968 and the *City of Los Angeles* by 1970. They required extra crew to run, and some cars needed mechanical work. Trains 103-104 and 9-10 (*City of St. Louis–City of San Francisco*) were combined across the Cheyenne–Ogden corridor on September 7, 1968, after the summer season. Early the next year the *City of St. Louis* became the *City of Kansas City*, when Norfolk & Western withdrew from through service out of St. Louis. That same spring the *City of Denver* lost its only sleeping car.

Not much juice remained to be drained from the *City* trains before they began expiring altogether. The last possible consolidation occurred September 7, 1969. The *City of Portland* and *City of Denver* joined the already combined *City of Los Angeles–San Francisco–Kansas City* east of Green River, Wyo. This, finally, was the "City of Everywhere" (never so labeled by UP, of course), a train that at its full 27-car length in the Cheyenne–Green River corridor stretched half a mile from E units to marker lights. In its scope and inclusiveness, this megaservice had no equal. The closest other railroads came to touching so many bases with one core train were Seaboard Coast Line with its *Champion* and Missouri Pacific with its *Texas Eagle* family. Cheyenne and Ogden remained the primary hubs. The Green River split of the *City of Portland* was made easy by the car order out of Cheyenne—uncouple the Portland cars from the body of the train, push them onto No. 105's locomotives and dome lounge, then highball out of town. (Sitting directly behind the locomotives, passengers in the dome lounge enjoyed a sensational view of what lay ahead.)

One last change: In early 1970 Southern Pacific was permitted by the Interstate Commerce Commission to run the *City of San Francisco* triweekly. Thereafter, on days the Oakland cars didn't run,

▲ *No railroad more closely identified with sleek E8 and E9 units of Electro-Motive than UP. Units ran four and five at a time in front of supersized trains. The place to find them in numbers during the late 1960s was Cheyenne, where the fleet was broken apart and rearranged morning and afternoon. On March 23, 1968, power for trains 9, 105 and 103 waits at the depot's west end while the trains are switched. (A. J. Wolff)*

▶ *In mid 1968, an Alco S2 shuffles the eastbound City of Los Angeles–City of San Francisco. (A. J. Wolff)*

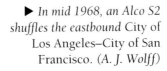

◄ UP's Prairie Dog: Eastbound No. 370 negotiates an S-curve along the northern edge of the Flint Hills, 20 miles west of Salina, Kansas, on an October noontime in 1967. Though technically a mixed train on this part of its run out of Ellis on the old Kansas Pacific main line, the train today is thoroughly first class—four lightweight baggage cars and a reconditioned heavyweight coach behind an omnipresent E9. Two more head-end cars and a second coach will be attached at Salina, en route to a sunset arrival in Kansas City. The sun is setting on this train in more ways than one. Soon reduced to three cars, it would last only until March 18, 1968. (Victor Hand)

▶ Three E units give all they've got lifting No. 10, the eastbound City of St. Louis, up Sherman Hill just west of Hermosa, Wyoming. But they're no match for two diesels and a single heavyweight coach of No. 28, which originated in Laramie just behind the streamliner and now slips past it on a parallel track. Soon, at Cheyenne, nameless No. 28, en route to Omaha, will add another coach and a string of head-end cars. Richard Steinheimer's stunning summer-of-1965 panorama illustrates better than a thousand words the breadth and intensity of UP passenger operations in the years just before cutbacks made such dramas unrepeatable.

▶ The North Platte–South Torrington mixed lasted in splendid obscurity along the North Fork of the Platte until Amtrak, across a dirt-track line that would later become UP's corridor to the Powder River Basin. Westbound No. 93 makes timetable speed—49 miles per hour—through Oshkosh on May 9, 1968. (Victor Hand)

▲ *Rare indeed is evidence that UP passenger trains were hauled by anything but E units. Here's proof otherwise: On August 6, 1967, GP9 233 and two cabless sisters await departure of No. 36, the* Butte Special, *from its namesake city. (John C. Illman)*

extra Los Angeles and Portland coaches adorned the train. You see diagrammed on the facing page an Oakland day in the summer of 1970.

Just creating a core train for Los Angeles, Oakland and Portland, with input from both Chicago and Kansas City, required a long train in any season of the year. In the winter of 1969–70, the City of Everywhere left Chicago with 21 cars and Cheyenne with 23. In the pit of winter the last car

became a baggage car whose interior hid a full-service boiler. The auxiliary boilers came to life when they sensed low pressure in the steam pipes.

The rest of Union Pacific's passenger network shrank almost to oblivion. Trains 27 and 28, the Omaha–Laramie locals, vanished in autumn of 1967, the Prairie Dog early in 1968. Gone almost overnight were the days when UP sent a minimum of 33 mail and express cars west from Omaha each

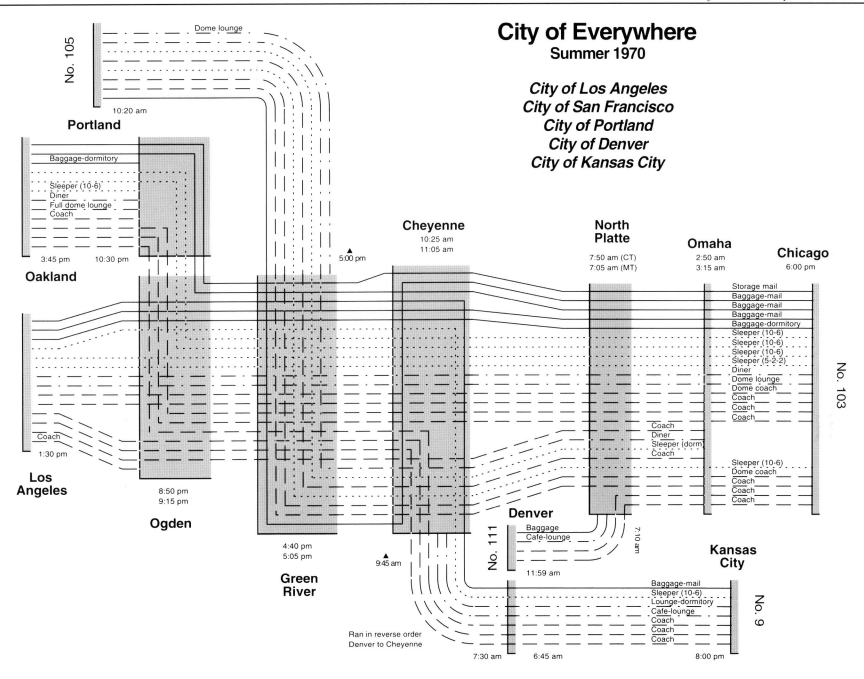

City of Everywhere
Summer 1970

City of Los Angeles
City of San Francisco
City of Portland
City of Denver
City of Kansas City

as always, is hypnotic. Reluctantly I go downstairs for a drink and some conversation.

We're a reflective and rather depressed lot this April evening, my fellow travelers and I, saying our goodbyes to a train that had held up to the onslaught of time and economics better than most. It's best we didn't know just now that the Milwaukee Road rails over which the *City* bounces toward Omaha at 79 miles per hour would be torn up scarcely a decade later; our funk would become unbearable. On this we are unanimous: The American passenger train is largely pathetic. We all hope for something better from the new Railpax that will soon start. Something, perhaps, as decent and workmanlike as the City of Everywhere.

▲ *For a big train, big engines! No fewer than six E units, arranged in classic A-B-B-B-B-A fashion, jump over Sherman Hill on August 24, 1970, with the westbound* City of Everywhere. *Those 13,500 or so horses are pulling 27 cars representing UP's entire timetable of City streamliners. Nowhere else in America could you see a show like this during the final pre-Amtrak summer. (A. J. Wolff)*

day; trains 5 and 6, the mail haulers, shrank to just a baggage car and two coaches, and succumbed altogether by early 1970. The *Portland Rose* lasted until Amtrak, as did the *Butte Special*, which operated triweekly.

A mere two weeks before its demise in 1971, I ride a 14-car, off-peak version of the City of Everywhere from Chicago. Served in the grand old manner, that complete sirloin steak dinner costs me $5. Later, from the dome lounge in the dark of an Iowa evening, I watch block signals turn green to red as our locomotive ahead rushes by. The effect,

▶ *Just past 3 a.m. on a warm spring morning, No. 103 awaits its departure from Omaha. Over the noise of ten 12-cylinder diesel engines comes the sound of steam blowing off from boilers. But most passengers are asleep now anyway. A pity they couldn't witness the moment: It's May 1, 1971, and this is the last westbound* City *streamliner to pass UP's birthplace. (William Kratville)*

SPOILER

Southern Pacific picked fights throughout the 1960s over the necessity of running passenger trains. And sometimes the railroad became its own worst enemy.

◀ *For one of the most charming railroad routes in the world, one of the most charming trains: Southern Pacific's* Coast Daylight. *Joining Los Angeles and San Francisco, it confronted coastal mountains near each end as well as in the middle and strode the length of the fertile Salinas Valley. But the poet in you would love most the 100 miles alongside the Pacific Ocean, half of that length almost removed from civilization. Here the San Francisco-bound* Daylight *skirts the sea with a nine-car train north of Ventura, California, on July 1, 1965. (William D. Middleton)*

No railroad was ever more up-front: Southern Pacific absolutely, positively wanted rid of passenger trains. Its obsession drove regulators to distraction, then retribution. And had you seen the wires to and from president Donald Russell on Election Day, 1956, you'd have seen the trouble coming.

Russell—a man brilliant, arrogant, endearing, dictatorial—has stopped in Houston en route to a vacation at Sea Island, Georgia. And he is in foul humor this morning because of the *Sunset Limited.* The westbound *Sunset* just left Houston with only 19 passengers in its four Pullmans and 57 people in the coaches. "I presume," Russell wires Claude Peterson, SP's passenger traffic manager, "your explanation will be that because of election people are not traveling, etc. But I notice large numbers at the airport. We have the finest equipment in the country and the best schedules on the *Sunset Limited*, but apparently to no avail."

Later this day, aboard the eastbound *Sunset*, the boss sends a second guided missile to Peterson in San Francisco. He recites the head count on this train: 18 people in four sleepers, 95 in three coaches.

"We are not handling sufficient passengers on these trains to justify their daily operation, even allowing for the Election Day period," Russell says. "If this trend continues, perhaps it will be necessary to operate these trains on a triweekly basis. Please carefully consider and let me have your comments."

Peterson sends his own passenger counts for the *Sunset* on this day. Russell dismisses them as "at distinct variance" from reality. "Misleading information or information that fools ourselves," he tells Peterson, "is the worst kind of information."

Diplomatically, Peterson waits almost a week before gently reminding Russell that the *Sunset Limited* is a mobile gold mine. In the preceding 12 months it earned almost $2.7 million over and above direct operating costs. Going triweekly, Peterson says, would forfeit $1 million in mail-hauling revenues and might doom the train's extra fare, which brought in another $700,000 annually. By 1960 the train's profits would reach almost $4.5 million. Yet the *Sunset*, like the rest of Southern Pacific's passenger trains, stands now and forever in the glare of Executive Office disapproval.

The man who called the shots

Southern Pacific's corporate persona directly reflected its strong-willed boss. Russell, who reigned from 1952 until he turned over the reins to Benjamin Biaggini in 1972, was ever the realist. His attitudes had been honed by years of battling nature in the Sierra Nevadas and Cascades as a track employee and later as an Engineering Department officer; there, wishful thinking could cost you your life. Russell never let himself be blinded by the beauty or romance of his passenger trains. "He recognized the business for what it was," says Richard Spence, SP's vice president of operations in the late 1960s (and later Conrail's first president). "He was very unabashed in the 1950s about saying that passenger trains were crippling the railroad, and that we had to bring them to an irreducible minimum."

Biaggini says of Russell that the old man was "seldom wrong, and never in doubt—once he got confirmation of his feelings, he pushed aggressively." As early as 1945 Russell foresaw the demise of the sleeping car. In the closing weeks of World War II nobody had ever heard of Boeing 707s or interstate highways. Yet Russell sensed that both airlines and autos would be brutal competitors for first-class business. "We should energetically get after the coach business and should go slowly in expanding Pullman operations," he advised A. T. Mercier, SP's president then. "In any forecast that can be made, we can always use coach equipment."

Trends of the mid 1950s played to Russell's worst fears. Between 1950 and 1953 SP passenger revenues exceeded solely related costs by more than $63 million—hallelujah years, to be sure. Then began a vicious reversal. Between 1952 and 1958, passenger miles plummeted 44 percent and passenger revenues 36 percent. Losses began in 1954. They peaked at $16 million in 1956 and tapered off through 1961. Those eight miserable years bled the passenger accounts to the tune of $82 million. Then in 1962 the passenger service began registering profits again, and continued doing so through 1966, at least on a direct-cost basis.

His suspicions confirmed in the mid 1950s, Russell seemed oblivious to the improved results. By words and deeds from which he never wavered, he signaled his distaste of passenger trains. "I started as a passenger agent on the *Coast Daylight* in 1954 and quickly realized the Passenger Department was a sinking ship," says William Settle, later SP's head of management training. "They were cutting off jobs at the top, as well as in the middle." Settle escaped by going to graduate school. In 1955 Russell rebuked passenger traffic manager Peterson for presuming that SP's almost-dieselized passenger trains would require additional locomotives. "If we are going to discontinue passenger trains," he wrote, "then we should be buying freight diesels and not passenger diesels, even though it is necessary to use freight diesels on some passenger services. . . . With business of the country generally almost booming and on the increase, our passenger occupancy and revenue are on the decrease. In other words, the two trend lines are getting farther and farther apart."

Was Russell deliberately putting passenger trains on the skids? His associates at the time reply that the truth is more complex. Robert Jochner, a career Passenger Department employee who became its last pre-Amtrak director, met with Russell weekly in the 1960s to review ridership, train by train. "He was probably the most knowledgeable person in American railroading on the passenger business," says Jochner. "He took a personal interest in it."

Philosophically, Russell couldn't bear to run a passenger train that lost money. And so, Jochner contends, many of the cost-cutting moves others interpreted as deliberate sabotage of Southern Pacific's passenger trains were meant to keep them economically viable as long as possible. Jochner remembers accompanying Russell on visits to Los Angeles Union Passenger Terminal. "Nobody ever made more detailed inspections. He'd spend hours going through the *Coast Daylight* before it was loaded, noting every imperfection. Russell was a watchdog for passengers. Nobody ever appreciated that fact." Adds Settle: "One thing Russell insisted on was that the service level be maintained. If you had a hamburger grill car, it had better work right and be clean and have good stuff. In those days that was a bit of a departure."

Donald Russell was prescient in anticipating the impact of air and highway competition years before they began to drain life from his passenger trains. If the man can be faulted, it's for his why-even-try attitude, which percolated through the ranks of the company. SP finished streamlining its premier trains in 1950, shortly before Russell succeeded Mercier. Thereafter, the railroad seemed to give up and begin a train-by-train death watch.

Tales of Form 3646

Were passenger trains' losses indeed strangling Southern Pacific? Form 3646, an internal management report, tracked revenue and outgo of first-class trains. Expenses included all direct operating costs, but excluded Passenger Traffic Department overhead (including advertising and ticket offices) and such indirect costs as delays to freight trains, track maintenance and indirect corporate costs. Form 3646, in other words, gave you a handle on what individual trains contributed beyond direct costs, or the money that might be saved by dropping those that couldn't match direct expenses.

A look at annual figures on Form 3646 from 1955 to 1960 reveals some interesting patterns:

❑ Long-haul trains, by and large, were in good shape. A few of them—the *Sunset* and the mail-heavy *Imperial,* Coast Mail, *Klamath* and Overland Mail—actually increased their earnings during 1955–1960.

❑ Trains run solely within California weren't so well off. The premier Los Angeles–San Francisco *Coast Daylight* and all-Pullman *Lark* were only mod-

Coast Route
Summer 1960

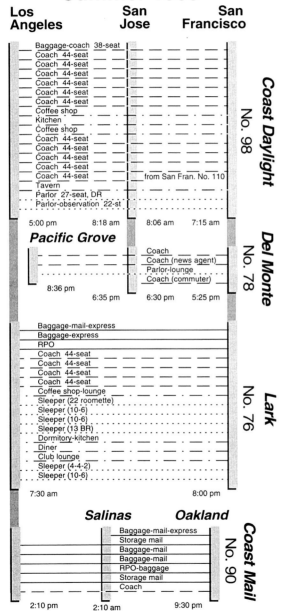

Los Angeles **San Jose** **San Francisco**

Coast Daylight No. 98

Baggage-coach 38-seat
Coach 44-seat
Coach 44-seat
Coach 44-seat
Coach 44-seat
Coach 44-seat
Coach 44-seat
Coffee shop
Kitchen
Coffee shop
Coach 44-seat
Coach 44-seat
Coach 44-seat
Coach 44-seat
Coach 44-seat — from San Fran. No. 110
Tavern
Parlor 27-seat, DR
Parlor-observation 22-st

5:00 pm | 8:18 am | 8:06 am | 7:15 am

Pacific Grove

Del Monte No. 78

Coach
Coach (news agent)
Parlor-lounge
Coach (commuter)

8:36 pm
6:35 pm | 6:30 pm | 5:25 pm

Lark No. 76

Baggage-mail-express
Baggage-express
RPO
Coach 44-seat
Coach 44-seat
Coach 44-seat
Coach 44-seat
Coffee shop-lounge
Sleeper (22 roomette)
Sleeper (10-6)
Sleeper (10-6)
Sleeper (13 BR)
Dormitory-kitchen
Diner
Club lounge
Sleeper (4-4-2)
Sleeper (10-6)

7:30 am | 8:00 pm

Salinas   Oakland

Coast Mail No. 90

Baggage-mail-express
Storage mail
Baggage-mail
Baggage-mail
RPO-baggage
Storage mail
Coach

2:10 pm | 2:10 am | 9:30 pm

est money-makers, the *San Joaquin Daylight* and all-coach overnight *Starlight* hovered around breakeven and the overnight *Owl* and *West Coast* on the Valley line were in the red.

☐ Short-distance trains—the three round trips between Oakland and Sacramento and the two pairs of trains between San Jose and Oakland—came nowhere near covering their direct costs.

The first conclusion that jumps out at you is that for all of Donald Russell's bellyaching about the financial bath his railroad was taking on passenger trains, they did just fine, thank you very much. By 1960, after some belt tightening, the 18 remaining pairs of intercity trains took in (according to Form 3646) $12.3 million *more* than their direct costs to operate. By the Interstate Commerce Commission's method of accounting, SP that year lost $7.2 million, based on solely related costs (similar to but not identical to Form 3646's direct costs). The ICC number included the Peninsula commuter service, whose results weren't reflected in Form 3646.

The railroad always referred publicly to only the fully allocated losses, which required that passenger trains be gigged a pro rata share of everything from track maintenance to train dispatchers' salaries to Russell's own fringe benefits. But it is altogether clear that management kept its eyes on the more-realistic numbers revealed by Form 3646. Beginning about 1955, almost without exception, as soon as a train became unprofitable by the generous yardstick of Form 3646 cost accounting, the railroad immediately sought to remove it from the timetable. Only then did SP puff up a train's purported costs to justify its desire before regulators. Says Ralph Kirk, who became Texas & Louisiana Lines general manager in 1965: "I never knew Russell to advocate getting rid of *anything* that made money. That was the thing with him—he wasn't interested in boxcars but rather in what revenue those boxcars produced."

Case in point: the Los Angeles-to-Sacramento *West*

San Joaquin Route
Summer 1960

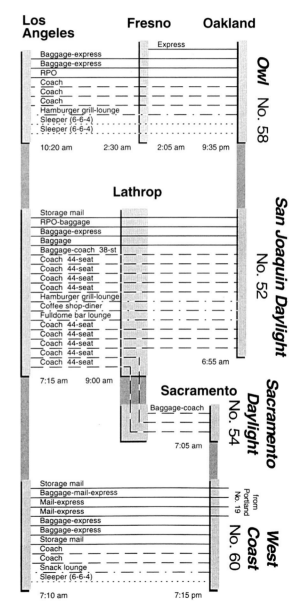

Los Angeles **Fresno** **Oakland**

Owl No. 58

Express
Baggage-express
Baggage-express
RPO
Coach
Coach
Coach
Hamburger grill-lounge
Sleeper (6-6-4)
Sleeper (6-6-4)

10:20 am | 2:30 am | 2:05 am | 9:35 pm

Lathrop

San Joaquin Daylight No. 52

Storage mail
RPO-baggage
Baggage-express
Baggage
Baggage-coach 38-st
Coach 44-seat
Coach 44-seat
Coach 44-seat
Coach 44-seat
Hamburger grill-lounge
Coffee shop-diner
Fulldome bar lounge
Coach 44-seat
Coach 44-seat
Coach 44-seat
Coach 44-seat
Coach 44-seat

7:15 am | 9:00 am | 6:55 am

Sacramento

Sacramento Daylight No. 54

Baggage-coach

7:05 am

West Coast No. 60 (from Portland No. 19)

Storage mail
Baggage-mail-express
Mail-express
Mail-express
Baggage-express
Baggage-express
Storage mail
Coach
Coach
Snack lounge
Sleeper (6-6-4)

7:10 am | 7:15 pm

Coast, an overnight train via the San Joaquin Valley. Its last year to cover direct costs was 1954. The train registered a $98,496 loss on Form 3646 for 1955, and the next year SP sought its removal. Interestingly enough, the railroad told the California Public Utilities Commission that the train's out-of-pocket loss exceeded $850,000. Getting approval to discontinue the *West Coast* became arduous, lasting until 1960. By 1958, SP told the CPUC the *West Coast* was losing $1 million; its Form 3646 distributed to management pegged the figure then at a more modest $328,207. Needless to say, SP didn't share Form 3646 numbers with anyone.

Disappearin' train blues: Part I

The diagrams on these pages depict the scope of Southern Pacific passenger trains at the dawn of the 1960s. Those trains stand, by and large, as magnificent icons of their time. But events of the coming decade were cruel. First to go were the money-losing locals. The San Jose–Oakland trains, tied to connections with the *Coast Daylight* and *Lark,* fell in May 1960. The *Senator,* last of the Oakland–Sacramento round trips, went two years later. (These routes were revived by Amtrak under state sponsorship 30 years later, with some success.)

One early case was particularly rough. Since a schedule change in 1955, the *San Francisco Overland* had been the Ogden–Oakland connection with Union Pacific's *City of St. Louis.* But the *Overland* existed on the cusp of profitability—barely in or out of the black—and hence was put on the death watch. Its schedule both ways closely matched that of the *City of San Francisco.* When UP told Southern Pacific that its *City of Los Angeles* and *City of San Francisco* would be combined east of Ogden after the summer of 1960, and that the *City of St. Louis* would pass Ogden at about the same time as the newly merged streamliner, SP moved immediately to combine the *Overland* with its own *City of San Francisco.* The ICC began an investigation—the *Over-*

land to continue running in the interim—but SP went ahead and shifted St. Louis cars to the *City* anyway, making the *Overland* a three-car stub (a coach, sleeper and hamburger grill) with no connection at Ogden.

Not smart. The Interstate Commerce Commission, angry that SP had ignored its request to keep through cars on the *Overland* pending its decision, ordered the *Overland* run as before for another year, until early 1962. The ICC largely rejected SP's cost estimates of operating both the *Overland* and *City* (trains 101 and 102). For 1959, here are profits or losses of the two trains as told by the SP to the commission, as shown on Form 3646 and as figured by the California Public Utilities Commission:

	SP to ICC	SP Form 3646	CPUC
Trains 27-28	-$1,338,000	$47,075	$147,600
Trains 101-102	-593,000	671,564	431,700

One reason for numerical discrepancy was that SP, in cost submissions to the ICC, threw into the kettle almost $2 million in indirect costs, such as track maintenance, general office and traffic expenses, and locomotive and car depreciation—costs whose recoverability was debatable, at best.

Southern Pacific dutifully rescheduled the *Overland* to again connect with the *City of St. Louis.* But in early 1962 it repeated its request to discontinue trains 27 and 28. This time no tricks occurred. SP said dropping the *Overland* would save $1.5 million—a claim that the ICC called exaggerated. But the commission granted Southern Pacific's wish anyway, with a twist: It required the *San Francisco Overland* to continue to run as a second section of the *City of San Francisco* from June 14 through Labor Day, and from December 22 through January 2. That requirement was honored in the breach.

The *Shasta Daylight* between Oakland and Portland wasn't so much killed as tortured to death. Inaugurated as a luxury day train in 1949 (and with

Russell's enthusiastic blessing), it became an instant success, in summer at least, swelling to 17 cars by 1954. Biaggini recalls it as one of his favorite trains. You'd find, besides 11 coaches, a triple-unit coffee shop-kitchen-diner, one of SP's Sacramento-built three-quarter-length dome lounges and a 22-seat parlor-observation. We're talking class.

But imagine Russell's discomfort because of off-peak loadings. Those 11 coaches shrank to five after summer, when patronage dropped off sharply. How inefficient! And proof, perhaps, to Russell that the public wasn't interested in his fine train. Over a year's time the *Shasta Daylight* was a good money-maker, contributing more than $600,000 above direct costs in 1955, $309,000 in 1956 and $550,000 in 1957. Yet in May 1959, after more than a year spent jousting with regulators, SP succeeded in having the train run on a triweekly basis, except during summer, when daily operation resumed.

This was one of the few instances of a still-profitable SP train being cut back. And the off-season curtailment ruined the train's profitability. Form 3646 showed a $292,220 profit above direct costs for 1958, but a small loss for the first year of non-daily operation and a larger one in 1960. By 1962 SP's infamous automat buffets supplied off-season food service. Soon thereafter the parlor-observations were axed.

▶ *As the Tehachapi Mountains cast their afternoon shadow, the* San Joaquin Daylight *scoots toward Los Angeles on March 18, 1971. An inland version of the* Coast Daylight *that originated in Oakland, it carries behind the baggage car an infamous automat diner. (Victor Hand)*

Then in May 1964, with patronage dwindling, the ICC let the *Shasta Daylight* become a summer-only train. A year later SP was back yet again, seeking to be rid of it altogether. The government said no. For the summer of 1966 the train was down to a baggage car, dome lounge, coffee shop-lounge and three coaches, in that order. In February 1967 SP told California and Oregon regulators it wouldn't reinstate the train that summer. This time the ICC wasn't interested in the *Shasta Daylight*'s fate.

Demise of the mail

Three pair of trains disappeared within a month early in 1965. First to go, on April 10, were trains 19 and 20, the old *Klamath* between Oakland and Portland, now a nameless local carrying only one coach behind the head-end cars. In 1964, its last full year, revenue from passengers amounted to less than $60,000. When storage mail was diverted to freights in a Postal Service economy move, the ICC let the inevitable occur.

Two days later came the last run of the overnight *Owl* from Oakland to Los Angeles via the San Joaquin Valley. Its second sleeper went in early 1962 and an automat car replaced the hamburger grill. Those two changes saved $20,000 per month in costs. Still, the *Owl* was vulnerable—a marginal train on a secondary route. What kept it alive was mail revenue, which vanished in the same Postal Service cost-cutting that killed trains 19 and 20.

The *Coast Mail* between Oakland, San Jose and Los Angeles via the Coast Line became the third victim of Postal Service economies. It was far more prosaic than the name implied—a head-end train that carried a single heavyweight coach for whatever unhurried passengers happened upon it, plus five or so storage mail or express cars and an RPO-baggage. The *Coast Mail* (never so named in timetables) left its terminals in late evening and consumed that night and most of the next day reaching the other end 466 miles away. Everything had superior rights. And it

was never a big moneymaker, the 1960 profit of $248,000 being perhaps its biggest in that decade. Excitement? Well, in strawberry season the Oakland-bound Coast Mail would collect strings of REA Express refrigerator cars at Watsonville Junction and Salinas for forwarding on No. 22, the eastbound Overland Mail. Otherwise it was slow, dull stuff—just the sort of lazy-day train you and I would kill to ride in the 1990s. Its removal on May 19, 1965, attracted little notice.

But the demise of the Ogden–Oakland Overland Mail (again, my name for it, not SP's) two years later was absolute catastrophe. In 1960 this train earned $2.8 million above direct costs. The Mail owed its good fortune to Union Pacific, whose own Overland Mail exchanged prodigious amounts of mail and express with Southern Pacific at Ogden. The Mail's minimum length was about 15 cars, its maximum sometimes three times as many. Eight or nine cars behind the locomotives came the RPO-baggage and a heavyweight coach for passengers, and on the rear another coach for the flagman.

Each way the Mail crossed Utah and Nevada deserts by day and California's mountains by night. Except for halts in Sacramento and nearby Roseville, it ran nonstop all 240 miles from Reno to Oakland in darkness, making it all but invisible on the most populous part of its route. But that was the schedule postal authorities wanted. In October of 1967 the RPO contract was canceled and the storage mail and express put on freights as part of the Postal Service's shift to regional distribution centers. "It came as a sudden move—a shock," says former Passenger Traffic Department boss Jochner. On November 15, 1967, after an unopposed 30-day notice, the Mail was no more.

Diners (and gloves) come off

Those were the easy ones for Southern Pacific. The other train-off cases would be hard fought and bitter, sometimes attracting the national publicity that

SP least needed. Most remaining passenger trains bore elite names and reputations, were the last on their routes, or both. Political sensitivity to the loss of passenger service was on the rise, too. But other railroads whacked away at first-class trains in the mid 1960s with as much or more vigor—Southern Railway is a prime example—without becoming targets in the gunsights of politicians or being held in public scorn. Southern Pacific suffered both indignities, and must take some of the blame.

Partly it was a case of earlier cost-cutting practices coming home to roost. If the articulated, triple-unit diners adorning the *Lark*, *Cascade*, *Shasta Daylight* and *Coast Daylight* spoiled the customers, then what followed was a living nightmare for people used to being pampered. On July 31, 1961, the first of what would become 17 "automatic food and beverage service cars"—automat buffets, for short—emerged from Sacramento Shops, rebuilt from a tavern car at a cost of $30,000.

"I think SP did some debatable things," concedes former VP-Operations Spence. "Because dining car losses were so horrendous, we built those damned vending cars." Their biggest booster, says Spence, was Russell. "The old man was deep in the planning of it and the idea of it. I was then division superintendent at Sacramento, and he'd come to the shops at night to inspect the work."

Automats boiled down to vending machines against both walls in the middle, and tables and chairs at either end, all of this adorned in wall-to-wall plastic and linoleum in neutral colors and manned by a bored attendant who must have yearned for happier days waiting tables in the diners. In 1966 the railroad installed microwave ovens. "Well, the cars looked great," recalls Spence, "and me, I was always a sandwich guy." But if cold sandwiches, hot casseroles in cans and machine-brewed instant coffee weren't your thing, you would definitely not have liked automat buffet cuisine.

By October of 1961 the first two automats were

Overland Route
Summer 1960

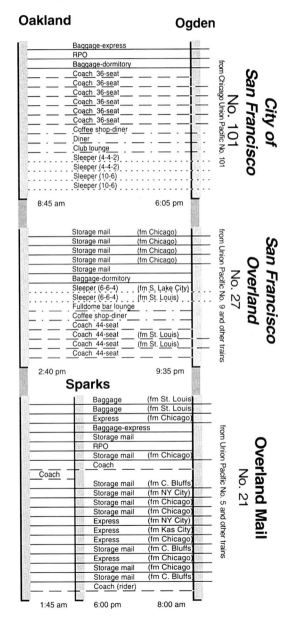

in service on the *San Joaquin Daylight,* replacing coffee shop-diners. Soon thereafter they showed up in place of diners on the off-peak *Shasta Daylight* and then the *Owl* and off-peak *Coast Daylight.* They were briefly used in 1962 on even the elite *Cascade.* By 1964 *any* SP train was fair game for an automat, either alongside a regular diner or in place of it.

Other less-obvious cost-cutting moves—some sensible, others pound-foolish—were adopted. Artificial flowers replaced the real thing in dining cars in 1960, to save $5,000 annually on the *Sunset* alone. The *Sunset* lost the shower and valet service in its lounge car in June 1961. That same year a 25-cent pillow charge for coach passengers began, promptly becoming 35 cents. The 10 percent commissions paid travel agents since 1946 ceased after 1964, for a saving of $123,000 a year but at a cost of perhaps ten times as much ticket revenue. The Form A timetable was cut in half, to 16 pages, in 1962, and eliminated altogether in 1965 in favor of a six-page folder. The railroad had long since ceased any meaningful advertising of its trains.

Then there were acts that seemed to rub Southern Pacific's disdain for passengers in the face of the public. For a decade, from October of 1956 until April of 1967, the railroad sold tickets for American, Trans World and United airlines—without commission or reciprocation—at its smaller stations systemwide. This was totally consistent with Russell's belief that the long-haul train was ultimately doomed. The railroad maintained that passengers would at least travel via SP to the nearest big city airport.

Attempts to educate the public to its way of thinking ended up repulsing potential riders. The railroad's ad in the October 1965 issue of *Sunset Magazine* was titled "The Vanishing American" and began: "The train traveler—a rare breed these days. What's happened to him? Where did he go?" To better forms of transportation, of course, the ad's copy concluded. Cuter but no more endearing to

Shasta Route
Summer 1960

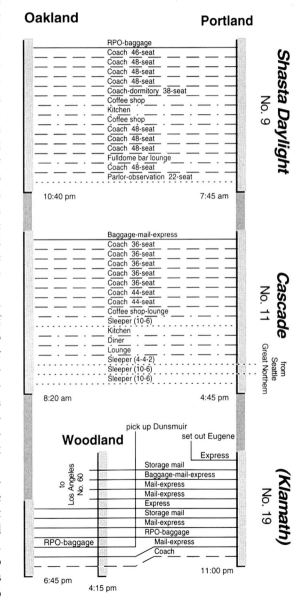

45

▲ *The conductor of the* City of San Francisco *couples his locomotive to the train in the Oakland coach yard in 1966. That summer was notable for the airline strike that packed this train and for the last stand made by SP's magnificent but aging Alco PA engines.* (Richard Steinheimer)

Stanford economists) were either naive or intentionally misleading in their use of numbers. They relied exclusively on passenger losses calculated by the fully allocated cost method, which the ICC itself had disavowed a decade earlier in favor of directly attributable costs.

This, then, was the stage on which Southern Pacific and its opponents fought brawl after brawl, until, in 1969, both sides seemed exhausted.

Disappearin' train blues: Part II

The *Imperial* had become plain old 39 and 40, and lost its diner and last sleeper, in a 1958 rescheduling that made this Kansas City–Los Angeles train (run by Rock Island Lines east of Tucumcari, New Mexico) a conduit for mail and express. One, sometimes two, coaches sufficed for passengers. Costs went down, revenues up and nobody complained. Strange, then, that it became the first true battleground of the decade between SP and regulators.

On September 1, 1964, the railroad asked to discontinue hauling passengers on trains 39 and 40 west of Phoenix. SP had just added piggyback flatcars and multilevel auto racks on this overnight run between Los Angeles and Phoenix as a means of meeting truck competition, and told the ICC that mixing freight and passenger service would injure its public image. Besides, only a dozen or so people a day rode west of Phoenix. Southern Pacific conceded the trains earned their costs and $40,000 more to boot without counting the new freight revenue; the ICC figured the real profit over this portion of the run at closer to $60,000. The commission in early 1965 ordered passenger service to Los Angeles continued.

Southern Pacific kept the mixed train service, using four locomotives and handling as many as 20 freight cars a night, in addition to half a dozen mail cars and a coach. But after eight months it knocked on the ICC's door again, wanting to discontinue trains 39 and 40 between Tucumcari and Phoenix.

customers and would-be customers was the ad in the *San Francisco Chronicle* on February 1, 1966: "The *Lark:* What future is there for a bird that can't fly?" Beneath that was the *Lark*'s symbol and the caption: "It never got off the ground."

And in 1965 the railroad commissioned an impressive-sounding tome from Stanford Research Institute—*The Future of Rail Passenger Travel in the West*. Its analysis reached the conclusion you'd expect: There was no future. But the authors (two

Dripping with anger, the ICC's decision of January 1966 rebuked the railroad for taking the train out of its public timetable, and noted that ticket agents seemed under orders to deny its very existence. Financial figures submitted by SP to prove that the train lost money were jumbled, contradictory and unintelligible, making evaluation simply impossible, the commission said. It added, in harsh words seldom directed at a railroad:

> Whenever it appears, as in this proceeding, that a carrier has deliberately downgraded its service in order to justify discontinuance of a train irrespective of the actual or potential needs of the traveling public, the Commission will order the service to be continued. . . . The Commission will not find burdens on interstate commerce within the meaning of section 13a to be "undue" if those burdens are voluntarily created by the carriers for the purpose of obtaining a favorable decision from the Commission.

When Southern Pacific came back a third time 15 months later, to drop the train all the way from Tucumcari to Los Angeles, much had changed. Rock Island's connection from Kansas City had just been taken off. So had the connecting Missouri Pacific–Texas & Pacific train into El Paso from Dallas and the east. The Railway Post Office contract had lapsed, too. The only tether tied to trains 39 and 40 was a Memphis–Tucumcari train of Rock Island's that furnished four or five storage mail cars. Ridership had dwindled to eight to 12 people a day per trip—and averaged just one person departing Los Angeles.

A contrite Southern Pacific, in the meantime, had restored this train to its timetable. The railroad arrived with reams of well prepared financial statements to back its claim of a $1 million annual loss. The train's plight was indeed hopeless. It finished August 18, 1967.

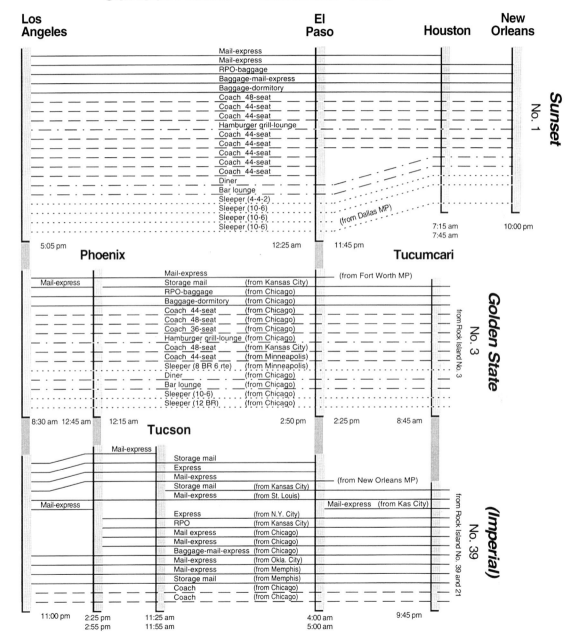

Sunset Route   Summer 1960

▲ *From the steps of Tower 121 in San Antonio's East Yard, J. Parker Lamb snapped the* Sunset Limited *coming and going through crossovers in July 1964. Already underway was the deliberate downgrading that would make the train a cause celebre.*

Sundown for the *Sunset*?

A mere month later SP and Rock Island asked to be rid of their jointly run, Chicago–Los Angeles *Golden State,* too. By then, trains 3 and 4 ran independently only east of El Paso. On April 19, 1964, the *Golden State* and *Sunset* had been consolidated into a single megatrain between El Paso and Los Angeles—without, it developed, any of the required notices to either the ICC or state regulatory commissions. The railroad got away with that feint, but the resulting *Golden State–Sunset* that summer was of such length that it usually ran in sections, somewhat negating the sought-after savings.

The expedient of consolidation didn't keep wolves away long. Rock Island, fading fast, was hurt by failure of the Oklahoma wheat crop in mid 1967. Then the Postal Service cancelled the Chicago–Los Angeles RPO car and most storage mail, robbing the train of most of its $3 million in mail revenues. And ridership in the first nine months of 1967 fell some 20 percent from the year before, averaging only 121 people per day westbound and 89 eastbound on the El Paso–Tucumcari segment. The two railroads maintained that they would lose a combined $1.8 million on the *Golden State* over the next year. Rather reluctantly, it seemed, the ICC sanctioned the removal of this transcon schedule, effective February 21, 1968. I rode the last eastbound *Golden State* into Chicago. Prophetically, lights in my coach failed five miles from LaSalle Street Station.

This set the stage for the *Sunset* confrontation. In 1960 the *Sunset* stood at the pinnacle of success, earning almost $4.5 million above direct costs and running 20 cars long in summer. Its downfall began in earnest in 1964, and within four years the debacle was complete—no sleepers, no diner, no lounge, no mail, a lot fewer happy passengers across those 2,033 miles to New Orleans and a whole lot of losses, by SP's reckoning.

The 1964 consolidation of the *Sunset* and *Golden*

State between Los Angeles and El Paso created a combined train of such size—27 cars in the summer of 1965—that it was almost unmanageable. No fewer than 14 coaches ran in an unbroken row on busy days (five for the *Golden State* east of El Paso, six for the *Sunset* and three in Los Angeles–El Paso local service). And it had five sleepers (three for the *Golden State* and two for the *Sunset*). Supporting this train, whose capacity was 725 people, were only the *Golden State*'s dining and lounge cars and an automat. East of El Paso the *Sunset* had a diner-lounge and an automat; the separate Los Angeles–New Orleans dining and lounge cars were swept away in earlier economizing.

Come early 1966, more unpleasant changes: On January 19, the El Paso–New Orleans diner-lounge and baggage-dormitory cars were removed—a $217,000 cost saving, the railroad figured. Only an automat provided food or lounge service east of El Paso. On February 1 seat reservations ended, but the extra fare did not. One of the two New Orleans sleepers had been cut the previous autumn, and on February 24 the other one vanished, too, making the *Sunset* coach-only in Texas and Louisiana.

Meanwhile, the states of Arizona, California and New Mexico got nowhere in efforts to undo the unannounced (and therefore technically illegal) consolidation of the *Golden State* and *Sunset* almost two years earlier. But the downgrading of the *Sunset* in 1966 supplied the lever they needed. At their urging, plus that of Texas and Louisiana regulators, the ICC opened a highly unusual investigation into the adequacy of service offered on the *Sunset*.

Hearings consumed months, after which 32 attorneys involved in the proceeding had a chance to write briefs. By the time the report of hearing examiner John Messer was issued on April 22, 1968, the *Golden State* was a recent memory, and the *Sunset* stood exposed as a rather pitiful five-car train east of El Paso and only slightly long to the west.

Messer's single-spaced, 60-page opinion showed Southern Pacific no mercy. He mocked the railroad's contention that the New Orleans sleepers were removed for lack of patronage, noting that the load factor on these cars had stood above 80 percent. He said the railroad vastly overstated costs of running the *Sunset*, and asserted that the train was more likely to be earning almost $700,000 than to be losing several million, as SP contended. He ridiculed the Stanford Research Institute study (*The Future of Rail Passenger Travel in the West*), paid for by SP, as naive. He called the automats inadequate for extra-fare clientele. And Messer concluded that SP had "downgraded its passenger-train service and that this has contributed materially to the decline in patronage."

Washington lowers the boom (sort of)

Remedies? "The time has come," Messer wrote, "when the Commission can no longer act like a county coroner and, acting upon death certificates in the form of [train discontinuance] notices, inquire by an inquest into the cause of passenger-train demise. . . . The urgent need is for preventative medicine." He recommended that the ICC impose minimum standards for passenger trains—for example, food service on trains traveling more than 250 miles, dining cars on trains operating longer than 12 hours, sleeping cars on all overnight trains, average speeds at least as fast as a railroad's fastest freight train and equipment clean inside and out and in working order.

"He went overboard," says Jochner, "but I can't say I was shocked. I'd attended or testified at all the hearings, and you could tell by his line of questions where this was going." The next day, April 23, 1968, SP removed the Los Angeles–El Paso sleeping and coffee shop cars it had kept on the *Sunset* after the *Golden State* was taken off two months earlier. Checked baggage was next to go. The California Public Service Commission ordered the sleeper and coffee shop cars restored, and SP complied—but only as far as Yuma, Ariz., with sleeping car passengers forced to vacate their rooms before crossing the state line at 2:20 a.m. This farce lasted three weeks before state regulators capitulated. One day later the railroad put the entire *Sunset* up for discontinuance. SP management, obviously angry, wasn't going to roll over and wag its tail.

Jochner is right—Messer *did* go overboard. His full set of recommendations tried to tell Congress, state legislatures, labor unions and mayors what to do to save the passenger train, even though he was asked to examine only one train. Ultimately, the ICC concluded it lacked authority to impose minimum standards of service.

But the commission did deal quickly with SP's train-off notice for the *Sunset*. Its decision in October 1968 acidly noted that the railroad provided sleeping facilities for food-service attendants but none for the paying customers, who averaged 220 per day on each train in the first half of 1968, and concluded: "The record is convincing that the Southern Pacific has deliberately set out to discourage existing, as well as new, patronage of the *Sunsets* by reducing what was once a convenient and comfortable railroad passenger service to a slow, unreliable, uncomfortable train without sleeping facilities, with only rudimentary dining facilities; a train on which a seat cannot be reserved, arrival and departure times cannot be easily ascertained by telephone, or by printed schedules because they are often unobtainable, and a train for which adequate station waiting room is frequently lacking." Keep running the train, SP was told.

Jochner says SP didn't get a fair hearing on the *Sunset* case. "That was true," he adds, "of most of our cases." But the passenger services chief should have ridden this train across West Texas night after night, as Rollin Bredenberg did in 1965–1968 as a young brakeman. Invariably, Bredenberg says, his eastbound *Sunset* would get train orders at Sanderson, Texas, giving the two sections of the westbound *Blue Streak Merchandise* freight train superior rights. "We bucked the *Blue Streaks*," says Bredenberg, later to become an SP vice president, "and invariably arrived late in San Antonio."

The westbound *Sunset* sometimes fared no better. E. L. (Buck) Hord, a San Antonio Division train dispatcher in 1969, began work on third trick one night to find every siding between San Antonio and Flatonia (90 miles to the east) plugged with freight trains, and three more eastbound freights ready to leave San Antonio. Meanwhile, the westbound *Sunset* was bearing down on Flatonia. "Where were you planning on meeting all those trains?" Hord asked the second-trick dispatcher. "You know, Buck, I've been wondering about that," the man replied as he went out the door. Hord buzzed the operator at Seguin, midway from San Antonio to Flatonia, to ask if the house track there was empty. "He came back on the line a few minutes later to say it was clear. So I issued a train order that read, NO 1 MEET FIRST 248 SECOND 248 AND THIRD 248 AT SEGUIN. NO 1 TAKE HOUSE TRACK." There the once-mighty *Sunset* sat, and sat, and sat.

Air-conditioning failed so often, Bredenberg says, that conductors kept one coach empty as a reserve when other cars became hot. Machines in the vending car were either empty of food by this part of the trip, or failed to function at all, causing the crew to take orders for food from passengers that would be delivered to the train by a cafe when the *Sunset* paused in Del Rio, Tex. His railroad's stance on the *Sunset*, Bredenberg concluded, "defined Southern Pacific's culture, Southern Pacific's priorities, Southern Pacific's attitudes toward its products. What we did was let standards go to hell, and then allowed the market to take care of the demise of the train."

A bird without feathers

Three months before the *Sunset* decision, the ICC sent yet another poisoned arrow toward Southern Pacific. The *City of San Francisco*, which had swelled to 24 cars in mid 1966, was nonetheless on the block. Bad news had swamped it like a tidal wave in 1967. Inexplicably, passenger revenues of the Chicago–Oakland train fell 30 percent from a year before (calls for space falling so drastically that SP dismissed some of the summer employees of its San Francisco reservations bureau). Cancellation of the RPO car in September cost the train another $450,000 a year in revenue. Diversion to freights of its storage mail in October meant $950,000 in additional lost income. From a profit of $318,100 in 1966, SP told the government, the *City of San Francisco* slid to a $284,800 deficit in 1967. The railroad predicted a 1968 loss of $1.4 million.

No matter. Evidence in hearings had been damning. One station pulled the plugs on its switchboard at 7 p.m., cutting off people in the midst of making reservations. Another closed its doors each night 11 minutes before the *City*'s arrival. There were complaints of dirty cars and discourteous employees, too. The ICC's denunciation went beyond the particulars of the trains:

> Reservations are denied to people when the space is available. Advertising of the train has been eliminated. Travel agents are not used despite their value in attracting revenue. But the greatest inhibitor of passenger revenues on the *City of San Francisco* is the attitude of Southern Pacific toward the passengers themselves. . . . Service on the *City of San Francisco* is more likely to drive passengers away than to attract anyone.

> A search of the record finds only one explanation for the deplorable conditions allowed, if not promoted, on these trains. Management admittedly does not want to retain passenger service. No other reasonable explanation found its way into the record.

Saying that SP had forfeited its right to claim that "the losses it helped to create" caused the rail-road hardship, the ICC ordered the train continued at least another year.

Still another bitter case ended in removal of the San Francisco–Los Angeles overnight *Lark*, on April 8, 1968, on SP's second attempt. On the first try, early in 1966, SP claimed a loss of $993,683 for the first 11 months of 1965, the California Public Utilities Commission a deficit of less than $300,000. The CPUC hearings made great theater. On one side was economist (and railfan) George W. Hilton, who said the *Lark* was the equal in luxury of any overnight train in America. "We are justified in concluding," he testified in supporting its discontinuance, "that if this train cannot survive economically, then no intercity train can." On the other side was comedian and advertising man Stan Freberg, who said the *Lark*'s $3.25 steak sandwich was "even tougher than the heart of an SP reservation agent" and offered to direct a pro-*Lark* ad campaign for SP for a year, gratis. CPUC commissioners unanimously granted the *Lark* a reprieve.

By the time of that decision in mid 1966 even Professor Hilton might have tempered his praise of the *Lark*. The all-Pullman train had added coaches in mid 1956, and its merger with the all-coach *Starlight* the next summer pumped up profits to almost $400,000 by 1958, according to Form 3646. But

▶ *In a last hurrah for Alco PA diesels, during the summer of 1967, four of the big beasts launch the* City of San Francisco *on its way to Chicago from Oakland's 16th Street Station. (Richard Steinheimer)*

◀ *Through cars to Sacramento had become a memory in 1969, but the* San Joaquin *and* Sacramento Daylights *still did a brisk interchange where they met, at Lathrop, a junction near Stockton, California. That's the* San Joaquin *at right in the top photo. (Ted Benson)*
Below, the day is fast fading as Sacramento Daylight No. 53 hustles toward its namesake city in late 1967. (Ted Benson)

thereafter, attrition of its business clientele to airlines slowly consumed the train's vitality. Its ten sleeping cars in 1956 become five by 1962, three by 1965 and two by 1966. In March 1966 the train's remaining signature cars—the triple-unit diner-kitchen-club lounge *Lark Club*—were replaced by separate dining and lounge cars. Eight months later a snack lounge (the former hamburger grill of the *Sunset*) supplanted these cars, and thus ended hot meals on the train—a $147,800-per-year economy.

On September 29, 1967, the train's last big ($271,000 per year) revenue-producer, the Railway Post Office car, made its final run. Four weeks earlier, citing a $560,000 loss in the first six months of the year, Southern Pacific again asked the CPUC to be rid of the *Lark*. Early in March 1968, after SP prodded California regulators by taking its case to the ICC, the utilities commission relented, setting the date four weeks in the future. In the end, Southern Pacific's ad was right: This bird couldn't fly.

Disappearin' train blues: Part III

There simply was no parallel, before or since, to the brittle, uncompromising tone of debate waged by Southern Pacific and its opponents. Railroads in other parts of the country could confidentially brief state regulators about their passenger problems and get a sympathetic ear. This wasn't possible in California's politicized atmosphere of the 1960s. Says Biaggini: "You couldn't take a CPUC commissioner to lunch without reading about it the next morning in the papers." Jochner concedes that the railroad might have done a better job of ingratiating itself with regulators. "But Russell was a stickler for handling things on their merits," he adds, "and that's what we did."

After all but a trickle of mail was taken off its trains in late 1967 there was precious little to support them but ticket revenue, and it declined rapidly, too. SP dutifully posted discontinuance notices on every passenger train but two in 1968. (The *Coast Daylight* acquired the distinction of being the only run SP never sought to end.)

The other schedule left alone in 1968 and thereafter was the *Del Monte*, a commuter train from San Francisco to San Jose and a two-car local the last 67 miles to Monterey, with parlor and bar space provided on a former *Golden State* lounge car. SP had learned its lesson in a 1964 attempt to remove this train. The *Del Monte* enjoyed a regular clientele so loyal that it dug into its collective pocket to charter an extra lounge car one day to honor the long-time parlor car attendant, who had retired. (Organizer and fund-raiser for that party was a high school student, Andrew Fox, who later became SP's superintendent of transportation.) Take off *our* train, these affluent riders asked? No way! "All the local people jammed auditoriums at hearings," Jochner says. "The hotels and tour people got behind the train to support it, too." It was a "rough and bitter experience" for the easy-going Jochner, who prided himself on having a tough hide. Southern Pacific lost that one, and never tried again.

After the *Golden State* and *Lark* came off in early 1968, in fact, SP never succeeded in pulling off another passenger train, anywhere. The best it could

The Del Monte *scoots through San Bruno. Its patrons were fiercely loyal, to say the least. (Ted Benson)*

do, on the very eve of Amtrak, was to achieve triweekly operation for three of its trains—the *City of San Francisco* (effective February 13, 1970), *Cascade* (August 1, 1970) and *Sunset* (October 1, 1970). And as part of the deal to reduce *Sunset* frequency, the railroad—glory of glories—reinstated both a sleeping car and diner-lounge, all the way to New Orleans. Furthermore, the sleeper became a coast-to-coast car run to New York City in conjunction with Southern Railway's *Southern Crescent* and Penn Central.

The lingering aftertaste

It's fair to say nobody welcomed the coming of Amtrak more than the long-suffering customers of Southern Pacific. Virtually all remaining SP passenger trains continued under Amtrak (the *San Joaquin Daylight* and *Del Monte* being the sole casualties). Their immediate growth of ridership under Amtrak was proof, if you needed it, that Donald Russell was not altogether correct in asserting that people deserted Southern Pacific passenger trains, rather than vice versa

I asked Biaggini whether—just perhaps—his railroad had been too trigger-happy in shooting down its passenger trains. "No," he replied, after thinking for a moment. "It would only have prolonged the agony." As Biaggini sees it, the railroad was a captive of its times. "Eastern railroad folks could find more or less sympathetic audiences among regulators. But we'd been kicked out of California politics by Hiram Johnson [a populist governor early in the twentieth century]. The California Public Utilities Commission wouldn't do a thing to help us." Southern Pacific, he implied, had to fight for every shred of relief it got from passenger losses. So fight it did.

But Biaggini realized SP ultimately paid a price for its behavior. He became convinced that the public relations fiasco it caused was an unspoken factor in the government's refusal to let SP and Santa Fe merge their railroads in 1986. "There were leftover antagonisms with no business being there," he says, "that Union Pacific and Rio Grande very skillfully exploited" in opposing the merger. Some of the roots of those antagonisms had names, and those names come easily to the lips—*Lark . . . Shasta Daylight . . . Del Monte . . . Golden State.*

THE TRUE BELIEVERS

The Santa Fe ethic: Run passenger trains as if your railroad would be judged by them. Of course, in this the railroad had certain natural advantages.

How well you do the hard things defines your character. The same is true of railroads. In the third quarter of this century Fred Gurley, Ernest Marsh and John Reed made Atchison, Topeka & Santa Fe synonymous with quality—a reputation that still burnishes the property. And they did it the old-fashioned way, running passenger trains.

President Gurley (president 1944–1957), Missouri-born and Burlington-trained, in the dozen years after World War II reclothed Santa Fe's fleet on a scale no other railroad west of Chicago matched—623 lightweight sleeper, coach, diner, lounge, baggage and mail cars. His boldest act, in 1955: spending $13 million of scarce capital to replace the equipment on the all-coach *El Capitan*—cars then only seven years old—with 55 revolutionary high-level cars. In a stroke, he improved passenger comfort, increased capacity and cut costs. Today every passenger aboard an Amtrak Superliner car, which is descended directly from those high-levels, owes a prayer of thanks for Fred Gurley.

President Marsh (1957–1966) cut away money-losing secondary trains and combined a few oth-

ers. But he never wavered. "We don't want to get out of the passenger business," he told Congress in 1958. "We are trying to hold on to the business." To prove it, Marsh in 1962 ordered 24 more high-level cars, this time for the *San Francisco Chief*.

It fell to president Reed (1967–1978) to dismantle the passenger traditions of Santa Fe, built by those who came before him. There's irony in this, for in his younger days John Shedd Reed was a railfan of prodigious enthusiasm and unbounded appetite. Reed did what had to be done in the best Gurley–Marsh tradition, but identified personally with the trains that remained. Eight days after his October 4, 1967, announcement that Santa Fe would seek to drop all but a handful of first-class schedules, he wrote to a Texas Tech University graduate student: "Our policy of being a leader with passenger service remains unchanged." If you wonder what he meant, you never rode a Reed-era Santa Fe train. Amtrak, for all its efforts and all its dollars, hasn't made passengers feel more wanted than Santa Fe, even after Santa Fe people realized that the time was up, the cause was lost.

In a class by itself

I don't mean to imply that a three-man band did it all. Santa Fe had been a drum-thumping, passenger-friendly railroad for decades before this trio came along, and enjoyed some powerful advantages. Most of all, it alone had the long, long haul. No other railroad stretched from Chicago to the West Coast. Union Pacific, Southern Pacific, Burlington Lines and Rock Island Lines all ran passenger trains against Santa Fe, and ran them well. Yet their transcontinental trains never answered to a single master. Santa Fe decided all by itself how to use the advertising dollars, when to invest in new equipment, where to peg fares and whether to take heart.

As years passed and the going got tough, the long-haul advantage became telling. *City* streamliners suffered from Chicago & North Western's deteriorating track and half-hearted commitment to the point that Union Pacific in 1955 "fired" C&NW and moved its passenger trains to Milwaukee Road, which within a decade was in no better shape than North Western. Southern Pacific gave up on the Chicago–Los Angeles *Golden State* years before Rock Island. The *California Zephyr* might have made it to Amtrak were Burlington a Chicago–Oakland railroad; but it wasn't, and partner Western Pacific demanded out and effectively killed the train.

Matters were much the same between Chicago and Texas. Santa Fe's additional good fortune was that the far destinations of its long-distance trains, California and Texas, became growth meccas. California's population grew 90 percent between 1950 and 1970, and that of Texas 45 percent.

But population growth and quirks of railroad development don't go to the heart of what put Santa Fe in a class by itself. To a degree, Santa Fe, under Gurley and Marsh in particular, worked to *build* a market for passengers, rather than merely maintain one. Its *San Francisco Chief,* new in 1954, exploited markets that didn't then exist—for luxury service from Houston or Dallas to San Francisco via through

cars, plus Wichita to Amarillo, and Kansas City to Clovis. In less than a decade the *San Francisco Chief* grew from a modest 12-car train to one carrying as many as 19. So Marsh bought more high-level coaches to maximize revenue at lower cost.

Okay, then, did Santa Fe's new 49-mile line to Dallas in 1955 really justify a separate Chicago-to-Dallas section of the Chicago–Galveston *Texas Chief*? Answer: No; the numbers just weren't there. Gurley's mistaken bet was that Dallas rather than Houston would become the megalopolis of Texas. But the railroad soon combined the trains north of Gainesville, Tex., and for the next dozen years filled three additional cars of the *Texas Chief* out of Chicago at relatively little extra expense.

What about those high-level cars for the *El Capitan* in 1956? Answer: At peak traffic periods, a conventional *El Cap* ran 16 cars, carried 438 people and weighed 1,069 tons. Fred Gurley's $13 million got Santa Fe a 13-car train (including the same head-end cars) that carried 130 additional people *and* weighed 110 tons less *and* required an on-board crew of four to six fewer people *and* freed some 65 almost-new coaches, diners and lounges for duty elsewhere in place of higher-maintenance heavyweight cars *and* kept the train short enough to be combined with the *Super Chief* more than eight months of the year. Passengers loved 'em.

The great comeback

Then by gosh (you must be getting exasperated by now), weren't Gurley, Marsh, Reed & Co. awfully brazen with the shareholders' assets, throwing around all this money for the sake of a good image and some congratulatory newspaper editorials? A fair indictment, if it were true. But that's the point: Its trains did well during the sixties, right up until the Post Office lowered the boom in 1967.

Using the Interstate Commerce Commission's method of fully allocating costs between passenger and freight traffic, Santa Fe went into the red on

passengers sometime before you or your parents were born. Using the ICC's other method of assigning to passenger trains only those expenses that are solely related to their operation—avoidable costs, if you will—an entirely different picture emerges.

The darkest hours came during 1954–1957, when a previously profitable operation (based on solely related costs) turned increasingly unprofitable, climaxing in 1957 with a deficit of some $10 million. During one period when the *Super Chief's* bookings nosedived, Reed remembers hearing Gurley proclaim, "Well, if this keeps up, I know exactly what I'll have to do. . . ." Recalls Reed: "Whatever he had in mind, it wasn't good."

Virtually all railroads saw business slump in the late 1950s. But few others recovered so thoroughly. In the midst of this downturn came those *El Capitan* high-level cars. The all-Pullman *Super Chief* and all-coach *El Cap* began running combined in non-peak periods on January 12, 1958. Trains dominated by heavyweight cars and some short-distance runs were pruned—for instance, the *Ranger* between Kansas

▶ *Photographer Patterson considers the* Chief *rather than the much-publicized* Super Chief *to have been Santa Fe's true flagship train. Westbound it needed but one night over the road to reach Los Angeles from Chicago, and accommodations (low-capacity coaches, dome lounge, sleeping cars) were the envy of competing railroads. Here the* Chief, *No. 19, nears Santa Fe's Argentine Yard in Kansas City, Kansas, in brilliant late afternoon sun on April 10, 1965. (Steve Patterson)*

City and Houston; the *Grand Canyon* section via Amarillo and Clovis; the eastbound *Kansas City Chief* and a matching Chicago–Kansas City local, and all but two of 16 branch line motor-car schedules that existed in 1953.

The effect: Passenger train miles fell 29 percent between 1954 and 1960. But passenger miles dropped only 13 percent, and passenger train revenues a mere 7 percent. By the ICC's solely related costs method, Santa Fe's passenger operations essentially broke even in 1959–1960, then earned $6.7 million in profits in 1961 and $5.4 million in 1962. Thereafter, until 1967, the passenger service generated either small profits or losses.

Finally, there's something intangible to consider, something you can't quantify. This railroad simply did not know how to run a substandard passenger train. It possessed the courage to buy new equipment in the mid 1950s and early 1960s to increase capacity and cut costs. It took ad-agency pioneer Leo Burnett on directors' specials, to soak up the sight and smell of Santa Fe territory as a lubricant to his creative inspiration. It included in every issue of *Santa Fe Magazine* letters of congratulation from satisfied passengers—letters naming names of exemplary employees. It applied silver paint to underbodies of cars and diesels before every backup move into Dearborn Station. Ever the class act, it

◀ *The San Francisco Chief was the last transcontinental train created from scratch. And from its start in 1954 it became wildly successful. Now a decade old, it tears eastward near Marmon, New Mexico, in 1964 with a set of smoky Alco PAs and a string of new high-level chair cars. (Jim Shaw)*

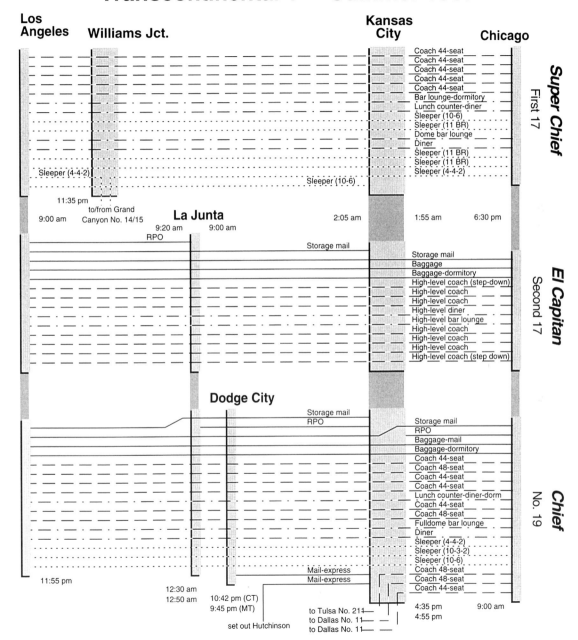

Transcontinental 1   Summer 1967

Super Chief / First 17

Los Angeles — Williams Jct. — Kansas City — Chicago

| Coach 44-seat |
| Coach 44-seat |
| Coach 44-seat |
| Coach 44-seat |
| Coach 44-seat |
| Bar lounge-dormitory |
| Lunch counter-diner |
| Sleeper (10-6) |
| Sleeper (11 BR) |
| Dome bar lounge |
| Diner |
| Sleeper (11 BR) |
| Sleeper (11 BR) |
| Sleeper (4-4-2) |

Sleeper (4-4-2)   Sleeper (10-6)

11:35 pm
9:00 am   to/from Grand Canyon No. 14/15   2:05 am   1:55 am   6:30 pm

La Junta
9:20 am   9:00 am
RPO
Storage mail

El Capitan / Second 17

| Storage mail |
| Baggage |
| Baggage-dormitory |
| High-level coach (step-down) |
| High-level coach |
| High-level coach |
| High-level diner |
| High-level bar lounge |
| High-level coach |
| High-level coach |
| High-level coach |
| High-level coach (step down) |

Dodge City
Storage mail
RPO

Chief / No. 19

| Storage mail |
| RPO |
| Baggage-mail |
| Baggage-dormitory |
| Coach 44-seat |
| Coach 48-seat |
| Coach 44-seat |
| Coach 44-seat |
| Lunch counter-diner-dorm |
| Coach 44-seat |
| Coach 48-seat |
| Fulldome bar lounge |
| Diner |
| Sleeper (4-4-2) |
| Sleeper (10-3-2) |
| Sleeper (10-6) |
| Coach 48-seat |
| Coach 48-seat |
| Coach 44-seat |

Mail-express
Mail-express

11:55 pm
12:30 am
12:50 am   10:42 pm (CT)
9:45 pm (MT)
set out Hutchinson   to Tulsa No. 211
to Dallas No. 11
to Dallas No. 11   4:35 pm   9:00 am
4:55 pm

made available a private dining room in the *Super Chief*'s dome lounge car. While he was Santa Fe's vice president of operations in the late 1960s, Larry Cena remarked: "When I look around for economies, I keep eyeing the passenger service. There are a lot of ways to cut corners on maintenance and save money. But I've never gone to Reed with those ideas because I know damn well he'd say no."

Single-track madness

People *did* complain. Timekeeping by Santa Fe's transcontinental trains was often a sometimes thing, made especially difficult by single-track operation by train orders across 668 miles of the northern line, between Hutchinson, Kansas, and Albuquerque. In the 1960s four to six 90-mile-per-hour passenger trains each way competed for space with several freights—four passenger trains most months, five in summer and at Christmas, and six one day a week in summer when a special train chartered by travel agencies ran as an advance section of the *Chief*. The worst of it occurred between Las Vegas, N.M., and Albuquerque, 131 miles. There you were apt, each summer afternoon, to find separate *Super Chiefs* and *El Capitans* going

◀ *The* Super Chief *and* El Capitan *ran separately each holiday season and summer through 1969. Most times, however, the* Super's *section carried four or five flattop coaches in front of its sleepers. But on this July day in 1968 the* Super Chief (top) *is a pure sleeping car train passing Lamy, New Mexico, while the* El Cap *carries the extra coaches. (John C. Lucas)*

Transcontinental 2 Summer 1967

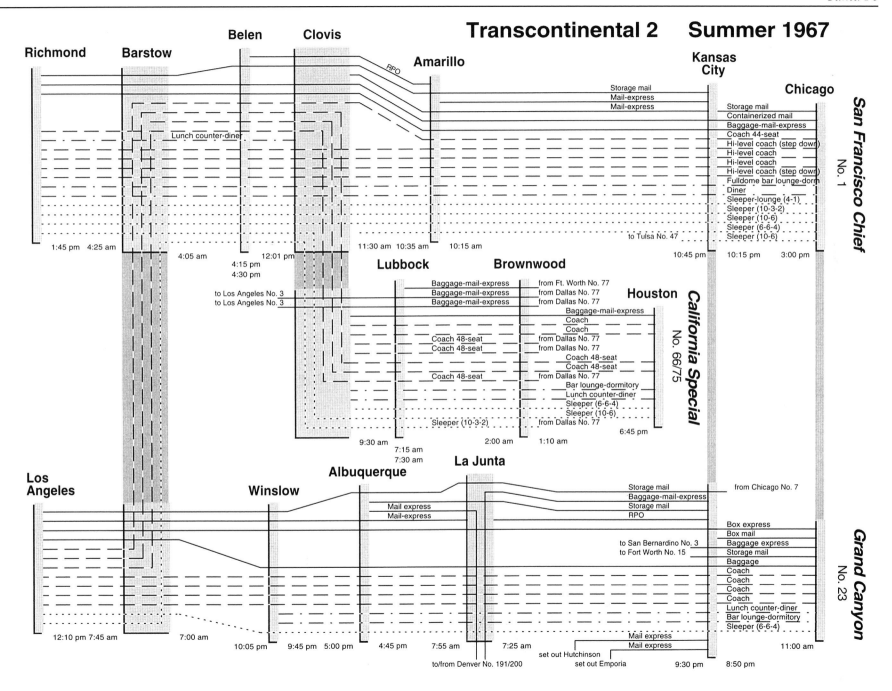

Richmond | Barstow | Belen | Clovis | Amarillo | Kansas City | Chicago

San Francisco Chief No. 1

RPO

Storage mail
Mail-express
Mail-express
Storage mail
Containerized mail
Baggage-mail-express
Coach 44-seat
Hi-level coach (step down)
Hi-level coach
Hi-level coach
Hi-level coach (step down)
Fulldome bar lounge-dorm
Diner
Sleeper-lounge (4-1)
Sleeper (10-3-2)
Sleeper (10-6)
Sleeper (6-6-4)
Sleeper (10-6)

Lunch counter-diner

to Tulsa No. 47

1:45 pm   4:25 am   4:05 am   12:01 pm   11:30 am 10:35 am   10:15 am   10:45 pm   10:15 pm   3:00 pm

4:15 pm
4:30 pm

to Los Angeles No. 3
to Los Angeles No. 3

Lubbock | Brownwood | Houston

California Special No. 66/75

Baggage-mail-express   from Ft. Worth No. 77
Baggage-mail-express   from Dallas No. 77
Baggage-mail-express   from Dallas No. 77
Baggage-mail-express
Coach
Coach
Coach 48-seat   from Dallas No. 77
Coach 48-seat   from Dallas No. 77
Coach 48-seat
Coach 48-seat
Coach 48-seat   from Dallas No. 77
Bar lounge-dormitory
Lunch counter-diner
Sleeper (6-6-4)
Sleeper (10-6)
Sleeper (10-3-2)   from Dallas No. 77

6:45 pm

9:30 am   7:15 am   2:00 am   1:10 am
          7:30 am

Los Angeles | Winslow | Albuquerque | La Junta

Grand Canyon No. 23

Storage mail   from Chicago No. 7
Baggage-mail-express
Storage mail
RPO
Mail express
Mail-express
Box express
Box mail
Baggage express
to San Bernardino No. 3   Storage mail
to Fort Worth No. 15   Baggage
Coach
Coach
Coach
Coach
Lunch counter-diner
Bar lounge-dormitory
Sleeper (6-6-4)

Mail express
Mail express

12:10 pm 7:45 am   7:00 am   10:05 pm   9:45 pm   5:00 pm   4:45 pm   7:55 am   7:25 am   set out Hutchinson   11:00 am
                                                                                                  set out Emporia

to/from Denver No. 191/200   9:30 pm   8:50 pm

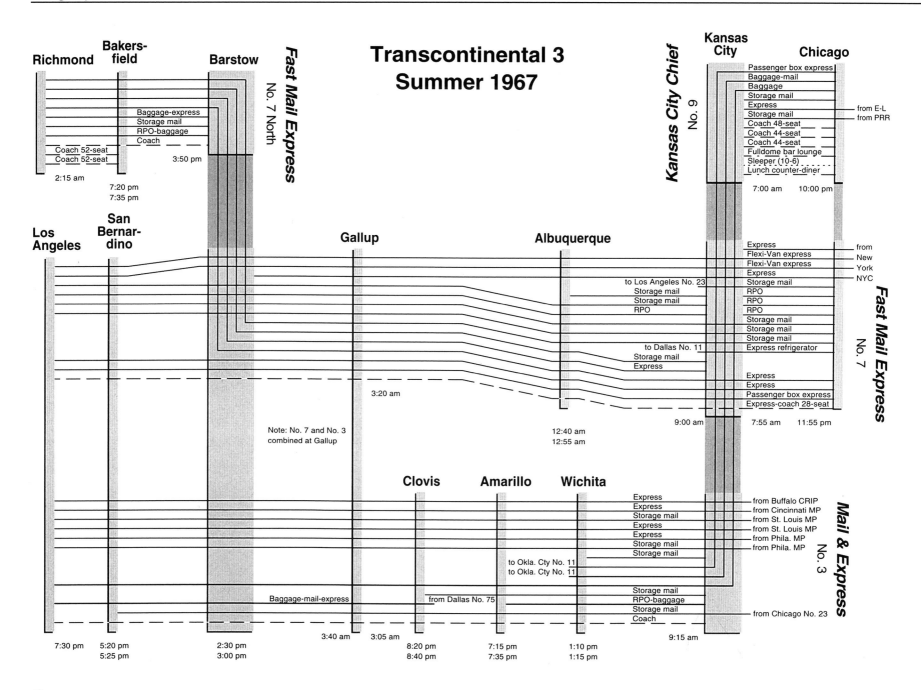

Transcontinental 3
Summer 1967

Richmond

Bakers-field

Barstow

Fast Mail Express
No. 7 North

Baggage-express
Storage mail
RPO-baggage
Coach

Coach 52-seat
Coach 52-seat

3:50 pm

2:15 am

7:20 pm
7:35 pm

Kansas City Chief
No. 9

Kansas City

Chicago

Passenger box express
Baggage-mail
Baggage
Storage mail
Express
Storage mail
Coach 48-seat
Coach 44-seat
Coach 44-seat
Fulldome bar lounge
Sleeper (10-6)
Lunch counter-diner

from E-L
from PRR

7:00 am   10:00 pm

Los Angeles

San Bernar-dino

Gallup

Albuquerque

Express
Flexi-Van express
Flexi-Van express
Express
Storage mail
RPO
RPO
RPO
Storage mail
Storage mail
Storage mail
Express refrigerator

Express
Express
Passenger box express
Express-coach 28-seat

from
New
York
NYC

to Los Angeles No. 23
Storage mail
Storage mail
RPO

to Dallas No. 11
Storage mail
Express

Fast Mail Express
No. 7

3:20 am

Note: No. 7 and No. 3
combined at Gallup

12:40 am
12:55 am

9:00 am   7:55 am   11:55 pm

Clovis   Amarillo   Wichita

Express
Express
Storage mail
Express
Express
Storage mail
Storage mail

to Okla. Cty No. 11
to Okla. Cty No. 11

from Buffalo CRIP
from Cincinnati MP
from St. Louis MP
from St. Louis MP
from Phila. MP
from Phila. MP

Mail & Express
No. 3

Baggage-mail-express

from Dallas No. 75

Storage mail
RPO-baggage
Storage mail
Coach

from Chicago No. 23

9:15 am

7:30 pm   5:20 pm
          5:25 pm

2:30 pm
3:00 pm

3:40 am   3:05 am

8:20 pm   7:15 pm   1:10 pm
8:40 pm   7:35 pm   1:15 pm

▶ *Trains 3 and 4 were mail trains running between Kansas City and Gallup via Wichita, Amarillo and Belen. Unlike the* Fast Mail Express *running via the Northern District, 3 and 4 accepted passengers in their single heavyweight coach. Here, 4 enters Kaycee in October 1966, a year before its demise. (Steve Patterson)*

east and west toward one another as each set of trains overtook the preceding *Grand Canyon* in each direction, perhaps as a 8,400-ton York Canyon coal train crept west toward Glorieta Pass. That's something like 18 meets and overtakes in perhaps 90 minutes, usually occurring in the 65 miles west of Las Vegas without train order offices to keep the train dispatcher abreast of things.

The railroad allowed zero tolerance for sloppy dispatching over this vast distance. What did a dispatcher do? Well, you laid out a plan, and prayed you could make adjustments when things went wrong, as they always did. Unless told otherwise, you stuck to the pecking order when plotting meets and deciding which train took siding, avoiding unnecessary delay to the *Super Chief, El Capitan, Chief, Grand Canyon,* hot freights, *Fast Mail Express* and drag freights, in that order.

Case in point: Wednesday, July 26, 1967, between Dodge City, Kan., and La Junta, Colo.—202.4 miles of 90-mile-per-hour speedway. No. 8, the eastbound *Fast Mail Express,* leaves La Junta with 11 cars at 6:34 a.m., nine minutes late, holding train orders instructing it to take siding and meet No. 23 (the westbound *Grand Canyon*) 27 miles east at Hilton, Colo.; First 17 (*Super Chief*) at Coolidge, Kan.; Second 17 (*El Cap*) at Syracuse, Kan., and Extra 236C West (symbol freight No. 35 to Denver) at Lakin.

The meet with No. 23 is perfection; No. 8's conductor later reports only a five-minute delay—the very least you'd incur entering and leaving a siding—and train 23's goes past unimpeded. But Second 17 is hung up at Dodge City by a steam-generator problem that roundhouse mechanics are wrestling with.

❐ 7:29 a.m. As first-trick dispatcher T. C. Hiestand sits down in front of trainsheet and microphone, the agent at Lamar, Colo., comes on the speaker: No. 8 just arrived with a broken airbrake pipe on unit 28B, the middle of its five Fs.

❐ 7:31 a.m. Lakin's agent reports First 17 by, kicking up a storm. If it maintains its scheduled speed, the *Super* will cover the 29.6 miles to Syracuse in 21 minutes. But it was 14 minutes late passing Lakin, so it will probably do even better. And

Syracuse is the last open office it passes before Coolidge, the meeting point with No. 8.

❐ 7:44 a.m. Hiestand dictates an order to First 17 at Syracuse and No. 8 at Lamar, resetting the meeting point to Barton, Colo., 13 miles west of Coolidge and 21 miles east of Lamar. That buys him time. Should No. 8 remain immobilized, he can change the orders again via the agents at either Coolidge or Holly, Colo., six miles west of Coolidge, without stopping First 17.

❐ 7:47 a.m. Second 17, its steam-generator problem solved, pops out of Dodge City with the *El Cap,* 89 minutes late, followed three minutes later by Extra 236C West.

❐ 7:51 a.m. First 17 passes Syracuse. It averaged 89 miles per hour from Lakin. Can you imagine the nerves of First 17's crew snaring that train order

from the delivery stand? At that speed, if you touch anything but the string that holds the order, you'll break a bone.

❐ 7:58 a.m. Eureka! The *Fast Mail*'s airbrakes again function. A hurried train order to it at Lamar and First 17 at Holly moves the final meeting point between the trains another 10 miles nearer Lamar from Barton, to Grote, Colo. It's a textbook meet; No. 8 will report a seven-minute delay getting in and out of the siding, without snagging First 17.

❐ 8:20 a.m. Looks as if Syracuse, the original meeting point between No. 8 and Second 17 (*El Capitan*) will hold up. Both trains took delays, and it sort of averages out. But uh-oh. A westbound drag freight distributing empty boxcars to grain elevators already sits on the siding at Syracuse. So Hiestand dictates a message to No. 8 at Holly: EXTRA 252C WEST ON SIDING SYRACUSE. MAY BE NECESSARY YOU TO BACK OUT AFTER MEETING 2/17.

❐ 8:30 a.m. Hiestand has second thoughts. He sends an order to Second 17 at Deerfield, Kan., and to No. 8 at Syracuse moving the meeting point one station and 12 miles east, to Kendall, Kan. Then Hiestand thinks better of that, and never completes the order for delivery. Good thing—he'd have stuck *El Cap* for seven or eight minutes. But the *Fast Mail* loses 23 minutes making maneuvers at Syracuse around Second 17 and the drag freight, leaving at 9:18 a.m., now 74 minutes late.

❐ 8:41 a.m. An order to No. 8 at Syracuse and

◄ *A timeless moment: The westbound* Fast Mail Express *drops the semaphore 12 miles west of La Junta, Colorado, as it rushes past at 90 mph late on the afternoon of October 1, 1967. Nobody knew it then, but 17 days later the* Mail *would run its last mile. (Victor Hand)*

Extra 236C West at Garden City resets their meeting point at Holcomb, Kan., just west of Garden City, instead of Lakin.

❐ 9:17 a.m. Oops . . . change that. Now that the magnitude of No. 8's delay at Syracuse is clear, Hiestand changes the meet with the westbound redball to eight miles west of Holcomb, at Deerfield. In retrospect, he should have left well enough alone. The *Fast Mail* is stuck another 15 minutes sittin' and waitin', and finally reaches Dodge City 56 minutes late. But there's slack in the *Mail*'s schedule, and it may yet make Kansas City on time.

Alas, Hiestand's troubles continue. That afternoon, the westbound *Fast Mail Express* loses power on one of its four Alco PA units while leaving the siding at Lakin, where it met the eastbound *Chief*. It lopes westward at about 55 miles per hour. Hiestand calls the diesel shop at La Junta, which sends an electrician by auto to meet No. 7 at Lamar. Result: 48 minutes of lost time. One of those days . . .

Eight across the continent

During the summers of 1966 and 1967 I sometimes go to Chicago's Dearborn Station in the morning to witness the loading of the *Chief* for Los Angeles. As much as the *Super Chief,* No. 19 embodies the Santa Fe ethic—luxury, speed and spit-'n-polish service. Outside, the 19-car train, led by five glistening F units, stretches far beyond the cool trainshed into the hot morning sun. Porters and car attendants stand beside their steps at the vestibules. Late mail is tossed into the stainless steel RPO car. Beneath Dearborn's bell tower on Polk Street just south of the Loop, the small waiting room can't begin to hold those waiting to board.

The gates open and a flood of humanity spills into the gloom of the trainshed. From the rear, you first pass the three Kansas City setout coaches, two bound from there to Dallas on the *Kansas Cityan* and the third for the *Tulsan*. Then come the three Los Angeles sleepers, the dining car and the

fulldome bar lounge. Now, as your shoulders ache from walking your luggage some 700 feet from the bumper post, you're alongside the Los Angeles coaches—six of 'em, spliced two cars up by a lunch counter-diner-dormitory. Still ahead of you are the baggage-dormitory, a baggage-mail car, the RPO and a car of storage mail. Finally, those F units. In all, a gleaming ribbon of stainless steel stretching more than one-third of a mile.

So savor the dimensions of this magnificent transportation machine. From Chicago in mid 1967 there were separate sections of the *Super Chief-El Capitan,* plus the *Chief, Grand Canyon* and *Fast Mail Express*— all to Los Angeles. The *San Francisco Chief* linked Chicago and Northern California, and nameless trains 3 and 4 joined it across the Southern District freight-train corridor between Kansas City and Gallup, New Mexico. From Houston and Fort Worth came a 16-car *California Special* to connect with the *San Francisco Chief* at Clovis. That's eight trains with continental agendas. Twice-daily service linked Chicago and Kansas City with Texas. There were two Kansas City–Tulsa trains each day, three *San Diegan* round trips from Los Angeles, a pair of passenger-carrying mail trains between Barstow and San Francisco Bay and branch line passenger trains to Denver; El Paso; Phoenix; San Angelo, Texas; Carlsbad, N.M., and Grand Canyon, Ariz.

All the while, management trimmed weak branches. The Houston–Galveston leg of the *Texas Chief* disappeared in mid 1967—in its last years, just a lightweight baggage car and coach connecting with the main train. On August 28, the Clovis–Carlsbad local made its last run. The *Golden Gate* trains between Richmond, Cal., and Bakersfield succumbed in 1962–1963, and the *San Diegan* streamliners were pared until the seven round trips of 1957 had become three. Rumor had it that the *Oil Flyer* between Kansas City and Tulsa would go next; late in 1966, to stimulate ridership, Santa Fe had added a snack diner-lounge (car 1396) and restored a

Chicago–Tulsa sleeper (taken off in 1965) to this coach-only train, but results weren't encouraging.

Disarray and retreat

Before Columbus Day, everything just collapsed. A quarter century later, Reed could recall few premonitions. "You could see it coming a little bit," he concedes, "because so many railroads were withdrawing trains that the Postal Service had used." But Santa Fe's own trends weren't encouraging, either. Coach revenues, which accounted for one-third of all passenger-service receipts and had remained constant at about $30 million annually for years, would end the year off 15 percent.

Fewer people showed up in 1967, and those that did tended to ride shorter distances. Ridership of the *Chief* dropped 10 percent in 1967 from 1966 levels, and the average customer rode 5 percent fewer miles. Ridership of the *Grand Canyon* fell 14 percent, and the typical trip length toppled 18 per-

cent, to 556 miles. When both passenger counts and trip lengths work against you, revenues retreat at double time. "I guess," says Reed in hindsight, "we were still hoping to make the best of it."

He lost all illusions right after Labor Day. The Postal Service informed the railroad that as of October 16 it would cancel the lucrative railway post office contracts. First-class mail would move by air on a space-available basis, and sorting would occur at regional distribution centers. Second- and third-class storage mail carried in the future would be at rates 20 percent lower than those then in effect. Given the option of hauling the remaining mail by either freight or passenger train, Santa Fe naturally chose the lower-cost freights.

September turned to October, yet not a word was said publicly about the scythe coming down on the passenger service. His associates say Reed simply couldn't give up hope. "He had a hard time with this," says Cena. "Knowing how much first-

▲ This matched set of E6 locomotives, fronting the Chicagoan *from Dallas, looks regal rounding a curve near Waukarusa, Kansas, with train 12 in October 1966. Santa Fe's fleet of Es worked this train, its sister train, the* Kansas Cityan, *and some branch line runs.*
(Steve Patterson)

class mail we carried, maybe he thought that moving it all by air simply would not work." Adds Jack Barriger, then the superintendent of transportation: "Reed was very reluctant to make decisions that affected Santa Fe's corporate being. We worked very hard on our image. I'm sure he thought in those terms."

John Reed, an intensely private, contemplative

Texas-Oklahoma streamliners
Summer 1967

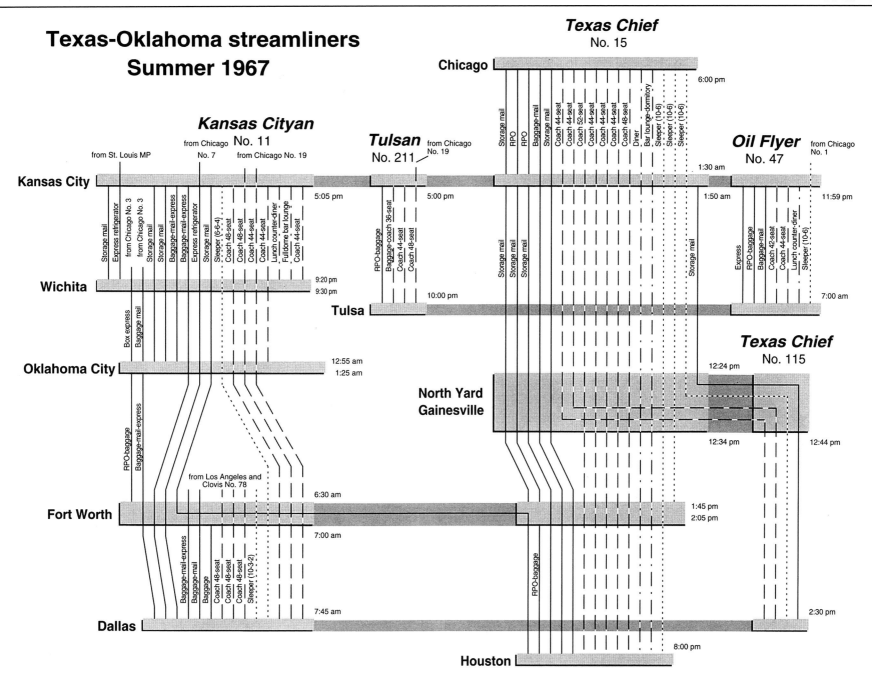

▲ *Passengers and baggage man await the southbound* Texas Chief *in 1965 as it pulls past the combination station and Southern Division office building in Temple, Texas. (J. Parker Lamb)*

◀ *Three years after the above photo, and 44 miles to the south, the* Texas Chief *snags train orders at Milano. Note the new General Electric power and off-season high-level coaches. (J. Parker Lamb)*

man, bided his time. "We didn't have a choice," Reed later explained. "The losses would be so devastating after we lost the mail. It wasn't fair to the company not to stop the flow of blood. All we could vow to do was to keep standards high on those trains that remained." Finally, on October 4, Reed called a press conference to lay it out: A "restructuring" would eliminate all but two of the transcontinental trains, leaving only the *Super Chief–El Capitan* and *San Francisco Chief*. Stated more bluntly, Santa Fe wanted to rid itself of everything but those two trains, the *Texas Chief* and the three *San Diegans*. Capitulation of the West's most pro-passenger railroad that day became a national news story.

Last departures of the *Fast Mail Express* from Chicago and Los Angeles were October 18. Trains 3 and 4, the *Fast Mail's* sister train between Kansas City and Gallup via the Southern District, went then, too. But train-off notices for the other trains didn't go up until after the Christmas-New Years holidays. Those days became a sort of last hurrah for Santa Fe passenger service. The *Super Chief* and *El Capitan* ran separately. The *Chief's* regular train was followed by a second section between Chicago and Kansas City. Out of Chicago went separate Houston and Dallas sections of the *Texas Chief*.

A *Chief's* untimely death

Come early 1968, public attention focused on the fates of the *Chief* and *Grand Canyon*. The Interstate Commerce Commission held hearings. Given the outpouring of testimony from governors, members of Congress, state regulators, businesses whose employees used these trains and ordinary passengers, it seemed possible that one of the two would be spared for a while—probably the more-traveled *Chief*. "We would rather have gotten rid of the *Grand Canyon*," says Reed. "It was our deadhead train and wasn't what you'd call great."

Evidence Santa Fe presented at the hearings was odd in the extreme. For the first nine months of

1967, latest date for which accounting was final, both trains had made money—$137,873 by the *Chief* and $221,418 by the *Grand Canyon.* (In 1966, the *Grand Canyon* had cleared its costs by $1.7 million, thanks largely to the mail carried aboard it.) But Santa Fe also calculated what the January–September results would have been without the mail and express revenue: a loss for the *Chief* of $1.2 million and for the *Grand Canyon* of $1.7 million.

The verdict on May 8: Drop the *Chief,* keep the *Grand Canyon.* I still cannot fathom the logic used to reach the tortured conclusion that the train losing the most money and carrying by far the fewer people should be the one to remain. The commission said the *Grand Canyon* stopped at more tiny towns than the *Chief,* and thus should be spared.

The wise men in Washington had spoken and that was that. The *Chief* made its last runs on May 13. People in the Passenger Traffic Department were stunned. "There was a fellow in the downtown ticket office named Max Strohm," relates Reed. "He went to Dearborn Station to see the last *Chief* leave, and the *Chicago Tribune* the next morning ran a front-page photo of Max with tears in his eyes. He died very shortly thereafter of a heart attack. I guess he sort of fell on his sword." (Footnote: The commission noted that it lacked authority to order Santa Fe to alter the *Grand Canyon's* schedule, cut its run-

▶ *In 1967, Santa Fe bought from Electro-Motive nine 3,600-hp passenger locomotives. Dubbed the FP45, most remained in service three decades later. Here in 1968 train 17, the* Super Chief– El Capitan, *crests the summit of Glorieta Pass in New Mexico, with FP45 101 in the lead. (John C. Lucas)*

◀ *Engine 102, at Lamy, New Mexico, carries green flags, indicating that Second 18, the* El Capitan *section, is on its way. Actually the* Super Chief *section has five coaches and lunch counter and lounge cars to serve non-first class riders on this August 1968 afternoon. (John C. Lucas)*

ing ideas continued as before. Reed became interested in a Taos, N.M., ski package linked to the *Super Chief–El Capitan* and wanted it promoted vigorously. During the summers of 1968 and 1969, that train ran yet again in two sections.

Remaining trains shared the best equipment. The *San Francisco Chief* got the fulldome bar lounges once assigned to the *Chief,* and the *Texas Chief* traded its flattop lounge-dormitory cars for fulldome bar lounge-dormitory cars given up by the *San Francisco Chief.* From September through May, high-level coaches were available to equip the *Texas Chief* in addition to the *El Cap* and *San Francisco Chief.*

The boss as devotee

What matter of man would consider his passenger trains the world's window on his railroad and retain his pride in them, no matter what? In 1969 I came to know such a person, John Reed. I was assigned by the *Chicago Sun-Times* to write a profile of Santa Fe's 53-year-old president. Reed consented and suggested that we talk aboard business car *Santa Fe* between Chicago and Lawrence, Kan., on train 23. I'd been told that Reed was a closet railfan. And true enough, as the interview progressed across the Illinois Division, I heard of a boyhood not much different from my own in one respect—a deep, uncompromising love of trains, to the exclusion of just about everything else.

ning time or restore its dining service, eliminated a few months earlier in favor of old-fashioned meal stops. But the ICC said it would be *nice* if Santa Fe did so. And Santa Fe—always the class act—within a month cut the Chicago–Los Angeles times of trains 23 and 24 by some three hours, adjusted schedules as suggested and added a lunch counter-diner.)

The Houston–Clovis *California Special* and its Fort Worth–Brownwood–San Angelo connection, the *Angelo,* made their last trips on July 18, 1968. Precisely three months earlier, the Kansas City–Dallas *Kansas Cityan,* the Dallas–Chicago *Chicagoan* and the Chicago–Kansas City *Kansas City Chief* were

dropped. Ultimately Santa Fe got its way with regulators on all the doomed trains but two: trains 23-24 and the La Junta–Denver local.

Another three years would pass from May 13, 1968, to the startup of Amtrak. Without the mail and express to support the trains, and with ridership slowly ebbing, losses became horrific. Figures the railroad gave regulators indicated an out-of-pocket deficit for the *San Francisco Chief* in 1969 of almost $4 million. Trains 23 and 24 (the former *Grand Canyon*) lost some $3.5 million that year. But I don't recall Santa Fe's people sulking about lost glories. Family fares, promotions and other revenue-build-

He was the grandson of John Shedd, a co-founder of Chicago's Marshall Field department store. "I guess my first awareness of railroads was from riding the old *California Limited*," Reed said. "We used to go out to California every year to visit my grandfather until he died in 1926. I think I was 4 years old when this started and we went every year thereafter until I was 9. The night before we would leave on that train I couldn't digest my food, I was so excited. And I remember having a temper tantrum at Pasadena because I didn't want the ride to end. I wanted to stay on the train and never get off."

After her husband's death—and the early, unexpected death of Reed's own father, who ran the Marshall Field store on State Street—grandmother Shedd chartered a Pullman and took her brood of grandchildren on a sort of Grand Tour of the American Northwest and Canada. Young John Reed was in heaven. "On the Northern Pacific they had just received their 2600-class 4-8-4 engines. [I made note of the fact that Reed knew his steam-era rosters exceedingly well.] They let me ride in one of these when our car was attached to the *North Coast Limited*. I also rode in the cab of a Canadian Pacific train going up Kicking Horse Pass in British Columbia. We almost stalled in one of the tunnels and I was about to pass out from the smoke. Then the fireman put his glove over my nose and I was able to breathe."

Back in suburban Lake Forest, Reed found a kindred spirit in Reuben deLaunty, his grandmother's chauffeur. They began converting anything with wheels into make-believe steam locomotives. When Reed was 12, they bought the real thing, a Stanley Steamer, at a South Side junkyard for $200 and converted it into a rubber-tired iron horse. "Reuben did the work on it and I . . . uh . . . I supervised. I

At the west end of Kansas City Union Station, No. 23 (Grand Canyon), Tulsan *and* San Francisco Chief *await highballs, on April 24, 1971. Six days later all would become footnotes in history. (Fred W. Frailey)

guess you'd say I studied locomotive design and told him where to put things. That was quite a job. All the controls had to be moved to the back of the car, where we built the cab. We even tried to add an air compressor and air brakes, but they didn't work well."

John Reed subsequently took a home-correspondence course on operating a steam locomotive, and upon completing his education (Chicago's Latin School, Hotchkis, Yale) in 1939 summoned his courage and got an appointment with John Purcell, Santa Fe's chief mechanical officer and a legendary figure who had, in his time, done just about everything on the railroad that involved getting your hands dirty. He asked Purcell for a job firing locomotives. Purcell just laughed. "Young fella," Reed quoted him as saying, "I've never seen a Yale man yet who could fire one of my locomotives well enough to get it from Chicago to Joliet." Reed never fired steam en-

gines. After service in the Navy during World War II Santa Fe made him a transportation inspector in Amarillo. Two decades later he was running the railroad.

That was quite a story. So are you, I asked him, the rarest of all rare birds in 1970—a railfan railroad president? I hoped he would admit as much. Frankly, in that era, for a railroader to say he enjoyed the sight of a passing train was a cardinal sin. As top gun, Reed could dispel the curse. But the man, conditioned as he was, didn't rise to the occasion. "I guess you can combine enjoying trains and operating a railroad. But railfans today have a different relationship to railroad managements than they did when I was a railfan. In my railfan days, I wasn't interested in the old locomotives or diamond-stacks. I was driving to Schenectady from Yale to see the new Mohawks and Mountains coming out of the Alco plant. But now the typical railfan—or at least the one who bugs me the most—is living in the past and wants to have everything maintained just the way it was in 1895. They would keep you from doing things any prudent management has to do.

"Maybe I'm being unfair to the railfans. I'll grant you there isn't much excitement to some new electric locomotives or diesels as compared to the old-style railroading. Still, when you have crazy people intervening in branch line passenger train-off cases . . . that's the kind of nut that gets in your hair. So am I a railfan? That's not the right word for me, because I think of a fan as a spectator and not as a participant. I'm a participant."

Well, okay. A few days later he sent to the *Sun-Times* a photo of his beloved Stanley Steamer of 1929—a 2-4-2 arrangement with whistle, pilot, feedwater heater, driving rods and number board. Then he consented to come to 18th Street coach yard to pose for a story-opening photograph in front of his railroad's passenger equipment. He could easily have said he wanted to be photographed at Corwith freight yard and gotten his way.

John Reed, all protests notwithstanding, was the real thing—as much a railfan in the president's office of a major railroad as we were likely to see for a while. In life, at least, he acted the part. Until Amtrak's arrival, Reed saw that his passenger trains were run as a railfan would want—for that matter, as Fred Gurley and Ernest Marsh would demand. That's Santa Fe for you. Or as Reed put it recently: "If you're going to run something, it had better be good. Otherwise, they'll be making jokes about you."

Super Chief postscript

The railroad came within a hair of dismissing Amtrak—of deciding (like Southern, Rio Grande and Rock Island) not to join the fledgling passenger train company in 1971. Santa Fe's corporate soul was inexorably linked to its passenger traditions, and to break that link was as difficult as for a mother to disown her child. "Reed didn't want *anyone* running passenger trains across Santa Fe but Santa Fe," says Bill Burk, head of public relations then. "Those trains were the pride and joy of the railroad—the pride and joy of the nation, as far as he was concerned. But when it came down to nut cuttin', he didn't have much choice."

Could he have run only the trains Amtrak chose to run—the *Super Chief–El Capitan*, *Texas Chief* and *San Diegans*—Reed says he could have convinced his board of directors to stay out of Amtrak. "John kept hoping there was another out," says Cena. "He wanted someone to reassure him we could dispose of most operations, keep a few trains and go it alone." But the law creating Amtrak didn't read that way. You'd be stuck with whatever you already ran, for at least three more years, and that also included the *San Francisco Chief* and trains 23 and 24 across the country, plus the *Tulsan* from Kansas City and the pair of trains between Denver and La Junta.

San Francisco Chief *conductor H. C. Dewey, going on duty in Richmond, California, personified all that was classy about Santa Fe passenger service. (Ted Benson)*

Reed, still undecided, named Jack Barriger to head a committee to recommend a course of action to the directors. Says Barriger: "He saw those trains as symbols of the railroad. And he, like myself, had a love for that part of the business." Barringer's group extrapolated current revenue and cost trends and concluded that Santa Fe's real, after-tax losses on passenger trains would exceed $35 million a year by 1975 if it didn't join Amtrak, but that its cash flow would rise an aggregate of $117 million by then if it did join. "It wasn't even a close decision," says

Barriger. "Within three years our passenger losses would wipe out the earnings of the entire company." Santa Fe signed up.

Reed found divorce from passenger trains hard to accept. Once, inspecting the Amtrak *Texas Chief* with Burk at Fort Worth, he remarked that Amtrak's purple-and-blue interior colors resembled "a French whore house." When *Business Week* quoted him to that effect (courtesy of a leak by Burk) Reed was genuinely upset—"I don't talk that way; maybe I said 'a French house of ill repute' "—until reminded by Burk that he had uttered the remark.

The Santa Fe president took to dropping by Chicago Union Station on his way from work to the commuter train, to walk through the *Super Chief* cars prior to boarding time. He didn't like what he saw. Santa Fe's Amtrak operations officer, E. L. Peterson, a man who never minced words, undoubtedly gave Reed an earful about Amtrak's lax standards. So, no doubt, did crews aboard the *Super Chief*, all of them Santa Fe veterans. In mid 1973 he had seen enough. Reed wrote Roger Lewis, reminding Amtrak's first president that Santa Fe held rights to the name *Chief* and saying that he could no longer sanction its use. Thus were interred, perhaps forever, the names *Super Chief* and *Texas Chief*.

That letter supplied the healing hand. Afterward everyone got along much better. Reed was, of course, absolutely right: Amtrak wasn't up to running a train as well as Santa Fe. But who was?

▶ *Just like old times: Five F units pull the last pre-Amtrak* Super Chief–El Capitan *through Apache Canyon in Glorieta Pass, New Mexico, on May 1, 1971. (John C. Lucas)*

KATY DID

This little railroad ran passenger trains in seeming defiance of economic realities. Too soon, the bills came due.

◄ Quintessential Katy: On a rainy April day in 1960, No. 5, the southbound Katy Flyer, pauses for lunch in Parsons, Kansas. Now a passenger carefully walks across a wet brick platform from the lunchroom to the comforts of the train's single coach. Today's mail is almost loaded aboard the 60-foot RPO car, so departure for Oswego and Chetopa, Vinita and Big Cabin, Eufaula and Stringtown, Atoka and Durant cannot be far off. Supper will be in the Denison, Texas, depot. The Katy Flyer, you see, was a creature of small-town America and its people. Thank David Strassman for this engaging scene, worthy of a Norman Rockwell portrait.

The finest show in Northeast Texas railroading begins at 5 a.m. in Denison. "OS Staley," reports a voice from the tower on the Oklahoma bank of the Red River, to the dispatcher. "Number 1, by at 4:59." A revolving headlight jabs across the dark northern sky. Then, topping a 1.3 percent grade from the river bottoms, appears the crown jewel of Missouri–Kansas–Texas—the San Antonio-bound *Texas Special*, now fewer than 12 hours out of St. Louis. Awaiting it is the whole *apparat* so common in pre-Amtrak days—the baggage wagons and express handlers, the car inspectors, the ice and commissary people, the mail and diesel-fuel folks, the yardmaster, the switch-engine crew for tearing the train apart and of course the outbound crew. From the second floor of the big brick depot, the North Texas Division dispatcher issues final train orders for No. 1 to the operator at Leigh Tower, a mile to the south. Couplers mate, break apart, remate. The blue flag comes down. By 5:25, the *Texas Special* is on its way toward Dallas and South Texas.

Close behind the *Special* comes No. 7, the *Bluebonnet* out of Kansas City, in custody of two red, cream and white Alco PAs. On an adjoining track, coaches, sleepers and mail cars from both No. 1 and No. 7 mate with a heavyweight coach, diner-lounge, railway post office car and two FP7s to form No. 21, a 10-car connection to Fort Worth and Houston. Just 15 minutes after the *Bluebonnet's* arrival, this train veers to the west toward the Fort Worth line. Then the *Bluebonnet* itself leaves for its appointment with the *Texas Special* in Dallas, where Seven Spot, the diminutive 0-6-0 switcher belonging to Dallas Union Terminal and perhaps the last working steam locomotive in Texas, will plume exhaust into the morning sky merging the trains for the trip toward San Antonio.

There's more. On the far track, an RPO-baggage and heavyweight coach, pulled by a Fairbanks-Morse roadswitcher, leaves at 6:15 a.m. toward a 9:40 a.m. arrival in Wichita Falls on Katy's dirt-tracked Northwest District. In all, four southbound departures from Denison in 50 minutes, as the town wakes up.

Don't you wish you'd been there? The year was 1956. Then you'd have thought that this routine would never end. But it did.

Life in the fast lane

Thus it went during the early Indian summer for MKT's passenger trains. By 1956, the season of plenty grew short for the Katy. Like other regional railroads—Lehigh Valley, Maine Central, Chicago Great Western, Florida East Coast, Boston & Maine, Monon and Jersey Central, to name but several—it could

not maintain its intercity passenger trains through the 1960s and into Amtrak's arms. Yet so downhome were Katy's trains that to tell the story of that decade and ignore the struggles of this woebegone southwestern railroad would be akin to shunning a sick aunt. God bless Katy! This little railroad, least able of all to afford a big show, didn't just run pas-

senger trains but whole fleets that intersected to touch every point on the main stems between Kansas City and San Antonio at least twice a day. Were Amtrak to attempt such switching acrobatics today, you could imagine the time it would allot. Katy's people did it as a matter of routine, in minutes.

The *Texas Special* of 1956, a joint venture with St. Louis–San Francisco Railway via the crossing of the two railroads at Vinita in northeast Oklahoma, was the pivot around which the other trains turned. On its point would usually be two E7 or E8 locomotives assigned by the Katy and Frisco to this service. And behind them came a (usually) unbroken string of silver-fluted, Pullman-made lightweight cars with red window bands and roofs and white lettering, capped by a classy observation car with a drawing room, two bedrooms and bar lounge. I say "usually" because Katy and Frisco erred in assum-

◀ *Soon before it was truncated to run only between Kansas City and Dallas, the southbound* Bluebonnet *approaches San Antonio; the sun gleaming off the side of its heavyweight cars and Alco PS Diesels. (Jim McClellan)*

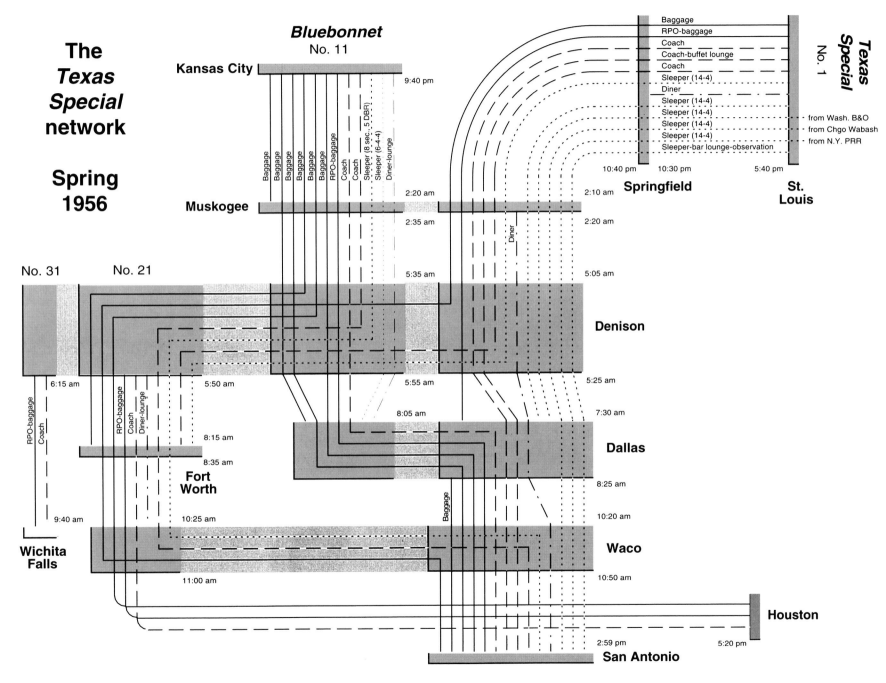

The
Texas
Special
network

Spring
1956

Bluebonnet
No. 11

Kansas City

9:40 pm

Baggage
Baggage
Baggage
Baggage
Baggage
RPO-baggage
Coach
Coach
Sleeper (8 sec., 5 DBR)
Sleeper (6-4-4)
Diner-lounge

Muskogee
2:20 am
2:35 am
5:35 am

2:10 am
2:20 am
5:05 am

Diner

No. 31   No. 21

Denison

6:15 am
RPO-baggage
Coach

5:50 am
RPO-baggage
Coach
Diner-lounge

5:55 am
8:05 am

5:25 am
7:30 am

8:15 am

Dallas

8:35 am
Fort Worth

8:25 am

9:40 am

10:25 am

10:20 am

Wichita Falls

Baggage

Waco

11:00 am
10:50 am

Baggage
RPO-baggage
Coach
Coach-buffet lounge
Coach
Sleeper (14-4)
Diner
Sleeper (14-4)
Sleeper (14-4)
Sleeper (14-4)
Sleeper (14-4)
Sleeper-bar lounge-observation

Texas
Special
No. 1

from Wash. B&O
from Chgo Wabash
from N.Y. PRR

10:40 pm   10:30 pm   5:40 pm
Springfield   **St. Louis**

Houston
2:59 pm   5:20 pm
San Antonio

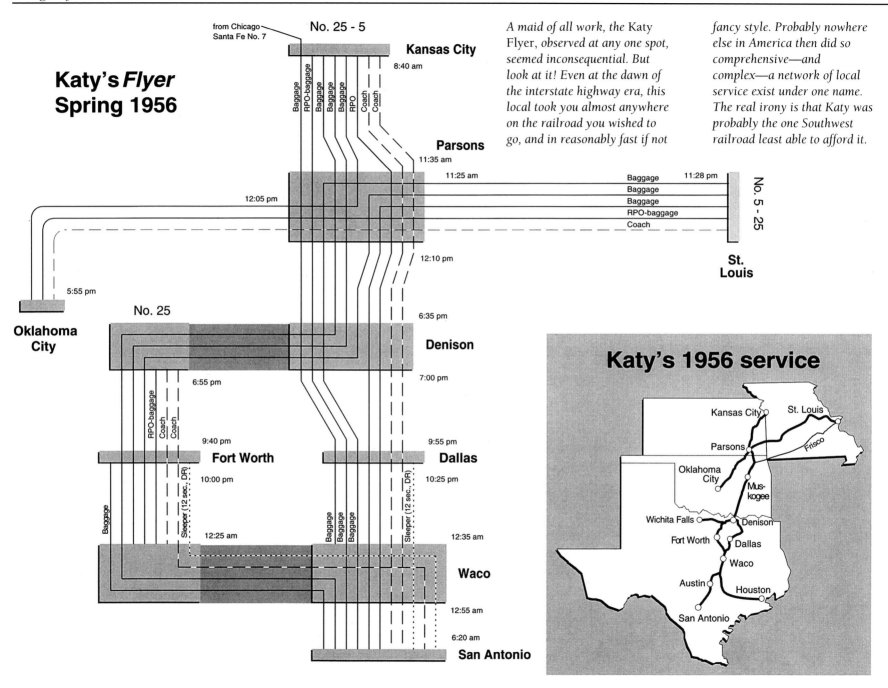

**Katy's *Flyer*
Spring 1956**

No. 25 - 5

from Chicago
Santa Fe No. 7

Kansas City
8:40 am

Baggage
RPO-baggage
Baggage
Baggage
Baggage
RPO
Coach
Coach

A maid of all work, the Katy Flyer, observed at any one spot, seemed inconsequential. But look at it! Even at the dawn of the interstate highway era, this local took you almost anywhere on the railroad you wished to go, and in reasonably fast if not

fancy style. Probably nowhere else in America then did so comprehensive—and complex—a network of local service exist under one name. The real irony is that Katy was probably the one Southwest railroad least able to afford it.

Parsons
11:35 am

11:25 am

12:05 pm

Baggage   11:28 pm
Baggage
Baggage
RPO-baggage
Coach

No. 5 - 25

**St.
Louis**

12:10 pm

5:55 pm

6:35 pm

No. 25

**Oklahoma
City**

Denison

7:00 pm

RPO-baggage
Coach
Coach

6:55 pm

9:40 pm

Fort Worth

Sleeper (12 sec., DR)

10:00 pm

9:55 pm

Dallas

10:25 pm

Sleeper (12 sec., DR)

Baggage

12:25 am

Baggage
Baggage
Baggage

12:35 am

Waco

12:55 am

6:20 am

San Antonio

Katy's 1956 service

Kansas City — St. Louis
Parsons — Frisco
Oklahoma City — Mus-kogee
Wichita Falls — Denison
Fort Worth — Dallas — Waco
Austin — Houston
San Antonio

▶ *The "MAIL" sign is displayed, the sack is hung on the delivery stand and in a couple of seconds the Texas Special will have this morning's southbound mail in its grasp. The scene is Garland, Texas, just northwest of Dallas, in the early 1960s. But it could as easily be any of the hundreds of communities that set its clocks by the passage of Railway Post Office cars. (John B. Charles)*

ing after World War II that a reequipped, high-speed *Special* would need but two sets of cars. Experience dictated otherwise. Extra lightweight coaches and sleepers ultimately fleshed out the trainsets. But thereafter every third day the diner and observation cars

◀ *The right of way, the train, the platform—even the water tower of Highland Park, a tony suburb of Dallas—had seen better days. The Texas Special makes ones of its final calls southbound in 1965. (John B. Charles)*

would be heavyweights—for a time, disguised beneath painted streamlined stripes.

The *Special* of 1956 still carried through sleepers from the Wabash (Chicago), Pennsylvania (New York) and Baltimore & Ohio (Washington, D.C.). This train equalled in quality, if not quantity, competitor Missouri Pacific's *Texas Eagle* fleet.

You'll see Katy's entire passenger service of 1956, including the multifaceted *Katy Flyer*, arrayed on these pages. The *Flyer* (actually, three distinct trains in all, from Kansas City to San Antonio, St. Louis to Oklahoma City and Denison to Waco, Tex.) wasn't in the *Special's* league. The Kansas City–Dallas dining car was long gone by then. What the *Katy Flyer* offered in 1956 was small-town service at a small-town pace. Those few people going long distances

▲ *The south siding switch at Caddo Mills, a village nine miles south of Greenville, Texas, was out of service when the northbound* Katy Flyer *showed up to meet a late-running* Texas Special *on a morning in 1964. So the* Special *stayed back while the* Flyer *pulled by and backed into the clear. That's done, and the main event unfolds. (William J. Neill.)*

on the train ate at station lunch counters in Parsons, Denison and Dallas as the *Flyer* was switched.

On paper, the *Katy Flyer*'s schedule seemed leisurely. In fact, given its mail and express business, to maintain the timings meant going full tilt between interminable stops. My introduction, in 1957, was watching the southbound *Flyer*, with two PA units, overtake our family car south of Stringtown, Oklahoma, at 75 miles per hour, as I begged from the back seat for my father to stoke his accelerator along potholed U.S. Highway 69. Pop had more common sense than his 13-year-old son. We overtook the *Flyer*, stopped at the Atoka depot, a few mo-

ments later. I was impressed by this train from the start.

You couldn't ask for a better cross-section of passenger power. While Electro-Motive E units ruled the *Special*, both the *Bluebonnet* and the Kansas City–San Antonio stem of the *Flyer* rated a pair of those boxy PAs in the mid 1950s. Usually a single E or one or two boiler-equipped FP7s headed the other offshoots of the *Flyer*, as well as the Denison–Houston spinoff of the *Bluebonnet*. As for the passenger cars, of 195 on the roster in 1956, all but those on the *Texas Special*, plus occasional lightweight coaches on the Kansas City-oriented *Bluebonnet*, were impeccably maintained heavyweights.

The big contraction

Then the ambitious network of 1956 vanished. That year, for every $1 in passenger revenues, MKT booked costs of $1.70. On passenger revenues of $2.8 million that year, this implies a passenger-service deficit of almost $2 million, although the real out-of-pocket loss was undoubtedly somewhat less.

Whatever the real loss, it was too much. Katy was going broke. Not having straightened out its finances through bankruptcy during the Great Depression, it entered the 1950s top-heavy with debt, which soaked up $3 million a year in interest payments. The railroad might have worked its way out of indebtedness had freight traffic blossomed. But from 1950 through 1956, a drought in Oklahoma

▶ *Plowing through weeds on unsteady track across classic central Texas landscape, the southbound* Texas Special *passes the abandoned depot at Eddy, between Waco and Temple, in the early 1960s. (Everett DeGolyer)*

and Texas stunted the wheat crops that were Katy's life blood and sapped the railroad's reserves. By the mid 1950s, you saw as many passenger trains as freights (and sometimes more) on MKT's Kansas City–Texas route. Profits topped out at $7.5 million in 1952. Then earnings relentlessly fell, turning to losses in both 1957 and 1958. Katy entered a fiscal starvation from which it never fully emerged before its purchase by Union Pacific in 1988.

Something had to give. Among other things, it was passenger service. In January of 1957, the *Texas Special* and *Bluebonnet* began merging in Muskogee, Okla., instead of Dallas. On April 30, 1958, the St. Louis–Oklahoma City edition of the *Katy Flyer* expired. That summer, so did the Denison–Fort Worth–Houston section of the *Bluebonnet* and the Denison–Fort Worth–Waco offshoot of the *Flyer*. The *Texas Special* out of St. Louis in late 1958 was pitiful: a baggage and RPO-baggage, two coaches, a

◀ *Just like old times: On July 14, 1958, the southbound* Texas Special *(top) nears suburban Dallas at Atkins, Texas. Note the heavyweight Denison–San Antonio coach for local Texas traffic, the heavyweight diner and the Frisco E units. Then a late* Bluebonnet *(bottom) follows. After early 1957, these trains consolidated at Muskogee, Oklahoma, instead of Dallas. But a delay this morning means a reprise of the two-morning-trains-to-Texas policy. (John B. Charles)*

Frisco diner to Springfield, Mo., and one sleeper. On January 5, 1959, Frisco dropped out altogether, and the *Texas Special* name was appended to the old *Bluebonnet* from Kansas City. The Denison–Wichita Falls local, represented since late 1956 by a new Budd RDC-3 railcar, lasted later into 1959.

Katy ran passenger trains another nine years after 1956. But what remained was a shell, not a structure. Bit by bit, both the trains and the track on which they ran sank from sight. William N. Deramus III, who became president early in 1957, adopted draconian money-saving measures beyond elimination of passenger trains. Replacement of ties beneath the rails—indeed, replacement of the rails themselves—fell to a level that assumed almost perpetual life; the maintenance of way payroll was cut in half almost overnight. Through the early 1960s, surviving trains, the Kansas City–San Antonio *Texas Special* and *Katy Flyer*, probably cost the railroad

▶ *At less than breakneck speed, No. 2 rocks and rolls its way north from Austin across verdant Texas hill country in July 1964, atop lightly ballasted track the Katy would abandon a few years in the future. The* Texas Special, *in fact, lives on borrowed time; it will cease to be seen south of Dallas within a few days. Behind the E8 and FP7 comes the standard train of that era— two baggage cars, two baggage-RPOs, two coaches (the first of them a heavyweight) and diner. (J. Parker Lamb)*

relatively little, thanks to Railway Post Office, storage mail and express contracts.

After the good years, the bad

Diagrammed here is the service in mid 1964, just before the *Special* and *Flyer* were cut between Dallas and San Antonio. I wouldn't have recommended these trains in the 1960s to my aunts and uncles; friends who rode the *Texas Special* from Kansas City into Texas told me it was like spending the night inside a Maytag washer-dryer. The rough ride, of course, arose from bad track. But inside Katy's trains, conditions had deteriorated long before. Ray George, son of the railroad's superintendent of transportation, rode the Fort Worth section of the *Bluebonnet* with his parents in 1958, and still vividly recalled his discomfort three decades later: "The cars were not well cleaned, the air conditioning was out of order, and we became very hungry on the trip." At the time, he found it hard to believe that this was the same train that had enveloped him in its comforts and delights only a few years earlier.

Growing up in Katy country in the 1950s, I too saw a lot of that railroad, though seldom from the interior of its passenger trains:

❑ In Fort Worth, a gigantic No. 21 enters the Texas & Pacific station used by Katy. This is not the little Dension–Houston stub of the *Bluebonnet* I'd expected. On this morning of its twilight months the train hosts several hundred fez-topped Shriners headed home from a convention. Even the engineer wears a fez. I see horse-baggage cars behind the locomotives, and a string of extra heavyweight sleepers—big-time stuff in July 1957.

❑ At Parsons, beside Katy's locomotive backshop, I find the uninterred remains of most of Katy's 14 Alco PAs. Years of exposure outside the backshop have bleached and chipped the red and cream paint. I debate whether to climb inside one of these dead units, but lack courage. That's August 1962.

❑ Outside the darkened country depot at

▶ *No-frills railroading: Katy by 1959 squeezed its passenger network into two bare-bones trains, and more or less ran them as shown for the next five years. Then the U.S. Postal Service said it would end Katy's contract for hauling mail south of Dallas (including mail trucked from Fort Worth to Waco each evening for loading aboard Katy baggage cars). VP-Operations Tom Carter rushed to Washington to seek a reprieve from Postmaster General Gronouski. Says Carter: "He put his big feet on the desk my tax dollars had bought and said, 'Our new system will deliver mail faster for less money.' He was wrong on both counts." Loss of that $1 million contract on July 1, 1964, had swift repercussions: The railroad immediately posted notice of discontinuance, and on July 26 of that year, the* Special *and* Flyer *were shortened to Kansas City–Dallas runs. A year later both were gone altogether.*

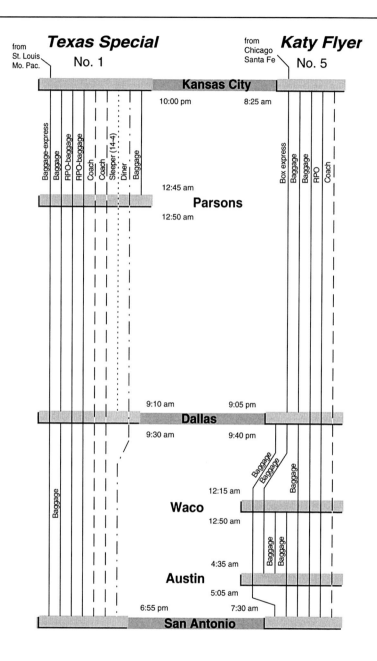

Summer 1964

Leonard, between Denison and Dallas, an elderly farm couple stands beside the tracks, just after sunset. Beside them is her suitcase. The southbound *Katy Flyer* soon comes into view, working power at about 60 mph. Leonard is a flag stop for the five-car train. The man waves his arms at the approaching headlight. Sparks dance from wheelsets as the train, unable to curtail its momentum, rolls by and disappears. But wait: A moment later the marker lights reappear; the *Flyer* backs to a proper stop. "Didn't think we'd leave you?" laughs the conductor, alighting with the footstep. That's November 1963. The last *Katy Flyer* and *Texas Special* would run just 19 months later. And wouldn't you know that a freight train derailment in Oklahoma would make the *Special* more than three hours late to its own funeral, at Dallas Union Terminal on July 1, 1965.

To me, Katy trains are not just lines on a page, but a way of life that slipped away—that era when business people booked Pullmans, when farmers flagged a *Flyer* at country depots, when mail went by rail, no questions asked. You undoubedly felt the same about the passenger service of some other railroad close to your experiences. Events of July 1, 1965, in Texas foretold other bittersweet last runs soon to come elsewhere, and with increasing frequency. I give Katy credit for doing the best it could, as long as it could. Some other railroads tried only half as much, or not at all.

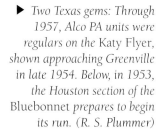

▶ *Two Texas gems: Through 1957, Alco PA units were regulars on the* Katy Flyer, *shown approaching Greenville in late 1954. Below, in 1953, the Houston section of the* Bluebonnet *prepares to begin its run. (R. S. Plummer)*

MISSOURI PACIFIC'S MR. CLEAN

Downing Jenks took over this railroad with his mind made up:
Passenger trains had to go. So why didn't they?

◄ *You look at this and wish
you could turn back the clock.
This is the* South Texas
Eagle, *the best little train in
Texas. No. 2 is rolling
downhill toward Austin behind
an improbable combination of
PA3, E3 and GP7, fronting a
seven-car collection that
includes a sleeper,
sleepercoach, dome coach,
diner-lounge and lightweight
RPO-baggage. The date is
August 1965. Very soon the
two lead locomotives will be
gone, and not long thereafter,
the train itself. (J. Parker
Lamb)*

You cannot imagine a greater contrast in style than that between Russell L. Dearmont and the man who replaced him in late 1960 as president of Missouri Pacific Lines, Downing B. Jenks. A handsome man, Dearmont got to the top via MoPac's law department, and suffered in the eyes of "real" railroaders. (Harold McKenzie, president of rival Cotton Belt, would many years later say of Dearmont that he was "a fine lawyer and a gentleman—but not a railroader.") Jenks, the son of Great Northern's vice president-operations and a railroad president twice over before he even got to Missouri Pacific at age 45, was *all* railroader.

As you might expect of such men, the passenger services each presided over were vastly different, too. In spirit it's as if there were two Missouri Pacifics, B. J. (Before Jenks) and A. J. Said Dearmont to a Voice of America interviewer in 1960: "I tell my associates and executives of other railroads that if they go out of the passenger business completely, they are taking the first step to going out of business altogether." What other railroad CEO in 1959 passionately urged shareholders at the annual meeting to ride passenger trains—to take their children and grandchildren, as well?

At various points along the St. Louis–Texas corridor in 1960, there were at least five, and as many as seven, trains each way, including a *West Texas Eagle* running on the markers of a nearly identical *South Texas Eagle.* Such profligacy! You could depart Wichita by Pullman going *west* on a three-car train that connected with the *Colorado Eagle,* or arrive by lightweight sleeper in El Dorado, Ark., aboard a two-car scoot that went down the 66-mile branch line from Gurdon into the heart of the old Smackover oil field, where billionaire H. L. Hunt in the 1920s made (and gambled away) the first of his several fortunes.

Was Jenks appalled by MoPac's extravagances? "Oh, absolutely," he replied three decades after the fact. By his way of thinking, in 1960 the verdict was already in on passenger trains. So the Dearmont heritage was immediately threatened. But for one who believed Missouri Pacific should leave the passenger business as quickly as possible, Jenks was darned slow to act.

A night at the casket company

What better way to introduce MoPac passenger trains at the dawn of the 1960s than to spend an evening—Monday, January 2, 1960, to be exact—just north of the venerable Little Rock depot. It's a mild winter day under a clear sky, and the view from the Cantrell Avenue overpass, adjacent to Capitol City Casket Co., lets you see everything. First in, at 3:17 p.m., is No. 220. It comes from Hot Springs, 58 miles to the south on one branch line, and will end up in Memphis, 149 miles to the northeast, on another secondary route. A shovelnose E6 (7002) leads an Alco PA3 (8032) and eight cars, including four Pullmans, two of them holiday extras. The diesels cut loose to be refueled while the south station switcher detaches the sleeping cars and the north switcher exchanges storage mail cars. Then No. 220 waits.

At 4:05, 45 minutes late, St. Louis-bound No. 8, the *Southerner*—which began as separate trains in El Paso, San Antonio and Houston, combining in Palestine, Tex., and Texarkana—arrives behind an E-E-PA combo and 18 cars. Like worker bees, the north and south switchers move in. Three of the four Pullmans taken from No. 220 go to the rear of No. 8; they'll leave St. Louis tonight on Gulf, Mobile & Ohio's *Midnight Special* for Chicago. On the other end, while the road units cut off for refueling, eight storage mail cars are pulled off, replaced by five other mail cars. Fifteen minutes after it arrives, No. 8 departs in a plume of exhaust and crosses the nearby Arkansas River, followed closely by No. 220 for Memphis. But for one sleeper from Hot Springs (*Eagle Rapids*, a 10-bedroom 6-roomette car) there wasn't a lightweight car on either train.

After a lull until 8:15, the *Texan*, No. 25, stops on track four from St. Louis with two PAs, an E7B and 18 cars, including four coaches and a diner-lounge. Its primary job is to advance mail from St. Louis to Texas. In Longview, Texas, at 2:45 tomorrow morning, the train will split into sections for Palestine and Dallas–Fort Worth. To Palestine will

Texas Eagles in the summer of 1956

This is what Frisco and Katy contended with out of St. Louis (see page 77): a competitor whose Eagle could take you almost anywhere in the Southwest, in style and comfort. As these diagrams demonstrate, the Texas Eagle was really an entire fleet of trains, all built around the late afternoon departures from St.

Louis of trains 1 and 21. Running against something so awesome as this, is it any wonder that the Texas Special folded its cards within two and a half years? Compare this also with the Eagle fleet nine years later, on page 94.

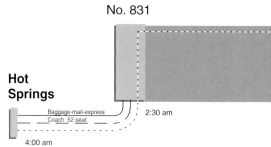

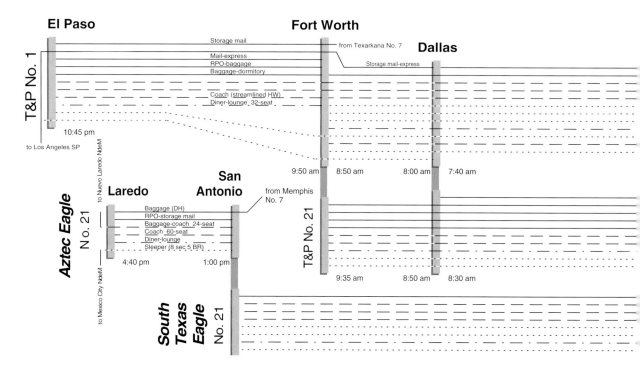

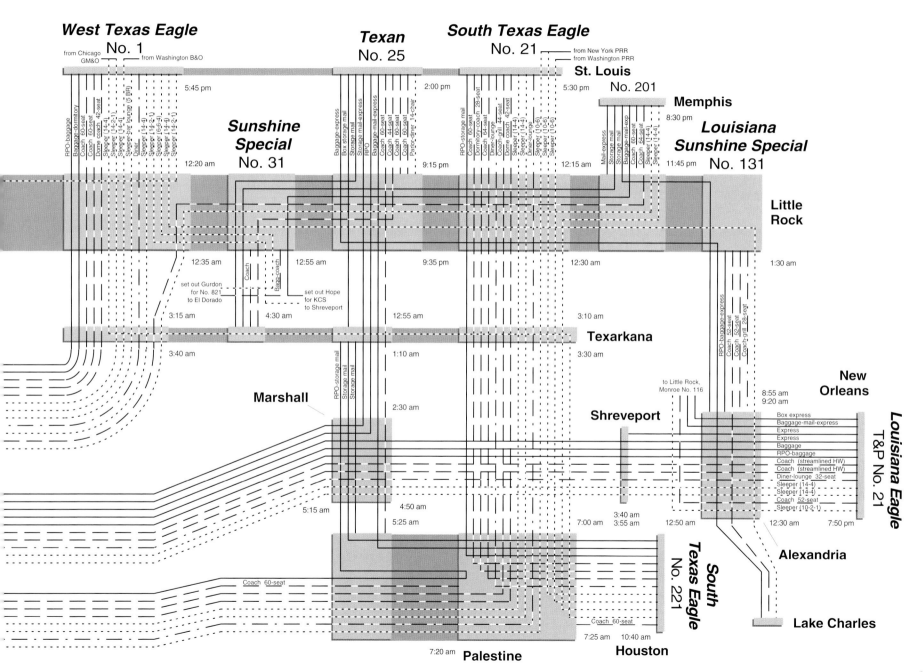

◄ *Viewed from beside the casket factory, the Little Rock station is abuzz this June afternoon in 1960. In the background are no fewer than three road engines and two switchers. Front and center, train 220 departs for Memphis behind two E3 locomotives. (J. Parker Lamb)*

▶ *J Parker Lamb specialized in getting such photos as this— one hand on the shutter, the other on his car's steering wheel. But this was made standing still: train 8, the* Southerner, *doing 80 near Newport, Arkansas.*

go storage mail for two sections of the *South Texas Eagle* that are following it by several hours. The Fort Worth section carries mail and express that would otherwise run on an already-long *West Texas Eagle.* At Little Rock, the diner-lounge and two coaches go off. No. 25 is on its way at 8:55, five minutes late.

You take a break now for supper in the depot restaurant, lingering over coffee and homemade pecan pie. When you emerge, the waiting room has come alive with college students and their belongings, servicemen and others young and old returning from holiday vacations. Lightweight sleeper *Cascade Drive,* which arrived from Hot Springs this afternoon, is now attached to a heavyweight coach and diner-lounge and all are accepting passengers. At 11 o'clock, No. 832, also from Hot Springs, arrives behind a steam generator-equipped GP7 with two rebuilt heavyweight coaches and sleeper *Eagle River,*

which joins *Cascade Drive* on the waiting track. Thirty minutes later comes No. 132 from Lake Charles, Louisiana, with sleeper *Eagle Divide* in tow, and it gets attached to the earlier arrivals.

Then, the deluge. At 11:53 No. 201 from Memphis passes under Cantrell Avenue with the E6 and PA3 that went north this afternoon and 13 cars, including four heavyweight sleepers with military personnel and lightweight sleeping cars and coaches for the *Texas Eagle* trains, the first of which arrives ten minutes later: First 21, the *South Texas Eagle*, pulled by E7 7012 and PA2 8021, with 12 cars. This is the San Antonio section. Even as the north switcher attaches sleeping car *Eagle Knob* from Memphis to the rear of First 21, Second 21 for Houston comes under Cantrell Avenue with E7s 7008 and 7015B and 12 cars. The switcher moves from First 21 to remove two sleepers from the back of the second section, for Lake Charles and Hot Springs, and add a Houston coach that arrived from Memphis on 201. First 21 is gone at 12:20, Second 21 at

12:49 and No. 131, the Louisiana section of the *Sunshine Special*, soon thereafter.

But in the meantime, First 1 is in the depot, at 12:40. This is the regular El Paso section of the *West Texas Eagle*, 16 lightweight cars behind a Texas & Pacific E7 and a MoPac E7 and PA1. It gets a coach and sleeper from No. 201. While this is happening, No. 32, the *Sunshine Special*, comes in. It originated in Texarkana, just 145 miles to the south, but has 17 cars and will require a lot of switching, including the addition of all those cars which have been collecting on the waiting track.

Now at 1:10 a third train joins the melee—Second 1, and it's a sight: a PA1, E7B and PA3 pulling 13 heavyweight sleepers and lightweight diner 742. This train gets the four extra heavyweight Pullmans from Memphis. First 1 is gone at 1:18, an hour late, and at 1:30 Third 1 rumbles past you into the station with a PA3, E3B, PA2, 18 heavyweight sleepers and two heavyweight diners. Second and Third 1 are really military extras carrying servicemen to Fort

Worth. Second 1 is out at 1:40 and Third 1 at 1:59.

There's lots more to happen tonight beside the casket company. No. 32 finally gets its act together and is gone at 1:50, by which time No. 2, the northbound *West Texas Eagle*, makes itself known. There will be two *South Texas Eagle* sections later. Trains will leave for Hot Springs and Memphis.

This was less than 12 hours in the Arkansas capitol city. A mere 10 years later, a single coach-only passenger train in each direction would survive. How could that be? You shall soon see.

Little birds in *Eagle*land

Besides the busy main line business, Missouri Pacific in 1960 still ran wonderful, quirky trains on the fringes. There was the "Pacific Eagle," what folks called the three-car commuter train that ran the 34 miles between St. Louis and Pacific, Mo., on the route toward Kansas City. Its revenues didn't cover the fixed costs of using Union Station. The cars themselves had open vestibules and five-across seat-

*◄ Uh oh, here comes trouble!
The brakeman of the* South
Texas Eagle *walks up to confer
about the Southern Pacific
local that is calmly switching
cars in his path at McNeil,
Texas, 18 miles north of
Austin, in July of 1965. Beside
RSD-15 5448, an SP
trainmaster chats with a signal
maintainer, while the rotund
station agent wearing the pith
helmet takes it all in, no doubt
with much amusement. Delay
to the* Eagle: *30 minutes. The
trains, the engines, the relaxed
way of life are long gone.
(J. Parker Lamb)*

ing. Its last run was December 15, 1961. Frank W. Bryan was along, and recalled years later in *The Eagle*, the publication of the MP Historical Society:

> The festivities occurred on the evening run: standing room only . . . an open (but private) bar for the regulars . . . black crepe on the exterior of the cars . . . H. E. Mack, passenger traffic manager, uncomfortable under the press flashguns, wishing he were elsewhere, any-where . . . pandemonium, songs . . . and a slightly tipsy trumpeter who got off and played taps at every stop (there were many).

Or, take locals 125 and 126. Until they were removed during Dearmont's final months, these nameless little trains trudged every day between Kansas and Little Rock—a 525-mile venture through rural southern Kansas, northeast Oklahoma and east-ern Arkansas over what was then a modestly active line but is today a major corridor for general freight, grain and coal. The whole trip took 15 hours, and lunch and dinner could be had during stops in Coffeyville, Kan., and Van Buren, Ark. The special touch: a four-mile backup off the main line to reach Fort Smith, Ark.— a round trip consuming 50 minutes.

Even more obscure: trains 221 and 222, over MoPac's most scenic route, the White River line between Pleasant Hill, Mo., just east of Kansas City, and Newport, Ark., between Poplar Bluff and Little Rock on the St. Louis-Texas main line—a 12-hour experience across 421 miles uninterrupted, I deduce from the *Official Guide*, by any stops for food. Nor was this *Eaglet* delayed by many freights.

Another train I should have taken: the Wichita leg of *the Colorado Eagle*. This three-car train—RPO-baggage, baggage-coach and lightweight sleeper, usually led by a steam boiler-equipped GP7—went west each evening at 10 o'clock. Ten stops and 88 miles beyond found No. 411 in Geneseo, a prairie village that could have been the locale of "The Last Picture Show." By and by came No. 11, which backed onto the Wichita Pullman and left for Pueblo and (via Denver & Rio Grande Western) Colorado Springs and Denver. About the time that owls get drowsy, the eastbound *Colorado Eagle* dropped its sleeper in Geneseo, and then No. 412 left for Wichita. Bryan made that trip once, soon before the Wichita train was removed in 1963, and described the scene in Geneseo: "A plains wind swept down the main street, unobstructed by traffic. The only man-made sound was the depot telegraph key, and the only illumination the glow in the operator's office."

The *Missouri River Eagle* was, in its time, something of a little gem, too. Possibly the shortest and least renumerative of the *Eagle* name trains, it typically carried in the late 1950s a dome coach,

diner-lounge and 32-chair parlor car between St. Louis, Kansas City and Omaha. Alas, Burlington's dominance in the Kansas City–Omaha corridor— three Q trains each way to MoPac's lone *Eagle*— drove MoPac out of this route in 1965, on its third try before the Interstate Commerce Commission. (The train stayed between St. Louis and Kansas City.)

All of this was the happy domain of Russell Dearmont before his retirement in the final days of 1960. In that Voice of America interview taped that year for broadcast overseas, he said, "It is easy enough to discontinue a service that is causing difficulty, but we want to improve our passenger service and thereby improve patronage." He wasn't mouthing platitudes, either. At about that time, MoPac had begun family-plan fares, budget-priced meals (breakfast 75 cents, lunch and dinner $1) brought to the seats of coach passengers from the kitchen and new low prices on sleepers

◀ The 14-hour, 533-mile journeys of locals 125-126, between Kansas City and Little Rock, was a tour through small-town America—places like Bucyrus and Durand, Kansas; Nowata and Fort Gibson, Oklahoma, and Mulberry and Russellville, Arkansas. In that world, in the 1950s, this attractive three-car train fit right in. In the summer of 1957, No. 125 arrives in Fort Smith, Arkansas, where a big load of express awaits it. The train would barely survive into 1960. (Louis A. Marre)

with upper and lower section berths.

You've got to hand it to the old man. Dearmont had bravely (and perhaps foolishly) lowered his head against the wind. But he was getting results. Passenger-train miles declined almost 9 percent between 1958 and 1960, primarily because of branch-line trains being removed. But passenger miles (one passenger carried one mile) rose by a like amount. And MoPac's solely related passenger loss, as defined by the ICC, fell from $6.1 million in 1958 to $4.1 million in 1960.

Mr. Clean comes to town

Ironically, in 1961, the first full year of the Jenks presidency, Missouri Pacific's passenger loss dissolved and became a profit of almost half a million dollars. If he remembers this, Jenks takes little satisfaction. His dour opinion of passenger trains was formed running the Rock Island Lines. "In 1952," he says, "there was a big wage increase

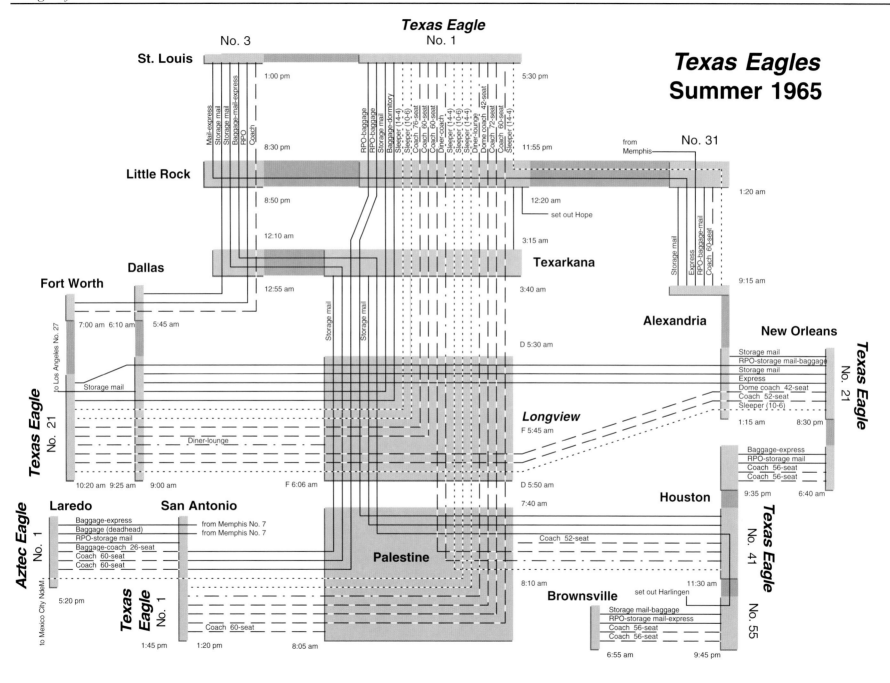

Texas Eagle

No. 3 No. 1

St. Louis

**Texas Eagles
Summer 1965**

1:00 pm

Mail-express
Storage mail
Storage mail
Baggage-mail-express
RPO
Coach

5:30 pm

8:30 pm

RPO-baggage
RPO-baggage
Storage mail
Baggage-dormitory
Sleeper (14-4)
Sleeper (10-6)
Coach 76-seat
Coach 60-seat
Coach 60-seat
Diner-coach
Sleeper (14-4)
Sleeper (10-6)
Sleeper (14-4)
Diner-lounge
Dome coach 42-seat
Coach 72-seat
Coach 60-seat
Sleeper (14-4)

11:55 pm

from Memphis

No. 31

Little Rock

1:20 am

8:50 pm

12:20 am

set out Hope

12:10 am

3:15 am

Dallas

Texarkana

Storage mail
Express
RPO-baggage-mail
Coach 60-seat

Fort Worth

12:55 am

Storage mail

Storage mail

3:40 am

9:15 am

Alexandria

7:00 am 6:10 am

5:45 am

to Los Angeles No. 27

New Orleans

Storage mail

D 5:30 am

Storage mail
RPO-storage mail-baggage
Storage mail
Express
Dome coach 42-seat
Coach 52-seat
Sleeper (10-6)

Texas Eagle
No. 21

Longview
F 5:45 am

Texas Eagle
No. 21

Diner-lounge

1:15 am 8:30 pm

Baggage-express
RPO-storage mail
Coach 56-seat
Coach 56-seat

10:20 am 9:25 am 9:00 am

F 6:06 am

D 5:50 am

9:35 pm 6:40 am

Texas Eagle
No. 41

7:40 am

Houston

Aztec Eagle
No. 1

Laredo

San Antonio

Baggage-express
Baggage (deadhead)
RPO-storage mail
Baggage-coach 26-seat
Coach 60-seat
Coach 60-seat

from Memphis No. 7
from Memphis No. 7

Coach 52-seat

Palestine

to Mexico City NdeM.

Texas Eagle
No. 1

5:20 pm

8:10 am

11:30 am

set out Harlingen

Brownsville

Coach 60-seat

Storage mail-baggage
RPO-storage mail-express
Coach 56-seat
Coach 56-seat

Texas Eagle
No. 55

1:45 pm 1:20 pm 8:05 am

6:55 am 9:45 pm

94

◀ *The St. Louis–Denver* Colorado Eagle *could not survive competition from jetliners and Union Pacific's* City of St. Louis. *But in August of 1959, when the train still took four sleeping cars west for Denver from St. Louis, you wouldn't have guessed the sorry end that awaited the train five years later. On this rainy afternoon in Kirkwood, Missouri, the westbound* Eagle, *trailed by a parlor-observation bound for Kansas City, gets underway. (J. Parker Lamb)*

Jenks to be vice president-operations (and later president) of MP, says there was a sort of "five-year plan" to take off trains. But the plan got behind schedule when long-haul business held up, says Lloyd. Besides, he adds, "We were willing to upgrade equipment. We wanted to maintain as good a public profile as we could."

One thing Jenks could do, without diminishing the choices of his passengers, was to combine the two *Texas Eagle* trains north of Texas. Most of the year, they were two trains doing the work of one. So in September of 1961, the *South Texas Eagle* and *West Texas Eagle* became one train between St. Louis and Texarkana, where they divided into Houston/San Antonio and Fort Worth/El Paso sections.

To the credit of the railroad, it expanded the train to its 23-car maximum—or ordered up two sections out of St. Louis—to satisfy seasonal demand. Bryan reports that on a bitterly cold Friday, December 22, 1961, the *Texas Eagle* left St. Louis in three sections (Fort Worth, San Antonio, Houston). Altogether, they had more than 50 cars and 1,500 passengers. Wrote Bryan in *The Eagle* newsletter: "Carmen thawed out steam connections under heavyweight section Pullmans (in coach service), heavyweight coaches and even a T&P 5 double bedroom-lounge car pressed into coach service. Some people sat up all night, but no one stood."

That day stands as a sort of watershed. Thereafter, MoPac ran the *Texas Eagle* in two parts frequently during summer and around the Christmas holiday. As late as the Christmas season of 1966, it mustered 23-car *Eagles* out of and into St. Louis. But never again did the railroad rise to such lengths to serve so many at once on these trains.

Trimming of the limbs

The years of the mid 1960s were a sort of holding pattern for the *Eagles* and kin. Jenks was unwilling to expend energy or very much money to sustain the passenger service, beyond ordering from Sedalia

for union people. Right after that we began to realize we were losing money hauling people." When he got to Missouri Pacific, Jenks says, he discovered that Dearmont "didn't have a handle on the costs."

In his zeal to create a neat as well as profitable railroad, Jenks acquired the nickname "Mr. Clean." But the moniker also applied to some of his cost-cutting measures. For instance, he discovered that six different colors of paint were needed to coat a passenger locomotive—blue, yellow, aluminum,

black and two shades of grey. "I said, 'Let's just paint 'em blue,' " and they did. When one of the Budd-built coaches had its fluted, stainless steel sheathing ruined on one side in a derailment, Jenks suggested it be replaced by plate steel and put back in service. "People said the car would look funny," he says, "and I replied, 'Nobody ever looks at both sides of a car at once.' " And he was right.

Jenks says his goal from the start was to phase Missouri Pacific out of the passenger business. In fact, John Lloyd, who came from Rock Island with

Passenger routes 1965

Shops some elongated boxcars to use in storage mail service and rebuilding some of the lightweight coaches for higher capacities. Certainly, the sort of enthusiasm that Dearmont had brought with him was missing. But Jenks didn't heave an axe into these trains, and the literature of experiences I've seen about Jenks-era *Eagles* is rather uniform in its conclusion that MoPac ran clean passenger trains with polite

◄ *Train 21, a nine-car* South Texas Eagle, *overtakes a local freight at Round Rock, Texas, just north of Austin, in 1965. Note the depot's two-level train order signal, necessary because the viaduct on which J. Parker Lamb stands would obscure its indication in one direction.*

crews, right to the end. Certainly that was my experience.

Rather, Jenks let nature take its course. As trains began to exhibit measurable out-of-pocket losses, the railroad went immediately to regulators to get them removed. In large part it succeeded easily. The *Missouri River Eagle* in 1965 and *Colorado Eagle* in 1966 (two tries) were exceptions to this rule.

The real devastation occurred in Texas. The pliant Texas Railroad Commission allowed MoPac by mid decade to drop twice-daily service between Houston and Brownsville, twice-daily trains between Houston and New Orleans, one round trip between Palestine and Houston (the overnight *Southerner* connection) and both the *West Texas Eagle* and *Westerner* west of Fort Worth.

As the 1960s progressed, Missouri Pacific hunkered down. The railroad's four lightweight parlor cars, bought from Chesapeake & Ohio in 1959, went into the Sedalia shops and came out as 60-seat coaches in 1962–1964. The parlors had been used alongside dining cars on St. Louis–Kansas City trains, and to eliminate a car in such trains, Sedalia in 1963 converted three diner-lounges to diner-parlors. The last modifications involved ten lightweight sleepers, which during 1964–1967 were converted into 76-seat coaches. A bitter pill was the sale in 1967 to Illinois Central of MP's six dome coaches, three of them built by Budd in 1948 for the *Colorado Eagle* and three in 1952 for the *West Texas Eagle*; all six last saw service on the *Texas Eagle* early in 1967.

From reign to ruin

I suppose that had the status quo stayed in place with the Post Office, that Missouri Pacific would have happily run trains into Texas—and west to Kansas City—into the 1970s, notwithstanding the attitude of Downing Jenks. The ICC later estimated MoPac's out-of-pocket passenger losses in 1966 to have been $2.1 million. That's real money, but less than half what Illinois Central and Great Northern lost on a

similar set of accounting rules, and one-third the losses incurred that year by Southern Railway. Other reasons to take heart:

❑ MP's Industrial Engineering Department in the mid 1960s had done preliminary planning for a new, compact St. Louis Union Station, to replace the Florentine white elephant whose costs were bleeding the tenants dry. Events overtook this project before it ever got beyond the study phase, but it implied a willingness to tough things out long term.

❑ Mail revenues more than held their own on the St. Louis–Texas corridor. To be specific, trains 7 and 8 to San Antonio (the old *Southerner*, now nameless) and connecting trains 27 and 28 between Texarkana and Fort Worth and trains 23 and 24 between New Orleans and Marshall recorded a combined profit of more than $750,000 on a direct-cost basis in 1966, thanks to $4.4 million in mail and express revenues. Similarly, nameless trains 3 and 4, which evolved from the old *Texan* and relayed mail cars to the *Texas Eagle* at Texarkana just as the *Texan* had a decade earlier, earned a $325,000 profit in 1966 on the strength of $3 million in mail and express receipts.

But mail business that sustained MoPac passenger service all but vanished, starting in October of 1967. Trains 7-8-23-24-27-28 lost their Railway Post Office cars that month, and the $575,000 in revenue that went with them. Within five months, $2.2 million in annual storage mail contracts for these trains were cancelled. Told by MP that it would seek to discontinue these trains, Railway Express Agency obligingly removed business that had contributed yet another $1 million in revenues. Passengers paid one-tenth as much revenue to these six trains as mail and express, so their discontinuance on July 11, 1968, was foreordained.

Mail trains 3 and 4 were next to go. That $3 million in mail and express business they enjoyed in 1966 was totally gone by early 1968, and on October 31 of that year, so were the trains themselves.

That left the *Texas Eagle* trains to Houston, San Antonio and Fort Worth, their New Orleans–Marshall and San Antonio–Laredo connections and two pairs of St. Louis–Kansas City trains. Virtually all mail revenue had vanished, and with it any pretenses that Missouri Pacific would willingly provide passenger service for anyone, anywhere. The railroad tried and failed to get rid of the Kansas City trains. But with the connivance of the Texas Railroad Commission, it sliced away the *Texas Eagle* network like pieces of salami. "We didn't go out of our way to make it better," Jenks said of his flagship train. "We thought we should get rid of these trains, and the *Texas Eagle* was at the end of our list."

Four sleeping cars in and out of St. Louis on No. 1 and No. 2 became none as of January 1, 1969, making the *Eagle* a seven-car train—a baggage car and coach for each of its three destinations, plus a San Antonio diner-lounge.

The last Palestine–Houston *Texas Eagle* ran April 1, 1969, and the Longview–Fort Worth section dissolved two months later. By the end of 1969 the *Eagle*'s New Orleans–Marshall arm was severed, leaving a St. Louis–San Antonio train and its connection to Laredo. Finally, in September 1970 the *Eagle* became a St. Louis–Texarkana baggage car and coach —reign to ruin in three years. "You couldn't cut out just pieces," said Jenks in a retrospective look at his passenger trains. "You had to maintain locomotives, shops and all this staff to sell tickets. When we got down to just hauling freight, we were able to do the job with a lot less people. As soon as we got rid of those passenger trains, we started making money."

ZEPHYRS AGAINST A HEAD WIND

Burlington defined the word 'streamliner' in the 1930s, and remained totally committed into the 1960s. Then came a superior force.

◀ *Of Burlington Route, you can truly say, it has sizzle. And no train exemplified the glamour better than the* California Zephyr, *shown here meeting a westbound freight near Chariton, Iowa, in 1960. The combination of dome cars and unbelievable views of the Colorado Rockies and California Sierras was sensual in the extreme. Even after partner Western Pacific dropped out, the CZ limped along as a Chicago–Salt Lake City train until Amtrak. (J. Parker Lamb)*

Louis W. Menk hit Chicago Burlington & Quincy with the force of the west wind after which its *Zephyrs* took their names. On October 1, 1965, he was Burlington's newest employee, just hired from the St. Louis–San Francisco Railroad as Burlington's president. That afternoon, bored, Menk wandered into Chicago Union Station to watch the passenger operation. Here's his account of what transpired:

"They were running a special to Colorado Springs—taking people there and back on this beautiful *Zephyr*-like train—and providing lodging and two or three meals, for the price of a one-way ticket, or about $75. I mean, here was this whole bunch of Burlington guys in red coats directing people onto the train. The mentality was that you lose money, but look at the advertising you get! I told them later, 'You're advertising to the wrong people. These folks don't ship anything.' I said right then that this would stop. We quit running those special trains. The passenger people simply had no sense of the economics of the business."

The intercity passenger train by 1965 had been through rough times. But Burlington in 1964 had carried more passengers more miles (820 million) than it had in 1949 (758 million). Burlington was a pro-passenger railroad—damn proud of it, too—and could claim to be making money at this.

Menk wasn't convinced, and set out to prove that the railroad was on the wrong course. In this culture clash, Burlington's passenger philosophy was altered from the top down, by executive fiat. Ultimately, of course, events proved Menk right. Within two years, superhighways, jet airplanes and wholesale loss of U.S. mail overwhelmed Burlington's passenger business, and no amount of positive attitude in 1965 could have held back those forces.

So you're left either to curse Menk as the grinch who turned out the lights early at the party, or to respect him as someone who saw through events of the moment and divined their eventual sorry conclusion. For his part, Menk has never doubted the wisdom of his beliefs. Declared this resolute man almost three decades later: "You couldn't make money then, can't make money now and won't make money ever on intercity passenger trains. That's all there is to it."

A different West Side story

No railroad ran passenger trains more exciting to watch, more fun to ride in the first half of the 1960s than Burlington. Its cupboard of lightweight cars seemed inexhaustible. Not only inexhaustible, but infinitely varied—a working catalog of the best rolling stock ever to leave Budd Co.

Come along to Chicago's West Side on a summer Sunday in 1964. Here are three nose-to-tail E7s accelerating a nine-car, fluted-side train that includes four domes—the normal *Morning Zephyr* of that era, bound for Minneapolis on what included America's fastest point-to-point schedule (82.3 miles per hour, from Aurora to Rochelle, Ill.).

By itself, the *Morning Zephyr* would be the magnificent flagship of any midwestern railroad. But it is almost obscured by what follows it west from Chicago. At 11, three hours behind the *Morning Zephyr*, comes the combined *Nebraska Zephyr–Kansas City Zephyr*, a colossus: four E units pointed forward elephant-style, 15 or so mail and express cars, the passenger-carrying cars of the *Kansas City Zephyr* and the five-unit, articulated Lincoln trainset, dating to the *Twin Zephyrs* of 1936 and punctuated by parlor-observation *Juno* or *Jupiter*. Seventy minutes later we see the immaculate, 16-car, Seattle-bound *North Coast Limited,* to be delivered 427 miles and 405 minutes later in St. Paul to Burlington's co-owner, Northern Pacific. Just after 2:30 appears another great Seattle train, the *Empire Builder*—14 squeaky-clean orange and green cars. As Q's other owner, GN also gets a 405-minute schedule to St. Paul for its premier train. (William J. Quinn, Burlington's last president, later remarked that both GN and NP demanded scrupulously evenhanded treatment for their premier trains while on CB&Q.)

The day is still young. The *California Zephyr* is out of Union Station at 3:10 and soon accelerating past us—six sleepers, five coaches, five domes and an observation car within its 15-car consist—on its way to Oakland. At 4:15, stand aside for the *After-noon Zephyr* to Minneapolis—the other half of Burlington's twice-daily *Twin Zephyr* service. Its trainset had arrived at 2:50 p.m. on the eastbound *Morning Zephyr* from Minneapolis. Then at 5 o'clock behold Burlington's pride and joy, the 20-car *Denver Zephyr.* On a Friday or Saturday, the train comes in two parts—a 15-car first section with the Denver sleepers and six cars for Colorado Springs (carried south from Denver by Rio Grande's *Royal Gorge),* and a 12-car, all-coach section.

That evening, there will be four more departures—the *Black Hawk* to the Twin Cities with West Coast coaches and sleepers for NP's *Mainstreeter* and GN's *Western Star;* the combined *Ak-Sar-Ben Zephyr–American Royal Zephyr* for Lincoln and Kansas City, splitting at Galesburg; nameless all-stops local No. 7 on its 31-hour odyssey to Denver, and the 1899-vintage *Fast Mail* to Omaha and a connection with Union Pacific.

Mixed signals

Yes, that was the glitter. The reality was that the *Zephyrs* were too big for their britches. Even after the *Kansas City Zephyr* had been separated in Galesburg, the *Nebraska Zephyr* might number 20 cars, double-stopping its way to Lincoln at platforms too small to contain it or other trains that follow. As for its overnight companion on the Chicago-Lincoln run, the *Ak-Sar-Ben Zephyr,* as early as 1960 one Omaha businessman complained: "The deterioration in service on your overnight trains has been steady and substantial." Once a swift streamliner, the *Ak-Sar-Ben* kept getting burdened with more—and longer—mail stops across Iowa that had once been worked by Q's truck subsidiary. The *Morning Zephyr* and *Afternoon Zephyr* were frequently saddled with heavyweight coaches during periods of heavy travel. The *Kansas City Zephyr* and *American Royal Zephyr* routinely surrendered their lightweight cars when demand built.

Timekeeping problems of the *Denver Zephyr* were legendary. Consider this: In 1960 and 1961, the westbound *DZ* was saddled with the job of picking up, in Brush, Colo., the three-car local from Alliance, Neb., and bringing it into Denver. The railroad calculated that this created a built-in 17-minute delay. And imagine the sight of Burlington's pride and joy arriving Denver with heavyweight cars on the tail. But this is indicative of what was happening everywhere on Burlington. At one extreme, the railroad gave birth to runaway successes, such as the *Denver Zephyr,* whose popularity created trains of such length that they destroyed the schedule trying to work the short-platform towns en route. At the other, it consolidated trains to save train miles and created monsters—the *Ak-Sar-Ben Zephyr* and *Nebraska Zephyr* are examples—whose schedules were dictated more by U.S. Postal Service concerns than by passenger convenience. By the middle of the 1960s, each *Zephyr* did the work that two used to do, and out on the road, they suffered for it.

For Denver, a new *Zephyr*

Of course, by the standards of the mid 1960s, ultra-long, mail-encumbered trains that didn't have quite enough good cars to go around seemed to be the mark of success in the railroad business, because they maximized revenue. Burlington was masterful in utilizing its primary physical asset: its passenger cars. As the public began deserting passenger trains in the late 1950s, keeping them full required total dedication. Burlington's dedication was personified by three men. One was President Harry C. Murphy, an Operating Department veteran who rose under the wing of Ralph Budd, Q's religiously pro-passenger president in the 1930s and 1940s. Murphy spent the 1950s ridding Burlington of doodlebugs, branch line locals and mixed trains. He removed, shortened or combined passenger and mixed trains more than 160 times during his 16-year tenure.

But Murphy kept the faith in his streamliners, and that faith went beyond lip service. He authorized purchase of two six-car *Kansas City Zephyr* trainsets, which began service in 1953 over CB&Q's just-shortened route across northern Missouri. Then in 1955 Murphy signed contracts for the 28 cars and four E9 diesels to reequip the *Denver Zephyr.*

Talking Murphy into spending $8,984,812.33 of pre-inflation-era capital to keep business his railroad already enjoyed was a hard sell, especially after the new *Kansas City Zephyr* wilted under Santa Fe's competitive pressure. The man who did it was Julius J. Alms, Q's passenger boss. "Julius Alms was the most dynamic, high-pressure person I've ever been around," says Jack Hammon, secretary to Alms in the mid 1950s. "He was a true believer in passenger trains. Had he lived [Alms died in 1964], there's no doubt he'd have been president."

As Alms saw things, a new *Denver Zephyr* domeliner was absolutely essential if Burlington were to remain a profitable carrier of passengers. The *DZ* was a phenomenal money maker, racking up profits above direct costs of more than $2 million, year after year. But the articulated cars were showing their two decades of wear and tear, and were difficult to expand during peak travel periods. Worse yet, in 1953 Union Pacific reequipped its *City of Denver,* which siphoned away *Zephyr* customers. In 1954, Chicago–Denver ridership sank 20 percent, and revenues of the CB&Q flagship fell $650,000. *Not* to act at once would be a major business blunder, Alms argued. He won the day

▶ *What kept Burlington in the passenger business? Trains like No. 11 (shown near Lisle, Illinois), which is really three trains in one: a 13-car mail and express train, a four-car* Kansas City Zephyr *and a five-car* Nebraska Zephyr. *(John W. Schultz collection)*

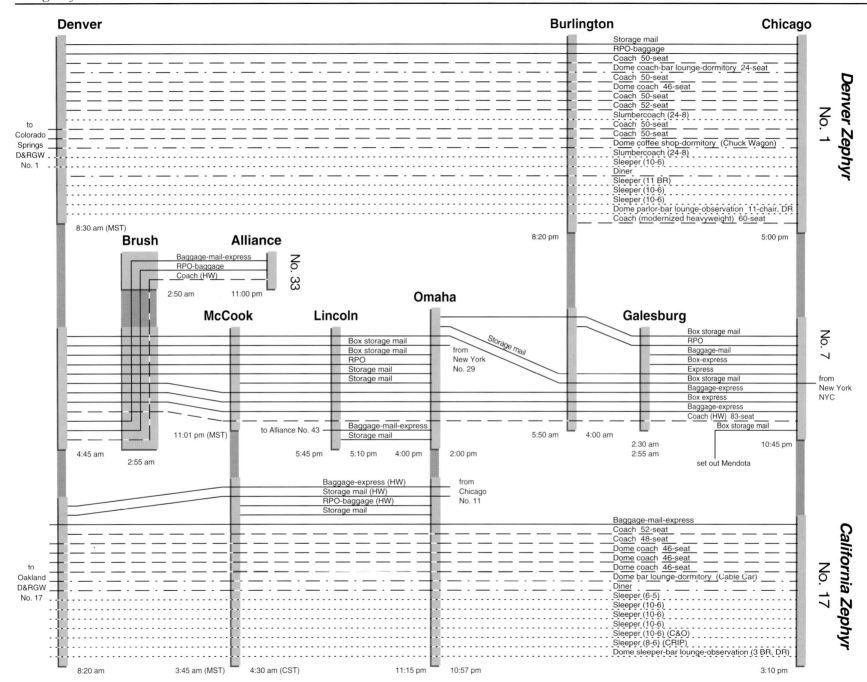

▶ *The flagship* Denver Zephyr *roars through Fairview Avenue station in Downers Grove, Illinois (and past a following dinky) on June 16, 1968. (J. David Ingles)*

and thereby fathered the last stem-to-stern streamliner commissioned in the U.S.

Filling the mighty Mississippi

But for sheer verve and bluster neither man matched Herbert C. Wallace, virtually unknown to the railfans who rode, admired and photographed his trains. On the masthead of the Passenger Traffic Department, Wallace was number two, behind General Passenger Traffic Manager Wilbur F. (Bill) Burke, who succeeded Alms as department chief. "Bill Burke was an auditor," says Wallace, with more than a hint of disdain. "I was a salesman."

Wallace, elevated to the top sales job in 1959, became the right man at the right time. Burlington decided then not to stand idly by and watch its passenger business, still profitable overall on the basis of solely related costs, slowly ebb. Wrote John W. Schultz, author of an authoritative history of the *Zephyr* era: "While the passenger department had maintained a creative traffic program for a number of years, 1959 signaled the beginning of an aggressive, bare-knuckled effort to keep *Zephyr* seats filled with paying passengers." It was the job of Wallace to put muscle behind those knuckles.

Wallace admits he was bored by the economics of passenger trains. But could he sell? Three decades after Wallace left to take an executive position at Hertz, the enthusiasm he brought to bear still resonated in his voice. "The idea was to fill our regular trains first. Did you ever see the headwaters of the Mississippi River? It starts out itty-bitty. By the time other streams have fed into it, the Mississippi is a

mighty river. By the same token, if you have all these tours going, they'll fill your trains."

And then some. In 1965, 201,000 adults and 180,000 schoolchildren rode organized Burlington Route passenger trips, and those who couldn't fit in scheduled trains spilled over onto specials. In those years there were "Springtime in the Rockies" specials ("I had 902 people on the first one" in 1960); weekend specials to the Broadmoor Hotel in Colorado Springs; "See or Ski" specials to Denver; one-day specials to historic Dubuque, Ia., Hannibal, Mo. and Prairie du Chien, Wis.; "Autumn Panorama" specials up the Mississippi; football specials in Iowa and Nebraska, and St. Paul Winter Carnival specials. Steam specials were pets of President Murphy, who kept 2-8-2 4960 and 4-8-4 5632 on the active roster for just such a purpose.

Every weekend, in other words, Herb Wallace motivated folks to leave home. "People are mobile," he says, "and we proved it by packaging things for them that were fun. One Saturday morning we had 10,000 people in Chicago Union Station going different directions on our special trains." The typical excursion price was a round trip for a one-way fare. "Herb used to go round and round arguing with the accounting people on costs," says Hammon. Wallace justified low fares by using suburban doubledecker coaches and diesels on weekends, or fully depreciated heavyweight coaches when lightweights were scarce.

The kiddie trains

Wallace, a man of many ideas, remembers as his best the one that came to him while riding the dinky to work from Aurora one Monday morning in 1962. His train passed Cicero Yard, and outside the window sat Mikado 4960, just in from a railfan excursion. "I looked at that engine as we passed and thought, 'What can we do with it?' And then it hit me: We'll run it with school kids! I knew we couldn't lose. I brought the salesmen in and told them to call every school superintendent in their territories to say we were going to run these steam trains, because it's a bit of Americana."

Reports came back negative—no interest. Unfazed, Wallace borrowed Murphy's stationery and penned a letter to hundreds of school superintendents over the signature of Burlington's boss. He pulled out all stops. He had the boss say that he'd just taken his grandkids on one of the steam trips. "Having seen the happiness of my grandchildren," Murphy/Wallace said, "it occurred to me that every boy and girl should have the same opportunity to relive our nation's history. I'm going to send my personal representative to talk to you and report back to me your reaction." The interest Wallace couldn't ignite via his staff, the Murphy letter did.

Thus began a two-year pilgrimage of the 4960 and 5632, from one end of the Q to the other, that put yet another 120,000 people inside Burlington passenger cars. The first year was tentative, the second wholehearted. The Mikado set off from Streator, Ill., on a branch line, working its way north, town by town, toward St. Paul, hauling hundreds of kids per day on brief trips for a nominal $1.50 or $2. The Northern started at Aurora and made its way to Denver, and then to Casper, Wyo.

"In towns where the school wouldn't cooperate, the merchants sold tickets," says Wallace. "All we had was an old engine and old cars we couldn't use anywhere else—the older the cars the better, in fact." Burlington's school specials generated hundreds of feature stories (including one in *Business Week*), made the railroad some $20,000 a month in profits, pleased the railfans and left behind an enormous reservoir of

goodwill. "The interesting thing is," says Wallace, "we didn't have to hire a single person to do any of these things. You motivated your people to become bigger and more creative. It was an exciting time on the railroad. Murphy said in 1965 that when everyone else was crying about the demise of passenger trains, they were adding $5 million to Burlington's bottom line."

Twin Zephyrs get a reprieve

William J. Quinn, who moved from Milwaukee Road's presidency late in 1966 to succeed Menk, is fond of quoting Harry Murphy: "Take away the passenger train, and a railroad is nothing more than a truck company." But even Murphy by the mid 1960s couldn't deny that some of his beloved *Zephyrs* were in trouble. "Sometime ago," he wrote in a January 1965 memo, nine months before his retirement, "I reached the conclusion we could not indefinitely continue the passenger service provided between Chicago and the Twin Cities. While I regret doing anything that will have the effect of lessening our status as a Carrier, I believe the time has come when we must consider a reduction in passenger train miles." As a first step, he suggested shedding the *Morning Zephyr* from Minneapolis and *Afternoon Zephyr* from Chicago.

These trains, of course, represented half of the twice-daily *Twin Zephyr* service dating to April 22, 1935. Since 1960 the westbound *Afternoon Zephyr* had been combined eight months of the year with the *Empire Builder,* and the *Empire Builder* with the *North Coast Limited* going east. Still, that was four trains each way eight months of the year, and five trains the other four months. By then, the *Twins,* the *North Coast Limited* and the *Empire Builder* lost a combined $700,000 a year in Burlington territory, based solely on direct costs.

As General Passenger Traffic Manager Burke began assembling paperwork for a train-off case, Wallace mounted a counterattack. In a biting memo

to Burke, his boss, Wallace said that abandoning these two trains would be "an indictment against this railroad, its policies and business methods, and against the Passenger Department itself." Continued Wallace: "We have let others take our customers away because we were railroad oriented instead of transportation oriented, product oriented instead of customer oriented. We should not be on the defensive but on the offensive." Wallace maintained that lost traffic could be regained, if the railroad tried harder. His position was buttressed by a study concluding that elimination of the eastbound *Morning Zephyr* and westbound *Afternoon Zephyr* would save a paltry $13,000 a year. So the trains remained.

But Burlington wasn't as willing as before to take risks to shore up weaknesses in the *Zephyr* network. Wallace's people generated more customers than the Burlington's big fleet of lightweight cars could carry. "WE NEED MORE EQUIPMENT!" pleaded Charles Able, assistant general passenger agent, in a 1960 memo to Burke. Burlington did scour the U.S. for good-condition secondhand lightweights, but aside from purchasing nine coaches from Chicago & North Western in 1963–64, did nothing. The railroad's board of directors, dominated by NP and GN, concluded the time had come to quit investing in passenger trains, and turned down subsequent deals. And in October of 1965, Burlington got a new president and the equation changed.

Burlington takes a new route

Tall, brown-haired Louis Wilson Menk, as pleasant to talk to as a small-town druggist, is a living Horatio Alger figure. Born the son of a Union Pacific trainman in Colorado, he worked three years for UP, starting as a telegraph messenger at night while attending Denver University during the day. Then in 1940, laid off by UP, Menk hired on as a telegrapher for the Frisco and slung Morse code dispatching trains over war-crowded tracks. Twenty-two years (and 21 moves from town to town) after his

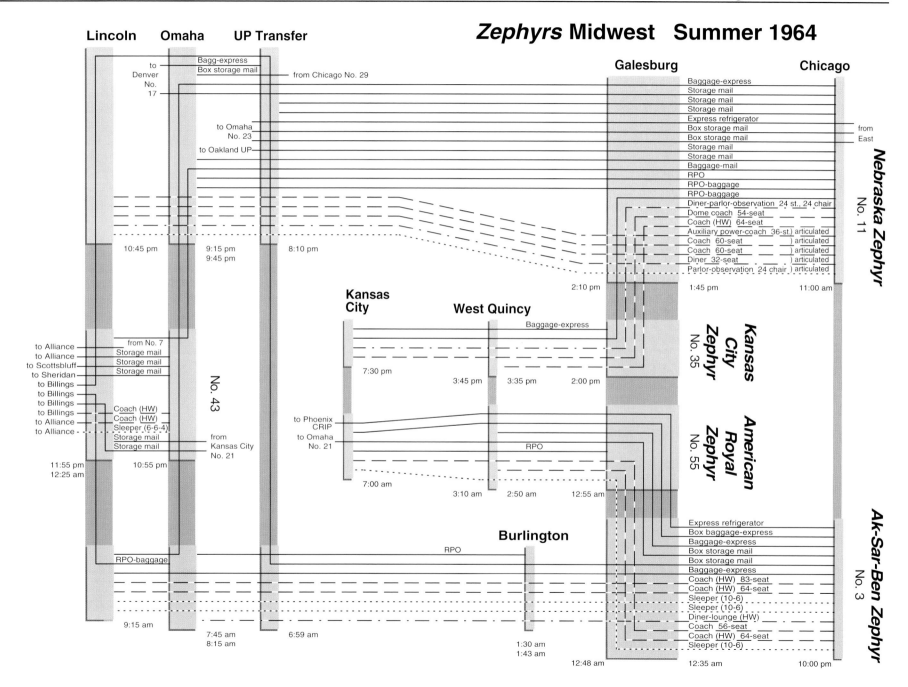

Lincoln **Omaha** **UP Transfer** ***Zephyrs* Midwest   Summer 1964**

Galesburg **Chicago**

Nebraska Zephyr No. 11

Bagg-express
Box storage mail
from Chicago No. 29

to Denver No. 17

Baggage-express
Storage mail
Storage mail
Storage mail
Express refrigerator
Box storage mail
Box storage mail
Storage mail
Storage mail
Baggage-mail
RPO
RPO-baggage
RPO-baggage
Diner-parlor-observation 24 st., 24 chair
Dome coach 54-seat
Coach (HW) 64-seat
Auxiliary power-coach 36-st.) articulated
Coach 60-seat   ) articulated
Coach 60-seat   ) articulated
Diner 32-seat   ) articulated
Parlor-observation 24 chair) articulated

to Omaha No. 23
to Oakland UP

10:45 pm
9:15 pm
9:45 pm
8:10 pm
2:10 pm
1:45 pm
11:00 am

from East

Kansas City
West Quincy

Kansas City Zephyr No. 35

Baggage-express

7:30 pm
3:45 pm
3:35 pm
2:00 pm

to Alliance
to Alliance
to Scottsbluff
to Sheridan
to Billings
to Billings
to Billings
to Billings
to Alliance
to Alliance

from No. 7
Storage mail
Storage mail
Storage mail

Coach (HW)
Coach (HW)
Sleeper (6-6-4)
Storage mail
Storage mail

from Kansas City No. 21

No. 43

to Phoenix CRIP
to Omaha No. 21

RPO

American Royal Zephyr No. 55

3:10 am
2:50 am
12:55 am

7:00 am

11:55 pm
12:25 am
10:55 pm

Burlington

Express refrigerator
Box baggage-express
Baggage-express
Box storage mail
Box storage mail
Baggage-express
Coach (HW) 83-seat
Coach (HW) 64-seat
Sleeper (10-6)
Sleeper (10-6)
Diner-lounge (HW)
Coach 56-seat
Coach (HW) 64-seat
Sleeper (10-6)

RPO-baggage
RPO

Ak-Sar-Ben Zephyr No. 3

9:15 am
7:45 am
8:15 am
6:59 am
1:30 am
1:43 am
12:48 am
12:35 am
10:00 pm

105

Zephyrs Northwest Summer 1964

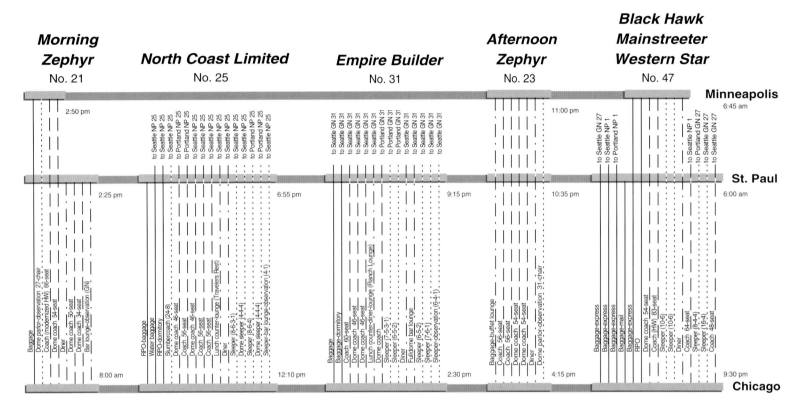

arrival Menk became president of the 5,020-mile railroad, half the size of Burlington. He would head three other Class I railroads. The first of those was as Murphy's successor at the Q, in late 1965.

"He crucified us, real quick," says Fred Clouse, a longtime CB&Q passenger sales officer. "It became rather depressing." But no one should have been surprised. Just before coming to Burlington, Menk sought to scuttle all of Frisco's six remaining pairs of passenger trains. I asked Menk recently if he thought Burlington's people expected him to do the same thing to the *Zephyrs*. "Certainly," he replied. "In fact, I told them I was going to. I told them we were

in the business of making money and returns on investment for shareholders."

Above all, says Menk, "There were way too many passenger trains." Harry Murphy must have loved those trains, Menk says, "because he did nothing about them. Burlington provided excellent service, and spent a lot of money doing so. Its strengths were trains like the *California Zephyr*—a beautiful train, well equipped and well run. But then you had trains to Quincy and Alliance and Billings and St. Louis that certainly weren't making money. In fact, none did on a fully distributed cost basis."

Or so Menk suspected. To prove it, he early on

brought in consultant William Carpenter, whose Silver Spring, Md., firm had helped Frisco on a freight-cost study. Menk's instruction to Carpenter: Provide the numbers that will convince regulators to let us get rid of these trains.

Wallace well remembers the tense meeting in Burlington's board room late in 1965 at which Menk introduced Carpenter to the Passenger Traffic Department officers. "I asked Carpenter," says Wallace, "whether he was sent here to do away with the Passenger Department, or to look at the facts. I asked this more than once. I'm sure everyone cringed in their seats. I was pretty proud of what we were

▶ *The distinctiveness of Burlington trains is evident at Dallas Union Station in 1962. Fluted-side E5 9953 has arrived with No. 7 from Denver, while sister 9952A waits to head south from town as No. 3,* the Sam Houston Zephyr. *(John B. Charles)*

doing, and Menk hadn't been there long enough to know. Menk interrupted Carpenter's reply to reassure us that he was only interested in gathering facts. But Menk went on to say that we couldn't maintain all the passenger services we then had, and I agreed. We had our weak spots."

Carpenter assembled his team, which included people from Burlington's accounting and operating departments. Two people involved in the project bear special mention. One was William Greenwood, a young trainmaster who went on to become Burlington Northern's chief transportation officer. The other was the man Greenwood reported to, a bald, heavyset, bespectacled fellow of intimidating demeanor named W. Edwards Deming. Deming, with a doctorate in mathematical physics, would later in his long life be hailed as the person who during the 1950s and early 1960s taught Japanese companies the gospel of quality manufacturing and thus helped spawn a decades-long economic boom for that nation. But in his own country Deming remained virtually unknown then and was hired by Carpenter to help build the statistical case.

"I'd meet Deming at the Whitehall Hotel on Sunday to get my assignment for the next two weeks," says Greenwood. "Deming designed a sampling study to be used in developing costs. I stopwatched every switching job involving a passenger train at every location a certain number of times. I'd spend four days in Casper and a week in

Omaha—all over the railroad. I even timed how long it took to wash the *California Zephyr* in Denver: 15 minutes. The engineer used a Dixie cup in the electrical cabinet to keep the Baldwin switcher from going into transition at low speed and jerking cars around."

Carpenter's people had a problem: The Interstate Commerce Commission would not consider indirect or apportioned costs—the passenger trains' share of the president's salary, for instance, or their portion of common track maintenance costs—when deciding whether to allow a train to be dropped from the schedule. So the consultants had to find every conceivable directly attributable cost, and switching

charges were an item sometimes overlooked by railroad managements.

The fact finding, which lasted six months, took longer than anticipated because the team had to keep going back to refigure the numbers. "The losses they expected weren't there," reports Greenwood. So some fudging ensued. Greenwood cites this example: He was told by Deming to count as time switching passenger trains from the minute the switch crew stopped doing whatever it was doing before working a passenger train until it resumed its previous task. At Casper, the switch crew customarily tied up for an hour to have a meal before the arrival of the Billings train. The actual switching

◀ *The Kansas City Zephyr, leaving its namesake city in 1966, never rose to much greater length on this end of the run than four cars; competitor Santa Fe need not fear. (Steve Patterson)*

WINNERS

Denver Zephyr	$1,653,005
Special trains	1,265,154
Fast Mail (trains 29-14)	1,110,685
Chicago–Denver locals (trains 7-8)	700,438
Nebraska Zephyr	543,010
California Zephyr	536,778
St. Louis–Twin Cities (*Zephyr-Rocket*)	148,659
American Royal Zephyr	114,303
Omaha–Kansas City trains (3 pair)	89,707

LOSERS

Empire Builder	$−412,237
Alliance–Casper	−168,459
N. Coast Limited	−166,125
Kansas City Zephyr	−152,409
Ak-Sar-Ben Zephyr	−113,867
Omaha–Billings	−101,896
Wendover–Billings	−100,779
Chicago–Galesburg (trains 15-2)	−88,909
Afternoon Zephyr	−80,550
Alliance–Brush	−57,597
Morning Zephyr	−41,058
Black Hawk	−39,827

out of a storage mail car or two took maybe ten minutes. But the train was charged for an hour and ten minutes worth of switching. Menk remembers the project as frustrating. "I wanted to know how we were actually doing," he said, "but accounting for costs was difficult. It was sort of like picking up a handful of jello. You'd get one fact and another would slip through your fingers."

"I wasn't a railfan"

Two things happened to stymie the Carpenter project. First, he lost his sponsor. Menk spent one year to the day at CB&Q before accepting the presidency of its half-owner, Northern Pacific. NP, GN and Q could smell success then in their decades-long pursuit of the merger that created Burlington Northern in 1970. "I would like to have stayed longer," Menk says. "I liked that railroad, and I think its people liked me. But then I'd be number three on the totem pole when the merger went

through, and at that stage of my life I wasn't going to do that." By the time Carpenter concluded his work on January 9, 1967, William J. Quinn was chief executive, after eight years running Milwaukee Road, and Quinn had no stomach for a big train-off campaign.

More important, Carpenter never made the case against the *Zephyrs*. The best he could do was report that in 1966 some trains made money on the basis of savable costs—what the railroad would save if a train no longer operated—and some did not. Train-by-train figures for his 1966 study have been lost. But Carpenter also presented profit-and-loss numbers on all Burlington passenger trains for the year 1964, attributing to passenger trains only those costs they directly bore and omitting common costs such as dispatching, rail and signal maintenance and the like. And on that basis, Burlington's intercity passenger trains, as a group, made more than $4.5 million:

Carpenter lamely recommended that all trains not covering direct expenses be discontinued. Inasmuch as the losers included all five pairs of Chicago–Twin Cities trains, including the flagship trains of Burlington's owners, this was not a very practical suggestion. Yet while Carpenter's work went for naught, Menk had a profound impact on Burlington passenger philosophy. Sent by Menk to the freight sales staff, Wallace resigned, and the railroad lost its most ardent passenger train proponent. Wallace felt betrayed by the turn of events. "The passenger trains were what made Burlington known," he says. "When everything else among railroads is the same, and they all lose their customers' freight cars in the yards, what sets you apart from the pack are your passenger trains. We were famous for ours."

But streamlined trains no longer mattered in Menk's scheme of things. The two steam engines were retired as quickly as he could order it done. Fred Clouse, who replaced Wallace as number two in the Passenger Traffic Department, lacked his predecessor's verve. "Most of us tucked our heads in our jobs and simply worked," says Richard Campbell, number three in the department then.

Did Menk feel he'd left unfinished business when he went to Northern Pacific? Yes, indeed, as it applied to passenger trains. "I'd have kept applying to take them off, one by one. On the Frisco we went community to community telling our story, and we even got support. It can be done."

C'mon Lou, I said, didn't you harbor an *ounce* of sentiment toward those beautiful trains? No, he replied matter-of-factly. "I made no secret that I wasn't a railfan. I never was a guy who had a [model] railroad in my basement." Menk fondly recalled riding with his dad between Denver and Ellis, Kan., on UP trains. "But somewhere along the line I became a businessman, and businessmen don't like to sit around and see something lose money. Even today I like to ride trains from here to there, to have fun. But I sure as hell wouldn't do it on business."

End of the *California Zephyr*

Menk missed an opportunity to practice what he preached early in his Burlington tenure. The *California Zephyr* was jointly owned by Burlington, Rio Grande and Western Pacific and had been a great money-maker from its inception in 1949. But

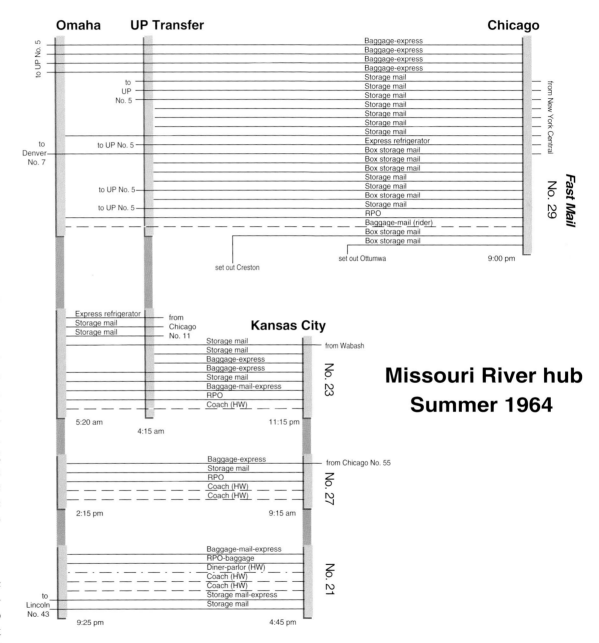

1956 became the last year that WP cleared a profit on the train, and increasing losses on its end exposed the Achilles heel of this *Zephyr:* If any one of the three owners opted out, the *CZ* was doomed.

Western Pacific President Myron Christy appealed to Menk in early 1966 for support in getting rid of the train, which lost WP $780,000 on an avoidable-cost basis the year before. In a "Dear Myron" letter on April 28, 1966, Menk turned him down, calling any effort by WP to be rid of the *CZ* "unwise, impractical and untimely."

Considering Menk's distaste for running passenger trains, the letter (unearthed by *Zephyr* historian Schultz) is remarkable. First, Menk reminds Christy that he tried to rid Frisco of all passenger trains. "I am, however," Menk continues, "a realist." Among other differences between the two situations, he says, Frisco trains were lightly patronized, the *CZ* heavily traveled.

Menk tells Christy that Burlington had already made concessions to Western Pacific to reduce the *California Zephyr's* loss. He says WP's claims of big losses from the *Zephyr* would be rigorously challenged at Interstate Commerce Commission hearings, and that the improved financial status of WP would be used against the railroad. He says that President Lyndon Johnson is arm-twisting railroad presidents to forestall train-off cases. He suggests that Christy examine troubles of Southern Pacific in taking off trains in California. Concludes Menk:

> We honestly feel that there is a future for this type operation if we maintain the quality of service and at the same time consider and make economies that appear to be possible.
>
> It is therefore my duty to inform you that Burlington will not support an application for discontinuance of your operation and while we would do so with great regret, we probably would take a formal adversary position in any such proceeding.

Menk doesn't say that the *CZ* had earned Burlington a $198,000 profit in 1965, based on direct costs. Train 17 and 18 did a brisk local business east of Denver—enough to often justify an extra flattop coach on its portion of the route. Discontinuance in 1960 of the *Coloradoan*, on schedules between Omaha and Denver substantially identical to those of the *California Zephyr*, brought new revenue to the transcontinental train. Each evening at Omaha, No. 17 picked up four head-end cars, two of which went to Denver and two (including a Railway Post Office) to McCook, Neb. Few passengers ever realized that under cover of darkness across the Great Plains, it carried (GASP!) Pullman-green heavyweight cars directly behind the silver-sided diesels. Eastbound, No. 18 handled three mail cars to Omaha, two of them regularly heavyweights.

Western Pacific in June 1966 went ahead and asked the ICC to let it be rid of the *Zephyr*, and got turned down. But the end was only a matter of time. Rio Grande had gone into the red on the train by 1964, and Burlington's last year to clear its direct costs was 1965. In 1966, when the Omaha–McCook and Denver–Omaha RPO cars were removed, the *CZ* had a $283,000 loss on Burlington. In 1967, when the last Omaha–Denver mail was removed, Q's loss mushroomed to $1.4 million. At the rate things were going in early 1968, Burlington would lose $2 million that year on this train.

If at first you don't succeed . . .

In January 1968, Western Pacific tried again. This time it claimed a loss for 1967 on its portion of the run of $1.2 million. Ridership had fallen 13 percent that year from 1966 levels—the first noticeable drop in the train's 18-year history. But even if the *California Zephyr* had run full every day of 1967 at its maximum summer length, WP said, it would still have cost that railroad $600,000 in losses.

Again the ICC turned Western Pacific down. Again the *CZ's* patronage dwindled. Again its costs rose.

Again the clock ticked, and when yet another year passed, Western Pacific came a third time to the regulators, now joined by Rio Grande.

Death rattles were audible. A measure of the costs WP bore: Its passenger service involved 252 employees—*all* chargeable to the *California Zephyr*, for this was Western Pacific's only passenger train. The *CZ's* loss on WP for the 12 months ending July 31, 1969, amounted to $2.2 million, and the railroad itself stood in danger of failure. Concluded a reluctant ICC: "Time has now run out on Western Pacific's *Zephyr*." Rio Grande, though still quite profitable, presented statistics no less sobering. From 1964 to 1968, the *CZ's* ridership over its line from Denver to Salt Lake City declined 25 percent, revenues fell 27 percent and expenses rose 33 percent. The avoidable loss shouldered by Rio Grande was now $1.8 million. This *Zephyr* had become a $6 million-a-year drain on its owners' profitability.

Through all three *California Zephyr* cases those three and a half years, Burlington remained mute. By 1969 it could have joined its partners in seeking a way out. Its own direct losses on the train by then were monumental. More than two decades later, Quinn himself couldn't recall why the Q remained willing to continue sponsoring this train.

But the source of Burlington's hesitancy isn't hard to fathom. It stood by the *California Zephyr* for the same reason that Santa Fe remained true to its

▶ *With a business car in tow, train 31, 36 miles out of Alliance en route to Casper, backs around the wye at Bridgeport, Nebraska, after leaving the depot, in October 1963. It was one of only two removed during the year that Louis Menk was Burlington's president. (Jim C. Seacrest)*

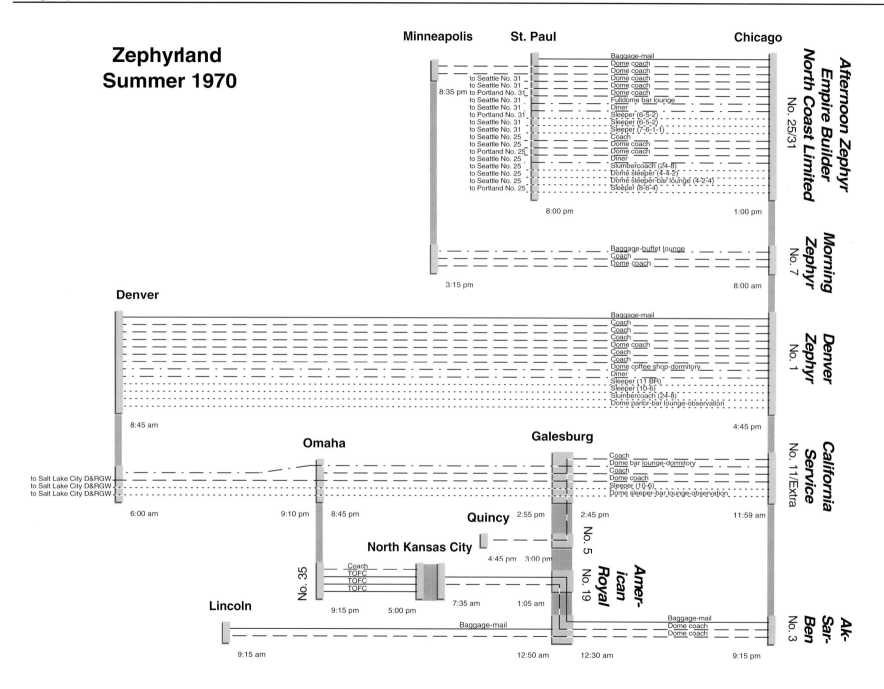

**Zephyrland
Summer 1970**

Minneapolis   St. Paul   Chicago

*Afternoon Zephyr
Empire Builder
North Coast Limited*   No. 25/31

Baggage-mail
Dome coach
Dome coach
to Seattle No. 31   Dome coach
to Seattle No. 31   Dome coach
8:35 pm to Portland No. 31   Dome coach
to Seattle No. 31   Fulldome bar lounge
to Seattle No. 31   Diner
to Portland No. 31   Sleeper (6-5-2)
to Seattle No. 31   Sleeper (6-5-2)
to Seattle No. 31   Sleeper (7-6-1-1)
to Seattle No. 25   Coach
to Seattle No. 25   Dome coach
to Portland No. 25   Dome coach
to Seattle No. 25   Diner
to Seattle No. 25   Slumbercoach (24-8)
to Seattle No. 25   Dome sleeper (4-4-2)
to Seattle No. 25   Dome sleeper-bar lounge (4-2-4)
to Portland No. 25   Sleeper (8-6-4)

8:00 pm   1:00 pm

*Morning
Zephyr*   No. 7

Baggage-buffet lounge
Coach
Dome coach

3:15 pm   8:00 am

Denver

*Denver
Zephyr*   No. 1

Baggage-mail
Coach
Coach
Coach
Dome coach
Coach
Coach
Dome coffee shop-dormitory
Diner
Sleeper (11 BR)
Sleeper (10-6)
Slumbercoach (24-8)
Dome parlor-bar lounge-observation

8:45 am   4:45 pm

Omaha   Galesburg

*California
Service*   No. 11/Extra

Coach
Dome bar lounge-dormitory
to Salt Lake City D&RGW   Coach
to Salt Lake City D&RGW   Dome coach
to Salt Lake City D&RGW   Sleeper (10-6)
Dome sleeper-bar lounge-observation

6:00 am   9:10 pm   8:45 pm   11:59 am

Quincy   2:55 pm   2:45 pm

No. 5

North Kansas City   4:45 pm   3:00 pm

*Amer-
ican
Royal*   No. 19

No. 35   Coach
TOFC
TOFC
TOFC

7:35 am   1:05 am

Lincoln   9:15 pm   5:00 pm

*Ak-
Sar-
Ben*   No. 3

Baggage-mail
Dome coach
Dome coach

Baggage-mail

9:15 am   12:50 am   12:30 am   9:15 pm

Not long before the California Zephyr's demise, a passenger happily relaxes in its observation lounge. (Ted Benson)

Not long before the California Zephyr's *demise, a passenger happily relaxes in its observation lounge. (Ted Benson)*

Super Chief, Illinois Central its *Panama,* Baltimore & Ohio its *Capitol,* Great Northern its *Empire Builder* and Seaboard its *Meteor.* These trains defined their railroads in the eyes of the public, employees and management. To have cast them aside, if such an act were avoidable, would have been corporate mutilation. Burlington in 1968 did consider combining the *Denver* and *California Zephyrs,* but did not because of schedule problems.

Nature took its course. On March 21, 1970, the *California Zephyr* was laid to rest. Western Pacific was rid of it altogether. Rio Grande was allowed to operate *Rio Grande Zephyr* just three days a week. Burlington filed a notice (which the ICC didn't oppose) to run a thrice-weekly *California Service* train west of Omaha in place of trains 17 and 18, to connect with the Rio Grande schedule. East of Omaha it combined with the remnant of the *Nebraska Zephyr.* Granted, the four-car *California Service* train was fully up to Burlington standards—dome coach, dome dormitory-buffet lounge, sleeper and the old *CZ* dome sleeper-lounge-observation. Still, things had come to a pretty pass on the railroad that had cradled the lightweight train three decades before.

The cruel 12 months

Burlington began in earnest to reduce passenger-train miles in 1967. First to go: The coach-only overnight train between St. Louis and the Twin Cities. The former *Zephyr–Rocket* was a joint effort of CB&Q and, north of Burlington, Ia., Rock Island Lines. Its last runs occurred April 8–9.

Next, on July 1, the railroad shed a pair of unnamed Chicago–Omaha locals—westbound, No.

7 (which kept running Omaha to Denver) and eastbound No. 14, a no-passengers counterpart to the westbound *Fast Mail.* In September the last trains between Denver and Dallas bit the dust.

The Chicago–Omaha *Fast Mail,* which regularly handled 20 or more cars of head-end traffic, was shorn of its business by postal authorities and discontinued on October 1, 1967, along with No. 8, the other half of the Chicago–Denver locals, east of Omaha. Both 7 and 8 were dropped west of Omaha on December 18.

Zephyrs went on the chopping block, too. In 1966 the railroad had rearranged service on the Twin Cities line, merging the *North Coast Limited* and *Empire Builder* both ways in eight lightly traveled months of the year. Both pairs of *Twin Zephyrs* ran independently. As of October 29, 1967, the *Morning Zephyr* from Minneapolis and *Afternoon*

Zephyr from Chicago were combined with the already-combined *North Coast* and *Builder.* All these trains had run rather closely upon one another's schedule. But an after-the-fact investigation by the ICC revealed that the two *Zephyrs* in 1966 carried some 155 passengers per train mile—a substantial number—and that ending their independent operation would overly inconvenience passengers, many of them college students. So the commission ordered the *Afternoon Zephyr* from Chicago continued as a separate train Friday and Sunday only. There was no eastbound counterpart.

Burlington also went after the *Kansas City Zephyr.* Since 1962, it had been combined with the *Nebraska Zephyr* east of Galesburg, and west of there puddled along at a sizable cash loss. Cancellation of the *KCZ*'s RPO contract in the fall of 1967 doubled the loss overnight. These trains, too,

were heavily used by students and were ordered continued east of Quincy, Ill., on the Missouri border. Last Kansas City runs were April 10, 1968.

Next on the block: the three pairs of Kansas City–Omaha trains. With their heavyweight coaches and strings of mail cars, they had been moderately profitable all through the decade. Again, loss of RPO cars and storage mail in January 1968 tipped the scales the other way. Three trains became two with loss of the overnight runs in June 1968, and two trains became one 17 months later. To cut costs, Burlington moved out of Kansas City Union Station and into North Kansas City.

The train-off wars

Some trains Burlington wanted rid of just wouldn't go. The *Nebraska Zephyr*'s prodigous mail and express revenue—$2.3 million in 1966—disappeared in stages during 1967 and 1968 (as did the articulated passenger-car sets, the five-car *Train of the Gods* and *Train of the Goddesses*, after 31-year careers spanning untold millions of miles). But when the Q sought to drop the train between Galesburg and Lincoln, the ICC only allowed it to discontinue the 55 miles between Omaha and Lincoln. Nor could the railroad scuttle the other Chicago–Lincoln train, the overnight *Ak-Sar-Ben Zephyr*. It had operated at a small profit right into mid 1969, when the loss of most mail (including one of two surviving RPO assignments on CB&Q) begat what Burlington calculated would be a $400,000 loss.

◄ *In this dramatic scene, Twin Cities–bound train No. 23, the* Badger, *has left Duluth and is picking up train orders at Central Avenue Tower in South Superior, Wisconsin. (William D. Middleton)*

The last sleeping car had been pulled in late 1968, and on average only 20 or so people rode the single remaining coach at any one time. But the ICC essentially said the train had not been unprofitable long enough to determine its losses.

The only clear-cut victory Burlington won in the train-off battles of 1968–69 turned bittersweet. The train in question was the Omaha–Billings local meandering almost 900 miles over a sleepy secondary route to southern Montana. Burlington's first effort to be shed of trains 42 and 43 in 1967 failed. In January 1969, on a second try, Burlington substantiated $844,000 in annual losses and prevailed. But a coalition of protesters sued to overturn the ICC judgment, and a federal appeals court ordered the train run pending a judgment.

When word reached the railroad early on August 14 that the lawsuit had been dismissed, Billings-bound No. 43 had just left Alliance. On advice of railroad lawyers, who wanted the train "dead" before CB&Q's foes could mount a new appeal, No. 43 was halted at the next station—Hemingford, Neb., population 909—and the 34 passengers were ejected to await a bus, while a switcher left Alliance 19 miles away to tow the empty train back.

All for naught. The Supreme Court reinstated the appeal and ordered 42 and 43 put back. Then Burlington learned that its abrupt act had stranded a Republican congressman and his son who had taken the train a few days earlier to a remote location for a fishing vacation, and held return-trip tickets. Worse still, the congressman sat on the House transportation subcommittee which oversaw all railroad legislation. Months later (long after trains 42 and 43 had finally been put to rest, for good), president Quinn had to face that congressman at a hearing, take the heat and publicly apologize for the "great embarrassment" caused by his railroad. "In hindsight," he said that day, "if I could erase the incident, I would certainly do it." *This* from the passenger-friendly railroad!

Mr. Menk meets his match

And where was Lou Menk by 1969? At Northern Pacific, where more than three years into his presidency of Burlington's co-owner, he was mighty frustrated. "I want out! Listen, we are losing money. Our ability to pay taxes, our ability to have competitive freight rates is being impaired." Menk was in fine form in the Rayburn House Office Building in Washington, D.C., on November 12, 1969, testifying to the transportation subcommittee on the passenger problem. "Our service is good," he said, "but nobody is riding our trains."

Northern Pacific in 1968 had lost $10.2 million on passenger trains, based on the ICC's narrow definition of solely related costs. Yet Menk got nowhere in removing the biggest money-loser of the bunch, the St. Paul–Seattle *Mainstreeter*. When NP first sought to discontinue the secondary transcontinental train late in 1967, soon after its RPO car was removed, trains 1 and 2 still handled as many as eight express and storage mail cars, two to three coaches in winter and five in summer, a slumbercoach between Spokane and Seattle and a crew dormitory (sleeping) car and economy diner between Mandan, N.D., and Spokane.

Undeniably, the *Mainstreeter* was costly. At 20 points en route some or all crew members changed. Each 1,892-mile run required 71 employees: 16 engineers and firemen, 18 flagmen, nine conductors, eight baggage messengers and mail handlers, and one cook, waiter, coach attendant and slumbercoach porter. On revenues of an impressive $6.3 million in 1966, NP still lost $1.3 million.

Here was what Menk could call an open-and-shut case. And he was turned down in May 1968. Cut away rhetoric in the ICC's 35-page opinion, and the reason boils down to this: Seven years earlier, Menk's predecessor, Robert McFarlane, had made a rash promise to run the *Mainstreeter* and *North Coast Limited* "until the public abandons them, if they ever do." Alas, McFarlane made the statement be-

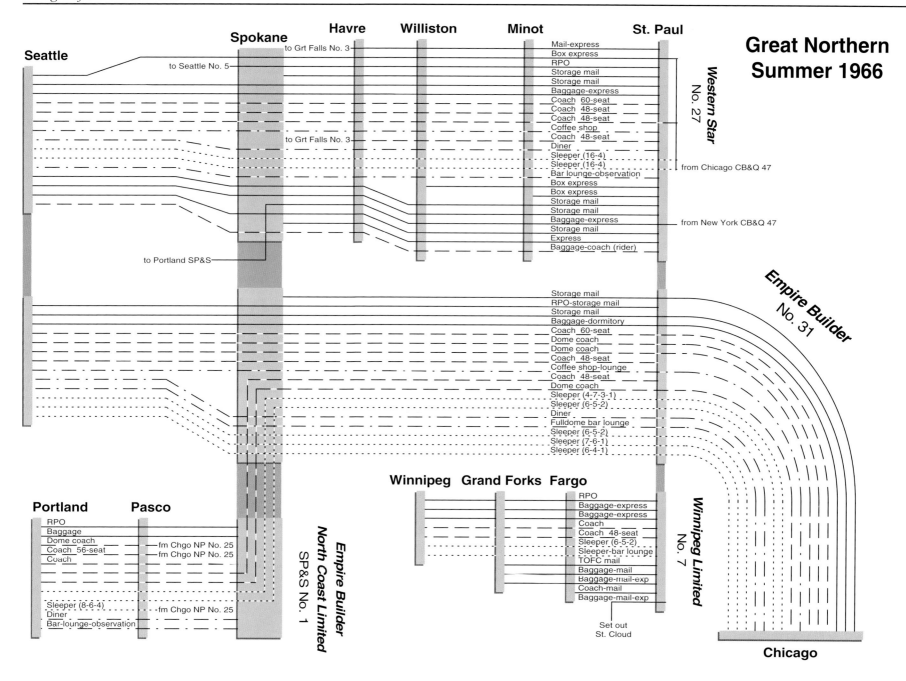

Seattle

Spokane

Havre **Williston** **Minot** **St. Paul**

Great Northern
Summer 1966

to Grt Falls No. 3

to Seattle No. 5

Mail-express
Box express
RPO
Storage mail
Storage mail
Baggage-express
Coach 60-seat
Coach 48-seat
Coach 48-seat
Coffee shop
Coach 48-seat
Diner
Sleeper (16-4)
Sleeper (16-4)
Bar lounge-observation
Box express
Box express
Storage mail
Storage mail
Baggage-express
Storage mail
Express
Baggage-coach (rider)

Western Star No. 27

to Grt Falls No. 3

from Chicago CB&Q 47

from New York CB&Q 47

to Portland SP&S

Storage mail
RPO-storage mail
Storage mail
Baggage-dormitory
Coach 60-seat
Dome coach
Dome coach
Coach 48-seat
Coffee shop-lounge
Coach 48-seat
Dome coach
Sleeper (4-7-3-1)
Sleeper (6-5-2)
Diner
Fulldome bar lounge
Sleeper (6-5-2)
Sleeper (7-6-1)
Sleeper (6-4-1)

Empire Builder No. 31

Winnipeg Grand Forks Fargo

Portland **Pasco**

RPO
Baggage
Dome coach
Coach 56-seat
Coach

fm Chgo NP No. 25
fm Chgo NP No. 25

Sleeper (8-6-4)
Diner
Bar-lounge-observation

fm Chgo NP No. 25

*Empire Builder
North Coast Limited
SP&S No. 1*

RPO
Baggage-express
Baggage-express
Coach
Coach 48-seat
Sleeper (6-5-2)
Sleeper-bar lounge
TOFC mail
Baggage-mail
Baggage-mail-exp
Coach-mail
Baggage-mail-exp

Winnipeg Limited No. 7

Set out
St. Cloud

Chicago

fore the ICC, under oath. And then McFarlane, who unlike Menk much admired his fine passenger trains, compounded matters by repeating his vow. In Missoula, Mont., he declared:

> Some people think that the passenger train service through Missoula is going to be changed. It is not going to be changed. I assure you that as long as the public will use our trains, the *North Coast Limited* and *Mainstreeter* will operate just about as they are at present.

Well, McFarlane in 1968 still held the (mostly honorific) position of chairman of NP. And the proposed merger which prompted these promises was, the ICC felt, about to be consummated. Moreover, the public had not forsaken the *Mainstreeter*. Ridership increased noticeably in both 1966 and 1967. Saying that the as-yet-unborn Burlington Northern had expressed corporate willingness to run the *Mainstreeter*, the ICC said NP could bear its burden a while longer. Menk must have rolled his eyes in disbelief. The BN merger wouldn't occur for another two years. So back came Northern Pacific a year later. Now it claimed a $2.5 million loss, and on the day of Menk's House subcommittee testimony in November 1969, the Interstate Commerce Commission spoke a second time: No.

This time the ICC didn't invoke McFarlane's promises. But it laid the blame for the *Mainstreeter*'s 30 percent drop in ridership during 1968 and the vastly increased loss at the railroad's feet. Northern Pacific, it said, discontinued sleepers in prime travel periods, altered schedules to send the train through key towns at inconvenient hours and missed connecting trains in Washington, provided poor on-board assistance and "extremely poor" reservation service and gave freights priority.

The commission's reasoning was hokum. The "altered" schedules represented a speedup that erased *seven hours* from the St. Paul–Seattle run,

Burlington co-owners Great Northern and Northern Pacific both operated extensive passenger networks to the west coast and upper Midwest from home bases in St. Paul. Right, in 1966, GN train 19, the Gopher, *passes Central Avenue Tower in South Superior, Wisconsin, on its way from Duluth, Minnesota, to the Twin Cities. Above, the* North Coast Limited *of Northern Pacific makes a servicing stop in Billings, Montana, in July of 1969. (William D. Middleton)*

putting eastbound passengers on Burlington's *Afternoon Zephyr* to Chicago rather the overnight *Black Hawk,* and got westbound riders to Seattle without having to endure a second night on the road. Kenneth Tuggle's written dissent noted that NP had cut expenses of No. 1 and 2 by $1.6 million in 1968; otherwise, the *Mainstreeter*'s loss would have been an intolerable $4 million. "As soon as a dollar is saved," he wrote, "the epithet of 'downgrading' is hurled. The majority shuts their eyes to the cost of maintaining the level of 1967 service." Tuggle then quoted from the *Bible:* "Woe unto you also, ye lawyers, for ye lade men with burdens grievous to be borne, and ye yourselves touch not the burdens with one of your fingers."

The kinder, gentler Great Northern

The third member of the triad that was to form BN lay low. Great Northern was run by John Budd, son of Burlington's legendary Ralph. The younger Budd, says Robert Downing, his second-in-command, was "a master of the art of not making people mad at him." And with the Northern Lines merger his dad had sought decades earlier within grasp, John Budd needed no enemies.

Geography played a part in Great Northern's passenger policy. Without the passenger train, northern Montana and North Dakota were prisoners of nature during bitter winters, due to the lack of all-weather highways and air service. "So Budd felt a greater sense of responsibility toward local people," says Downing. The policy that crystallized in the late 1950s: Avoid committing new capital, but run the best trains possible.

Great Northern shouldered without audible discomfort a direct-cost passenger deficit of roughly $5 million annually through the first half of the 1960s. "The *Empire Builder* remained profitable through 1966," recounts Downing. So, perhaps, did the *Western Star,* which had inherited the considerable head-end business of Great Northern's old *Fast Mail* earlier in the decade. From St. Paul each morning in mid 1966, a mega-*Star* hurdled itself toward Seattle with 24 cars: six head-end cars, five coaches, coffee shop, diner, two sleepers, full lounge and eight more mail and express cars.

John Budd's *noblesse oblige* was sorely tried after the *Builder* lost its RPO in late 1967, passenger volume began trailing off and mail starting leaving the trains. The direct-cost loss in 1968 rose to $8

million. "John had periods of depression about the whole picture," says Downing. "He'd say, 'What we ought to do is take off the *Empire Builder* and keep the *Western Star* so long as the post office gives us a decent amount of business. That way we're rid of the high-cost train and take care of local people.'" The *Builder*'s time was approaching, Downing says. "That was to be the last step."

But the *Empire Builder* never met its maker. Nor did the *Western Star,* or Lou Menk's millstone the *Mainstreeter,* or NP's *North Coast Limited.* Instead, the extraordinary lengthy effort to unite the Northern Lines finally leapt over its last barrier. Burlington Northern began March 2, 1970. Tying together the pieces, while calming shareholders after Penn Central's spectacular bankruptcy that June, kept management busy. By summer's end, Amtrak was on the horizon.

▲ *Running on time, but running out of time, the* Texas Zephyr *makes its way north near Walsenburg, Colorado, in October 1965. (Victor Hand)*

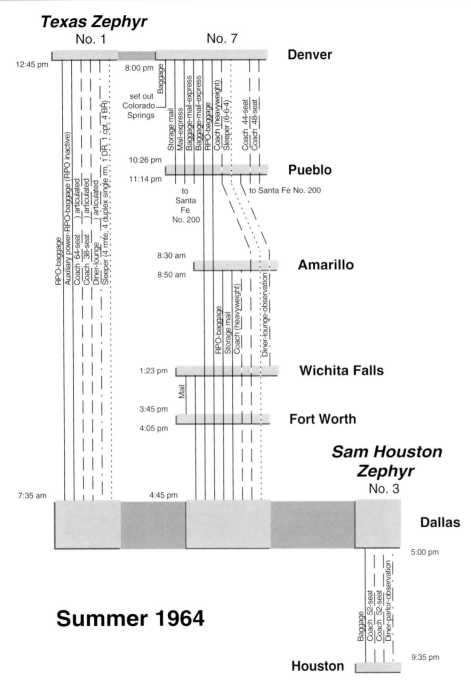

Texas Zephyr

No. 1   No. 7

Denver

12:45 pm

8:00 pm

Baggage

set out
Colorado
Springs

10:26 pm

Pueblo

11:14 pm

to
Santa
Fe
No. 200

to Santa Fe No. 200

8:30 am

Amarillo

8:50 am

1:23 pm

Wichita Falls

3:45 pm

Fort Worth

4:05 pm

Sam Houston Zephyr

No. 3

7:35 am   4:45 pm

Dallas

5:00 pm

Summer 1964

9:35 pm

Houston

Car labels No. 1: RPO-baggage · Auxiliary power-RPO-baggage (RPO inactive) · Coach 64-seat (articulated) · Coach 38-seat (articulated) · Diner-lounge (articulated) · Sleeper (4 rmte, 4 duplex single rm, 1 DR, 1 cpt, 4 BR)

Car labels No. 7: Storage mail · Mail-express · Baggage-mail-express · Baggage-mail-express · RPO-baggage · Coach (heavyweight) · Sleeper (6-6-4) · Coach 44-seat · Coach 48-seat

Wichita Falls label: Mail

Amarillo label: RPO-baggage · Storage mail · Coach (heavyweight) · Diner-lounge-observation

Houston (Sam Houston Zephyr No. 3): Baggage · Coach 52-seat · Coach 52-seat · Diner-parlor-observation

Zephyrs to Texas: Diminishing returns

The Texas trains of Burlington subsidiaries Colorado & Southern and Fort Worth & Denver (they joined at the Texas–New Mexico border) were distinctive. Their classic signature: a small fleet of slant-nosed E5 diesels that bore both stainless-steel sheathing and Silver-series names on their flanks. Alas, the Texas trains fared poorly in the 1960s.

The Texas Zephyr in 1957 inherited the low-slung, articulated cars of the original Denver Zephyr, but it was simply too much train. By 1960 the off-season TZ had shrunk to eight cars. First to go were a pair of articulated sleepers, each with 12 sections, and the dinette-coach at the front of the train. Next went a second pair of articulated sleepers, one with sections and the other all-room. Then the distinctive 10-chair parlor-bar lounge-observation disappeared except in summer and over the Christmas holidays. The obs left the train entirely after the summer of 1963, leaving the abbreviated Texas Zephyr depicted at left. Cracked truck frames began appearing in late 1964, and the 28-year-old cars were taken out of service in January 1965 in favor of regular lightweight cars (including diner-lounge-observations Silver Tray and Silver Bowl from the original Texas Zephyr of 1940).

Meanwhile, nameless numbers 7 and 8 put on quite a show, too. Between Denver and Pueblo they carried cars of Santa Fe's Denver–La Junta local. Out of Fort Worth, the Sam Houston Zephyr until 1963 rode at the end of No. 7 to Dallas, where its cars were attached to an E unit and sent on their way to Houston. (The northbound Sam Houston hitched a ride from Dallas on No. 2.) The Sam Houston Zephyr, last of Burlington's short-distance streamliners, was discontinued in January 1966. Next to go was the southbound Texas Zephyr and No. 8, on December 15, 1966. The previous April, a Time magazine correspondent had accompanied president Menk and Menk's dad aboard No. 1. Menk counted a mere dozen coach passengers—equal to the size of the crew—and exclaimed: "This is not only amazing; it's tragic." Two months later C&S/FW&D went to the Interstate Commerce Commission, claiming losses of more than half a million dollars a year on trains 1 and 8. As part of the deal to be rid of them, No. 7 would regain the sleeping and dining cars it had lost in 1965, and assume with No. 2 the Texas Zephyr name. In the early months of 1967, the reconstituted Texas Zephyr ran with as many as seven head-end cars and a lightweight coach, 6-6-4 sleeper and diner-lounge-observation.

But as mail revenues evaporated that year, these trains, too, went on the block. They expired on September 10, 1967, ending a colorful era of Zephyr history in the Lone Star State.

SOUTHERN'S HOSPITALITY

How a railroad drove away so many passengers that upon creation of Amtrak, it could afford to stand aside and run its own trains—this time to universal acclaim.

◀ *What have we here—the branch line of some Third World railroad? No, merely the entrails of the* Augusta Special *after it had been filleted by Southern Railway. The Southern, as was its habit, took advantage in 1966 of a loophole in the regulatory net to amputate this secondary train at both ends of its run, leaving it a train going from nowhere (in this scene, Warrenville, South Carolina) to nowhere (Fort Mill, S.C.). After some months of operating solely within South Carolina with virtually no revenue, it was a cinch to get state approval for its removal. Here the train—an RS3 roadswitcher, heavyweight coach, baggage car (its Railway Post Office apartment unused) and steam heater (a decommissioned FT diesel) while away the four-hour layover in Warrenville. (George Weiss)*

You can say many things about William Brosnan, who was president of Southern Railway from 1962 through 1967: That he pioneered mechanized track maintenance. That he midwived innovative services, such as the Big John covered hopper that undercut trucking rates. That he forever sought ways to increase the efficiency of his railroad and thus ensure its survival in the nation's poorest region. At these things he was very good.

But you can't call Bill Brosnan nice. He'd fire people on a whim (or drive them away), only to undergo a change of heart and beg them to return, which some of them did. "Brosnan was a strange mixture of genius and ruthlessness," remarks James Bistline, a Southern Railway attorney in the Brosnan era. "You couldn't have a long conversation with him. He saw through problems right away and acted. It was great for the railroad, but not for the people who worked for him." William Moore, Southern's VP-operations in the final Brosnan years, said flatly: "The man was Adolph Hitler."

Nor was the Brosnan era good for folks riding Southern passenger trains. Just ask those who boarded the *Augusta Special* in Charlotte, N.C., on October 16, 1966, en route to the train's namesake city 191 miles away. They never made it. At tiny Warrenville, S.C., the *Special* was halted by Southern officers without prior notice to anyone, even the crew—*especially* the crew, whose union attorneys would have been in court that minute seeking a restraining order. Passengers were put in taxis while mail from the postal car went into trucks.

Voila! Another Brosnan Trap had just sprung. From that day on, trains 31 and 32 would operate only within South Carolina, between Fort Mill (17 miles south of Charlotte) and Warrenville (12 miles north of Augusta). And it was all perfectly legal, though utterly mean-spirited. Southern had amputated passenger trains before and would do so again.

This wasn't all Brosnan's doing. He got excellent advice from his vice president-law, a brilliant tactician who plotted a strategy that virtually stripped Southern of its passenger trains in five brief years, and did so without scarring the railroad's reputation. That man? W. Graham Claytor Jr., later to be widely acclaimed as Amtrak's fourth president.

Name-train railroad

If you knew Southern in the 1960s from the pages of the *Official Guide of the Railways,* it must have seemed like heaven: Eight trains in and out of Washington Union Station as late as 1966, with names redolent of a honeysuckled South: *Piedmont Limited, Crescent, Carolina Special, Peach Queen, Tennessean, Southerner, Birmingham Special, Pelican.* On the railroad's west end, from Cincinnati toward Atlanta and Florida, ran the likes of the *Royal Palm* and *Ponce de Leon.*

Reality was quite different. It's true that as late as 1961, Southern reeled off almost as many passenger train miles as neighbors Atlantic Coast Line and Seaboard Air Line combined, and grossed half again as much more in mail revenue as ACL/SAL. But the typical Southern train carried only half as many passengers as those of the other two railroads. And the equipment was, by and large, old. Southern wasn't a rich railroad. In the 1940s its purchases of lightweight cars from Pullman-Standard and Budd didn't go far beyond equipping the *Crescent, Southerner, Tennessean* and *Royal Palm.* As late as 1964, *Trains* editor David P. Morgan would go out of his way to ride the last heavyweight section Pullman in regular service in America—on the Southern, of course, between Atlanta and the south Georgia coast at Brunswick. Southern's workaday car, right through the 1960s, was a green steel coach built during the presidency of Calvin Coolidge.

Another reality for Southern: Its routes as of the early 1950s were liberally peppered with passenger service—26 pairs of main line trains in 1950, for instance, and another 26 sets of locals. The main line trains were, as a group, enormously profitable. According to Southern's own internal records, the *Southerner* cleared its direct costs by $2 million in 1950, the *Crescent* and *Tennessean* by $1.2 million apiece, the *Piedmont Limited* by $1.1 million and, on the Cincinnati–Florida axis, the *Ponce de Leon, Royal Palm* and *New Royal Palm* by a combined $1.7

million. All told, the main line trains covered their direct costs and contributed $11.8 million to Passenger Department and corporate overhead.

But those locals were another matter. Only three of the 26 pairs earned their direct expenses in 1950. The others—running between such towns as Richmond and Danville, Va., Sheffield and Parrish, Ala., Danville, Ky., and East St. Louis, and Greensboro and Barber, N.C.—lost a collective $1.1 million.

Missionary work

And they were hell to get discontinued—a lesson not lost upon Brosnan during the 1950s, when he was Southern's vice president-operations. Way back in 1947, Southern established a Train Committee to oversee strategy in getting rid of unprofitable passenger trains, and through 1950 it succeeded in eliminating or shortening the routes of 17 pairs of trains, plus another seven mixed trains. But the going had gotten harder. In March 1951, no fewer than 11 train-off cases were being pressed by Southern, and in most instances the railroad got the runaround from state regulators and courts.

Management concluded it had to do a better job. The architect of a new approach—one followed all through the 1960s, with some modifications—was Charles Clark, a staff attorney in Washington, D.C. In a 1951 memo to President Harry DeButts, Clark coined a new term: missionary work. Clark envisioned having the resident vice presidents in each state marshal Southern's "missionaries"—division superintendents, trainmasters, freight agents, road foremen of engines and other officers—to preach the railroad's gospel in towns along the route of a forthcoming train-off case. The missionaries would call upon mayors, city council members, county officials, state legislators and business leaders, to explain the economic realities and ask for support. If nothing else, you'd at least identify your enemies. All this would occur before any public move by the railroad to axe a train. "A mere unannounced and

unprepared appearance before the Chamber of Commerce would not amount to a hill of beans," Clark wrote DeButts. But many of Southern's employees, he emphasized, "stand particularly well in their home towns or, in the broader sense, in their territories. Their assistance initially is what we need to get the missionary work properly underway."

Clark's plan worked well enough to become a model for other railroads in forestalling opposition to train discontinuances. When DeButts retired in 1962, the locals were history, and just 16 pairs of main line passenger trains remained.

Brosnan's turn at bat

Upon becoming president, reducing Southern's passenger train miles became a mission unto itself for Brosnan. The passenger network in 1962 was built around a giant X, with Washington–New Orleans as one axis, Cincinnati–Jacksonville as the other and Atlanta in the center. Following the Southern south from Washington, five of the eight departures ran to Atlanta, dropping Pullman and mail cars at Greensboro, N.C., for the *Ashville Special* and at Charlotte, N.C., for the *Augusta Special.* The other three trains veered west at Lynchburg in southern Virginia to run 203 miles on Norfolk & Western

▶ *Southern wasn't given to lavishing attention on its passenger trains. The only two it tried to do well by were the* Crescent *(top), pausing on its way north in June 1965 in Greenville, South Carolina, and the* Southerner, *pictured as it nears Atlanta in 1964. (Curt Tillotson Jr., top, and David W. Salter)*

◀ *Leaning on the superelevated curve, train 36, the Atlanta–Washington local, heads out of Atlanta in May 1965 with freight cars tacked onto the rear. (J. Parker Lamb)*

before rejoining Southern in Bristol in the extreme southwest corner of Virginia, en route to Chattanooga, and from there to Memphis to the west or Birmingham and New Orleans to the south.

Two trains from Cincinnati went down the left-hand arm of the X toward Atlanta and Jacksonville. The *Ponce de Leon* split at Oakdale, Tenn., to create the *Carolina Special* to Ashville, N.C., and eventually to Columbia, S.C. Rounding out the fleet: a pair of overnight Atlanta–Birmingham trains, a Birmingham–Atlanta–Brunswick train descended from the *Kansas City–Florida Special* and an all-mail-and-express schedule between Washington and Atlanta.

Of these, only two could qualify as class acts. One was the *Crescent*, whose beginnings traced to January 4, 1891. With New York City cars brought to Washington by the Pennsylvania, it operated overnight to Atlanta, running all-Pullman from Charlotte to Atlanta. From Atlanta, the *Crescent* was property of the Atlanta & West Point as far as Montgomery, Ala., and of Louisville & Nashville from Montgomery to New Orleans. Going north, the *Crescent* ran overnight out of New Orleans, by day through Atlanta (returning to Southern Railway) and overnight again into New York.

The other full-fledged streamliner was the *Southerner*, which left Washington three hours behind the *Crescent*. Beyond Atlanta, it kept to Southern tracks, first to Birmingham and then southwest to New Orleans via Meridian and Hattiesburg, Miss. Northbound, it left New Orleans in early morning, arriving

Washington at breakfast the next day and (via the Pennsylvania) New York that afternoon.

The political finesse required to be rid of money-losing passenger trains was light years beyond Brosnan's abilities. Raised in Albany, Ga., the son of its fire chief, he had advanced through Southern's ranks by virtue of his wits and intelligence. Brosnan didn't manage or even rule. He preferred to terrorize. "If anything went wrong," says Clark Hungerford, a division superintendent under Brosnan, "he'd try to find a scapegoat. If he couldn't find one, then the officer in charge would have to go." *Have to go,* you ask? "Fired," replies Hungerford. Attorney Bistline says Brosnan was notorious for firing people one day and hiring them back the next, at a higher salary if necessary. The man Hungerford replaced as Birmingham terminal superintendent in 1962 had been fired three times (and rehired the third time as VP-operations, only to be let go yet again). Hungerford himself quit in 1965 when "too many other officers tried to out-Brosnan Brosnan."

By then, says Hungerford, Brosnan distrusted any Operating Department officer with a college degree, believing them not tough enough (although Brosnan himself was a Georgia Tech grad). He leaned more and more upon the Special Services Department, to whose policemen he assigned sensitive missionary work on train-off cases. Says Hungerford: "He could keep his thumb on those people easily." Moore, as Western Lines general manager in the early 1960s, "couldn't even go to a picture show without telling Brosnan's office where I was."

Brosnan finds his Svengali

By 1964, two years into his presidency, Brosnan had scarcely made a dent in the passenger timetable. True, he was rid of a local between Greensboro and Goldsboro, N.C. Pullman cars on this train or that had gone, and dining cars (which operated at a cash loss of $700,000 in 1962) became scarce.

His big achievement was the first Brosnan Trap.

In 1963 Southern amputated the Cincinnati–Jacksonville *Ponce de Leon* just shy of the Florida border, at Council, Ga., a village described by attorney Bistline as "two or three houses on the edge of a swamp." Somebody within Southern Railway—nobody I spoke to professed to know who—had found a loophole in federal laws governing passenger trains. A train crossing state lines could be severed at the border if its only stop on the other side of the state line was its origin or destination. Jacksonville was the only Florida point served by the *Ponce.* By halting it at Council, the final flag stop within Georgia, Southern made it all but impossible for passengers to reach their Florida destinations.

Huge losses resulted from amputations. So you went to state regulators where the forlorn train still operated, pleaded insuperable deficits and asked to be rid of the nuisance. If a state proved obstinate, a railroad could appeal to the federal Interstate Commerce Commission, which in the early 1960s turned a blind eye toward amputations.

But opportunities for amputations were rare. And Brosnan couldn't march his Special Services Department troopers into state capitals in the Carolinas, Georgia, Louisiana, Tennessee and Virginia to handcuff uncooperative politicians and regulators. Brosnan needed someone who could steer him through the political white waters. Someone who could devise a course that would keep the politicians in the state capitals quiet. Someone who would not arouse the ICC's wrath or the Postal Service's irritation, yet peel off those damnable passenger trains. Plus, his aggressive rate-cutting initiatives for freight business had aroused a regulatory firestorm that needed a cooling hand.

The answer to his dream was W. Graham Claytor Jr. Claytor grew up in Roanoke, the son of an electric utility executive. His credentials were impeccable: University of Virginia, Harvard Law School, president of *Harvard Law Review,* law clerk to legendary jurists Learned Hand and Louis Brandeis,

World War II naval commander and senior partner of one of Washington's most prestigious law firms.

"Get me a lawyer—I want brains," Brosnan is quoted as saying in 1964, in Burke Davis's book, *The Southern Railway.* He found his brains in Claytor, a railfan from his youngest days, who agreed to become Southern's vice president-law. But Brosnan's reputation as a boss had traveled far, and Claytor insisted on simultaneously retaining his partnership in the Washington law firm of Covington & Burling.

Claytor told a Lexington Group audience in 1992 that Brosnan fired him and rehired him four times in the next few years. But he really needn't have worried. Compared with his less-polished fellow Southern executives, Claytor's people-handling skills were superior. Besides, Brosnan had driven away so many talented people by then that a sort of power vacuum existed within Southern. Claytor would have Brosnan's ear, and become one of the few to keep his respect. On ratemaking cases so vital to the railroad, Claytor was superb. But he was just as effective on the passenger problem.

"The trains must come off"

But wait a minute: What passenger problem? Like every other railroad, Southern Railway kept a private set of ledgers for its passenger trains that recorded revenues on one side, and the direct, identifiable costs of operating each of them on the other. By the ICC's formula of calculating solely related costs, Southern in 1964 had lost $4.6 million on passengers. By Southern's own books, these same passenger trains earned a profit of $5.2 million, and increased those earnings to $5.3 million in 1965.

Because its own figures measured only how much each individual train contributed above its direct costs to offset the common costs of passenger service—station expenses, advertising and salaries of the Passenger Traffic Department managers and salesmen, for instance—Southern didn't really earn a $5.2 million profit on passengers in 1964. But it probably came close to breakeven, thanks to prodigious amounts of mail and express, whose revenues were twice as large as those from ticket sales. On the typical railroad then, the ratio of mail and express to passenger receipts was 1:1.

Yet Brosnan behaved as if his passenger trains would bring the railroad to ruin, and peppered his executives with brief handwritten notes:

❐ Beside a recap of Pullman revenues and expenses for September 1964 that showed a modest sleeping car profit: "We must get rid of these cars as quickly as possible."

❐ On the margin of a *Washington Post* article in early 1966 regarding the decline of Northeast Corridor train ridership: "We are *not* getting rid of ours fast enough."

❐ Upon seeing a train-by-train profit and loss statement for September 1966, on which he circled eight pairs of trains failing to cover direct operating costs: "We must get rid of these. Let's be about it."

❐ Across a *New York Times* editorial in mid 1966 on train-off proposals by New York Central: "We should *push* our train discontinuances."

❐ After reading a newsletter's discussion of the passenger problems of railroads: "There is only one answer, as much as we may dislike it—the trains must come off. Our progress is scarcely discernible—it must be speeded up." This last note was written on March 24, 1966. By then, his vice-president-law was doing just what Brosnan wanted.

End of the *Tennesseean*

Southern's first streamliner, begun May 18, 1941, between Washington and Memphis, had long since lost most distinctive touches. The flat-end lounge-observation was gone. So were all but one of its sleepers, which by late 1965 attracted fewer than three persons each night between Knoxville and Memphis. That year, No. 45 and 46 averaged just 111 passengers per trip on their 929-mile, 24-hour

runs. A diner ran on No. 45 from Bristol to Knoxville (131 miles) and on No. 46 from Knoxville to Roanoke (282 miles), serving about a dozen meals per day each way. Except for that 10-roomette, 6-bedroom sleeper, cars were normally heavyweight.

The *Tennesseean,* however, thanks largely to mail revenue, not only cleared its direct costs but made a tidy profit—$334,000 in 1965, to be exact. In fact, all three pairs of Washington–Tennessee trains were profitable on a direct-cost basis. The *Birmingham Special* in 1965 cleared $492,000 and the *Pelican* made $734,000.

Claytor's goal, enunciated November 19, 1965, in a memo to VP-operations Moore, was to eliminate the *Tennesseean* all the way to Memphis, while retaining the bulk of its mail revenue on remaining trains. In one year to the day, he accomplished most of his goal. His first step, achieved early in 1966, was to get the Post Office to agree to let the other two pairs of trains handle the *Tennesseean*'s mail, provided that schedules were adjusted slightly—a big plus, inasmuch as mail accounted for 70 percent of its revenue. Claytor then strategized:

Accordingly it seems to me that the best chance of getting these changes made quickly would be to join with the N&W [which ran the *Tennesseean* between Lynchburg and Bristol] in requesting discontinuance . . . from Alexandria to Bristol. We may have to work to eliminate or cut down some opposition in Lynchburg and possibly Charlottesville, but I do not believe that this will be too severe. Once Trains 45 and 46 are off in Virginia, I would recommend that we file a petition with the ICC to remove them all the way from Bristol to Memphis. Since these trains will no longer have through connections and will carry no mail or express, I believe there is some chance that we could even get them off without a hearing.

As of January 5, 1966, the Knoxville–Chattanooga sleeper was discontinued. Six weeks later, heavyweight diners 3164 and 3168 came off the *Tennesseean,* to be replaced by a $1.55 box dinner put aboard No. 45 in Johnson City, Tenn., and a $1 breakfast for No. 46's passengers in Knoxville. Six weeks later Southern's Special Services Department reported that its missionary work with 98 political and civic leaders along the train's Virginia route had uncovered no serious opposition.

With the way now cleared, Southern and N&W could have jointly sent the usual request to the Virginia Corporation Commission to discontinue trains 45 and 46 east of Bristol. Instead, Claytor employed a politically influential Richmond attorney to write the request on his law firm's letterhead, on behalf of the two railroads. The attorney's letter argued that present service was "excessive," that mail commitments "are not being met successfully" and that a "rescheduling" would provide "more satisfactory service" while saving a purported $640,000 for Southern and N&W. No mention was made of the $207,000 profit earned by the three pairs of Tennessee trains in January of 1965; the *Tennesseean* itself had cleared its costs by $20,170.

On June 10, 1966, Virginia's regulators approved removing the *Tennesseean* in that state. Wrote Brosnan to Claytor upon getting the word: "Thanks. Now let's consider other needed changes and reductions in passenger service." Claytor replied that he would move quite soon to be rid of the train west of Bristol: "Since the Chattanooga–Bristol segment of the train will be carrying no mail, no express and practically no passengers, I am hopeful that we can obtain ICC approval to discontinue . . . without a hearing."

He was right. On October 19, 1966, Southern told the ICC it would drop the one-car *Tennesseean* on the Bristol–Chattanooga segment 30 days later, because of losses accumulating at an annual rate of $300,000. The loss was self-induced, but the ICC heard no groundswell of opposition and declined to order hearings. The *Tennesseean's* Chattanooga–Memphis leg, which connected now with the Washington–New Orleans *Pelican,* retained its mail revenue and lasted another two years.

The Claytor style

Perhaps you've sensed by now Claytor's way of getting rid of passenger trains: Move the mail away first. Take a train off state by state. Don't hint at your ultimate intentions. Smooth the political waters; make it seem like a small thing. Avoid putting state regulators on the spot by going instead to the ICC whenever possible; if not possible, then so cripple the train—by stopping it at state borders, for instance—that states have little choice but to grant your wish. With one case won, move quickly to the next.

All of these elements were present in the *Augusta Special's* demise, which began late in 1966. Trains 31 and 32 originated in Charlotte and leisurely ambled 191 miles in 385 minutes across South Carolina to Columbia, and then to Augusta, in the eastern end of Georgia. It handled a sleeper from New York City and two coaches from Washington that ran north of Charlotte on the *Crescent,* plus the usual Railway Post Office and baggage cars. Military business in and out of Fort Jackson, near Columbia, had kept its sleeping car profitable, to the tune of $68,130 in 1965. Overall the *Augusta Special* was a marginal branch-line operation, losing $33,550 on an out-of-pocket basis in 1965, then earning $63,835 in the first half of 1966.

The *Augusta Special,* in other words, wasn't helping Southern's cash flow but wasn't hurting it, either. But Southern's executives saw a perfect Brosnan Trap begging to be sprung. Trains 31 and 32 had no stops in North Carolina after leaving Charlotte and none in Georgia before terminating in Augusta. So without notifying either state or federal regulators, it could legally begin running the train only within South Carolina, between the

first stop at Fort Mill on the north and the last stop at Warrenville on the south.

On July 22, 1966, J. B. Addington, assistant vice president-operations, wrote William Moore to point out one problem with the plan: The Post Office required a 72-hour notice of discontinuing an RPO run. "To do this," Addington said, "would delay the adjusted assignments, which, of course, would give our hand away to the labor people and all likely protestants." Claytor reported to Brosnan on August 5 that Addington was trying to persuade the Post

▲ *On a happier occasion, before it was severed at both ends of its run in a Brosnan Trap, the Augusta Special is seen beneath the graceful trainshed of its namesake Georgia city. This is the day after Christmas, 1965, and the coming year will be this train's last. (Victor Hand)*

Office to cancel the RPO run, "after which there would be no difficulty in moving on this train as previously planned."

The postal service didn't oblige, but a Brosnan Trap was sprung anyway in mid October, without warning. "I got a call to see to it that passengers were all accommodated" that day and not left stranded in Warrenville, says Lou Sak, Southern's passenger traffic manager. Trucks came to cart the mail from the RPO into Augusta.

According to the *Columbia State,* public officials in three states remained unaware of the truncation for two and a half weeks. When they awoke, state regulators admitted they had no basis for ordering the train reinstated. The ICC wasn't interested, either. The next year South Carolina let the Fort Mill–Warrenville appendage be discontinued.

By October of 1966, with both the *Augusta Special* and *Tennessean* all but eliminated, Claytor had plunged into his next project: the Birmingham–Atlanta–Brunswick locals. As the *Kansas City–Florida Special,* trains 7 and 8 had carried a through coach and a lightweight sleeper for Jacksonville, exchanged with the Frisco at Birmingham and the Atlantic Coast Line at Jesup, Ga., 40 miles west of Brunswick. Frisco withdrew from the through service in May of 1964, but Southern continued the heavyweight Pullman between Atlanta and Brunswick that had beguiled the editor of *Trains.* But only one person a day, on average, rode the car and it was dropped in December, 1965.

Unquestionably, trains 7 and 8 were losers. On an out-of-pocket basis, they failed to cover costs by $49,000 in 1964, $143,000 in 1965 and $189,000 in the first nine months of 1966. Still, Claytor wanted to show an airtight financial case to the ICC. So he arranged to artificially increase the loss by moving its three Birmingham–Atlanta storage mail cars to the *Southerner* and transferring to freight trains the cars of liquid fertilizer regularly carried on the westbound train between Jesup and Atlanta.

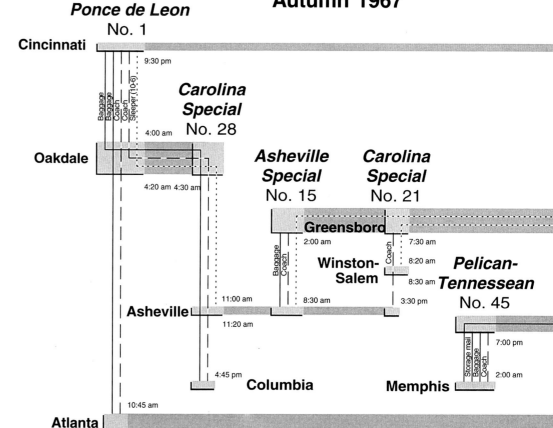

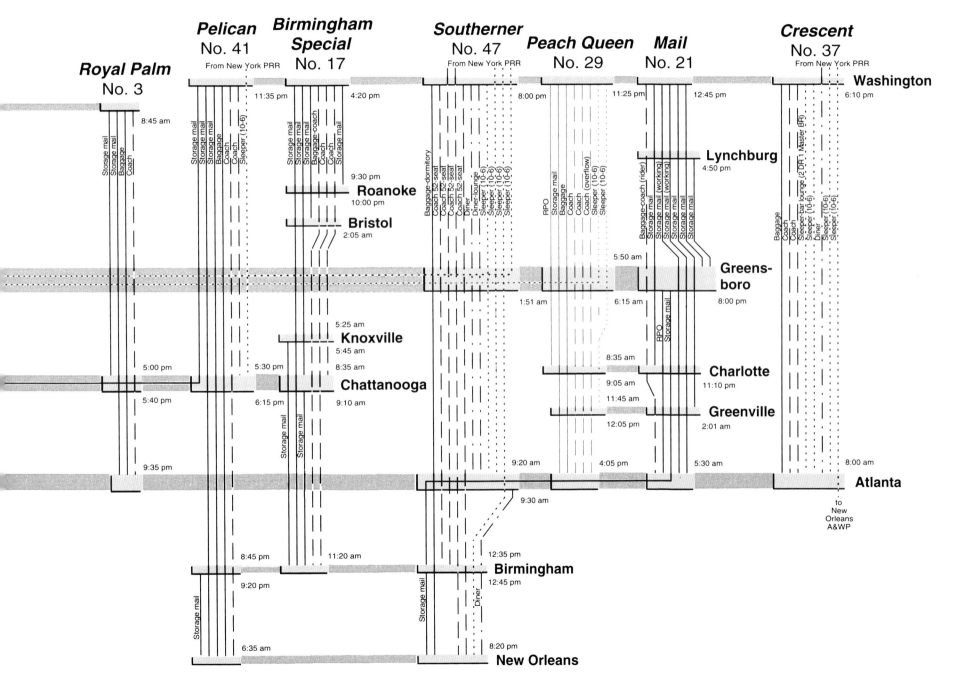

These moves completed, Southern on December 9, 1966, sent the ICC a 30-day discontinuance notice for trains 7 and 8. Less than three weeks later, Claytor wrote Brosnan that the ICC had decided not to intervene, and said he would immediately file his *next* 30-day notice—on trains 35 and 36, the last remnant of the *Tennessean*, between Chattanooga and Memphis. (The ICC didn't intervene in that case, either.) Wrote Brosnan to his VP of law: "Many thanks for the splendid job."

Enter the *Southern Crescent*

Decades later, Claytor (who replaced Brosnan as CEO in December 1967) said he'd done the right thing. "You'd have a train-off hearing at which witnesses showed up to admit nobody rode the train but that they liked to hear the whistle," said Claytor in a 1992 interview. "It was one hell of a job to get trains off, because it was all politics, not the merits of the case, that mattered."

Claytor's argument boiled down to this: The trains didn't carry many people. The system was rigged against Southern. So, living in a mean world, you did what you had to do. "Actually," he related, "we got them off, by every conceivable way. Pretty soon the only way was to break the trains at state borders. That was standard operating procedure. We did that. There was no other way, dealing with these

◀ *Two RS3 roadswitchers team up with a pair of F7 units to move No. 33, the southbound* Piedmont, *out of Duncan, South Carolina, in July of 1962. Note the piggyback flatcar on the rear of this 15-car train—a very early instance of mixing intermodal and passenger traffic. (Curt Tillotson Jr.)*

politicians. Then, instead of eight people on a train, you had nobody."

Yet Brosnan exhibited a soft spot toward the streamlined *Southerner* and *Crescent*. It helped, of course, that as of 1966 both trains covered their direct costs of operation. Early in 1966, for instance, the Pennsylvania said it would no longer operate the signature car of the *Crescent*—its mid-train sleeper-bar lounge that contained a master bedroom, two drawing rooms and shower—between New York and Washington. The A&WP and L&N had dropped this Pullman line on their parts of the run, south of Atlanta, in 1964. So the question was whether to take the car off the *Crescent* between Washington and Atlanta. Argued Sak, the passenger traffic manager, in a memo that worked its way up to Brosnan: "To remove this car entirely from the *Crescent* would severely downgrade the train and result in considerable loss of traffic in other Pullman cars as it would leave the train completely without lounge facilities."

Sak recommended that the car be withdrawn from Pullman use but kept on the train, Washington to Atlanta, for lounge use. The rooms could be used by deadheading railroaders. Wrote Brosnan in reply: "It should probably be cut off. Temporarily, the suggested arrangement is approved."

Then in mid 1967, Brosnan and Claytor had to devise a quick fix. Patronage on the *Crescent* and *Southerner* fell by approximately 30 percent. The Post Office by mid year was cancelling mail contracts for the trains. What had been modest operating profits blossomed into losses that the railroad figured would amount to some $700,000 a year for just the southbound *Crescent* and *Southerner*.

"I urged that they be combined," says Claytor. "Brosnan was dubious, because he had quite a feeling for the *Crescent*. But neither one was carrying many people. I said, 'These two trains are doing the same job. Let's make one good train out of two.' "

What occurred in late November 1967 was a

The *Southerner at speed, near Meridian, Mississippi, in 1969. (J. Parker Lamb)*

consolidation of the southbound *Crescent* and *Southerner*, which had left Washington within two hours of one another. Northbound, they ran separately for another two years; the railroad cut nameless northbound local No. 36 to balance the schedules.

Home free

True to his word, Claytor made one good train out of two. Plus, he gave the train his personal attention. "I got together with Lou Sak," said Claytor later, "and we agreed we'd make it absolutely first rate and keep it that way. And we did." The southbound *Southern Crescent* had critical mass: in mid 1969, three sleepers, the master room sleeper-lounge, as many as seven coaches, and diner, plus a few head-end cars—all an unbroken streamlined flow, led in prime season by four E units (which by 1972 sported the train's name on their flanks).

The deification of the *Southern Crescent* really

occurred in the 1970s, after Amtrak had helped by making a homogenized mush out of most other passenger trains, after Claytor had begun a spirited steam-excursion program on Southern and after a generation of Americans who had never ridden Southern's pre-Amtrak heavyweight trains had forgotten how ordinary they were. Meanwhile, Claytor and his people kept chopping off trains. The eight trains out of Washington in 1966 became three just four years later. The entire Cincinnati–Atlanta–Jacksonville corridor became freight-only.

I asked Claytor how Southern could run fairly shoddy trains and use underhanded methods to get rid of them, and still emerge with its reputation intact. Southern Pacific never sprung a Brosnan Trap on anyone, and put its passengers on spiffy-clean lightweight cars, yet stood condemned by both railfans and politicians throughout the West for playing dirty tricks. "I don't call what we did dirty," replied Claytor. "I call it the only way you could do it. I'd have done that anytime I could. When you run against this kind of political problem, there's only one way to do it, and that's to do what you can to get trains off."

Claytor and others made much of Southern's "political problem." The fact is, neither Claytor nor anyone else I interviewed could cite a single instance of obstinance by the supposedly backwater state railroad regulators. And in reading several reams of internal memos written by Southern executives to each other in the 1960s regarding passenger trains, not once did I find them complaining about specific mistreatment by the states. Certainly, after Claytor's arrival in 1964, Southern was extraordinarily successful in shucking passenger trains like so many ears of corn. You're left to conclude that Southern used experiences of the 1940s and 1950s to justify its own acts in the 1960s. Moreover, the majority of its coach passengers were blacks, who lacked a strong political voice in the South during that decade.

▲ *This is what the* Southern Crescent *looked like in August of 1972, after Southern decided not to join Amtrak, but to run itself. The northbound* Crescent *is approaching Meridian, Mississippi. (J. Parker Lamb)*

◄ *Old confronts new at Camp Austin, Tennessee, near Oakdale, in November of 1968. The Atlanta–Cincinnati* Royal Palm, *living on borrowed time, meets a southbound freight fronted by new Electro-Motive power. (Victor Hand)*

The legacy they left

Come 1971 Southern Railway was down to next to nothing—the *Southern Crescent* to New Orleans via Birmingham, triweekly south of Atlanta; the *Piedmont* to Atlanta; the *Birmingham Special* to its namesake city via the N&W route to Tennessee, and the triweekly *Ashville Special* leg of the *Piedmont* from Salisbury, N.C., to Ashville.

As the startup of Amtrak neared, the railroad had to decide whether it wanted to be a part of a nationalized passenger train network. The price of being rid of its obligation to run passenger trains under its name was a $9.8 million, one-time payment to Amtrak. Or, Southern could stay out, and be obligated to run these four pairs of trains until at least 1975. "I looked over the situation," said Clayton in 1992, "and it was clear to me that we didn't have to sign up with Amtrak. We could afford to keep our primary train and make it the finest in the country. If we turned the *Crescent* over to Amtrak, I

knew what would happen. It would go to hell, very fast."

At that, Claytor was true to his word. The *Southern Crescent* was everything that most of Amtrak's trains at that time were not: clean, punctual, organized and consistently pleasing to customers. In the diner you ate real food with real silverware on real china over real tablecloths. Southern Railway, in other words, possessed a discipline in running this service that Amtrak sorely needed.

Ultimately, in 1978, Southern did join Amtrak. And W. Graham Claytor Jr., upon his retirement from the railroad in 1977, became Secretary of the Navy under President Jimmy Carter and, in 1981, president of Amtrak. You've doubtless sensed the irony of this turn of events. The railroad that treated its passengers so shabbily in the 1960s spawned what would become America's best passenger train in the 1970s and contributed the leadership that took Amtrak through the 1980s. Life's funny that way.

MOST LIKELY TO SUCCEED

Atlantic Coast Line and Seaboard Air Line were two of the most successful passenger train operators. Joined together, they became the passenger train's last friend.

◀ *Train time down south. The era is July 1961, when you could still plausibly call a train the* Havana Special. *The locale is small town Selma, North Carolina, and the train is No. 75, an hour out of Rocky Mount as it brakes to a halt beside the ornate depot that also serves Southern Railway. There are passengers to load, plus mail to throw up—and no time to waste. In the lead is one of Atlantic Coast Line's venerable slant-nose E6 locomotives. This is one of J. Parker Lamb's most oft-published photos, and deservedly so.*

The marriage made in heaven, from the point of view of railroad passengers, was that of Atlantic Coast Line and Seaboard Air Line, on July 1, 1967. At this late-late date in the chronology of the pre-Amtrak passenger train, here were two railroads at the altar who loved each other's children. They had proven their commitment to streamliners not only by staying the course, but by investing new money during the 1960s—ACL to rigorously rebuild its Pullman-built lightweight cars, Seaboard by buying the fleet of lightweight cars declared surplus by strike-affected Florida East Coast.

Virtue was not its own reward. Almost at once the new Seaboard Coast Line found its passenger business threatened. The U.S. Postal Service stripped the railroad of most storage mail and Railway Post Office revenue by early 1968. At the stroke of a postmaster general's pen what been a bearable burden became intolerable—made more so by the fact that the density of intercity passenger operations by Seaboard Coast was unequaled anywhere outside of the Northeast Corridor. For the next three years SCL concentrated on what

was important to its success, the Florida trains, and let nature take its course with the rest. At the same time the railroad eagerly participated in research and test runs of a striking new idea: a train that would take people *and* their cars to and from Florida from the Northeast. This was the incubator of the *AutoTrain*.

Right to the end, Seaboard Coast Line never made people feel unwelcome. Numerous times in the late 1960s I rode its Florida streamliners, and the level of friendliness and service would stand today as a model for the entire travel industry. A quarter of a century later SCL's first chairman, Tom Rice, would say of Amtrak that it was "bred in iniquity and born in sin," and you could almost feel the pain in his voice. His contemporary Graham Claytor, who was the chief executive of Southern Railway, later remarked that Rice was bitterly disappointed SCL couldn't afford the luxury given Southern to run its own passenger trains after May 1, 1971, outside of Amtrak's network.

Needless to say, ACL, Seaboard and Seaboard Coast Line were out of the ordinary. Geography and climate made them so. This is their story.

Just the right place and size

Nowhere else in America stands a long-distance corridor to rival that between the Northeast and Florida. It's the right length—one night out, or long enough to create a delicious trail of revenue if you can fill the trains, but not so long that it would discourage people from travel. It goes the right way—north and south, against the grain of roads and other railroads alike. Its two ends have almost magnetic attraction for one another—moneyed and pleasure-seeking people in the cold Northeast, and warm and spacious Florida coastlines. Had Amtrak never come along, this would probably have been the nation's last long-distance passenger train route. It may yet be, inasmuch as the *AutoTrain* is Amtrak's only indisputably profitable long-haul train.

To grasp just how lively a business this was, consider that it flourished despite the fact that a traveler between New York City and Palm Beach had to contend with as many as four railroads, all of which had to agree on schedules, capital spending, fares and all the other little details, and sometimes could not agree. Not only that, but one of the partners (the Pennsylvania Railroad and its successor Penn Central) grew increasingly disinterested and finally almost hostile toward Florida trains as it tottered toward its own demise. And another (Florida East Coast) spent the middle third of this century in receivership and two years upon leaving bankruptcy abruptly terminated passenger trains (five each way at the time) as it entered a bitter strike that would drag on for years. In other words, there was indifference at one end and no service at all on the most popular line through Florida.

All this, and *still* the people came. As the 1960s progressed and Eastern Air Lines DC7s ate away some of the sleeping car business, the coach traffic to and from Florida grew, and in summer its volume was such that weekend editions of the *Silver Meteor*, *Silver Star* and *Champion* swelled to the 16-18 car sizes you associated with winter seasons.

You have to give credit where credit is due, and throughout the 1960s the railroads that really kept the passenger trains full and the passengers happy were SCL and the two railroads that joined in its creation, Atlantic Coast Line and Seaboard Air Line, and the short, 113-mile-long Richmond Fredericksburg & Potomac, on whose tracks trains of both railroads operated between Washington and Richmond. Pennsylvania had done its bit in the 1930s by electrifying the route north of Washington, and Florida East Coast's Henry Flagler created a century ago the beach resorts (including Miami) that established Florida's reputation as a playland. But the SCL lines bought most of the expensive lightweight cars, set the service standards and ceaselessly promoted the trains.

Atlantic Coast Line got to Florida first. Seaboard, in fact, didn't build to Miami until the eve of the Great Depression, and the financial strain of its southward push quickly sent it into receivership for almost two decades. ACL had the better structure—mostly double track and relatively straight alignments—whereas Seaboard went up, down and around through the Carolinas on single track. Yet surprisingly, ACL had the longer route between Richmond and Jacksonville (680 miles to SAL's 640), mostly because it veered out of its natural path to visit Charleston, S.C. But once in Florida, ACL's partnership with Florida East Coast gave it a shorter way to Miami, so that the New York–Miami mileages of both railroads were virtually identical, at just under 1,400 miles. Separately, the two railroads served Florida's west coast in a honeycomb of routes, two apiece on both railroads.

Parting of the ways

The first of three seminal events in the 1960s was the Florida East Coast strike. The FEC left bankruptcy on January 1, 1961, in not very good physical or financial shape, having lost money all but one year during the preceding decade. Take away those

five passenger trains in each direction, and FEC was incredibly overbuilt, with double tracks that supported only three or so freight trains each way. To judge by photos, those double tracks were not well maintained, either. During reorganization in the late 1950s, Seaboard Air Line and Southern had attempted to gain control of the FEC, while allowing it to operate independently, in order to thwart Atlantic Coast Line's own competing bid for the railroad. But the ultimate owner of Florida East Coast became St. Joe Paper, controlled by the Alfred I. DuPont Estate, whose trustee was short, bald, crusty and indomitable Ed Ball. Under Ball's direction, St. Joe Paper had bought FEC's defaulted bonds, and the terms of reorganization gave bondholders the railroad's common stock.

Mere months after leaving receivership, the railroad took the heretical step of refusing to join other Class 1 railroads in national wage negotiations with the 11 non-operating unions. And when a national accord was reached in 1962, the FEC declined to sign "me-too" contracts with the brotherhoods. Instead, it pursued separate talks with each of the unions, to no avail. The FEC wanted terms unique to its property, whereas the unions were adamant that national standards had to prevail. Both sides had too much at stake to compromise.

Thus it was that the non-op unions struck FEC on the morning of January 23, 1963. At that time, the railroad ran a 16-car *Florida Special* (18 cars on weekends), a 15-car *East Coast Champion* (17 on weekends), a 16-car *City of Miami* or 14-car *South Wind* on alternating days, a 14-car overnight local *East Coast Special* (a successor train to the *Havana Special*) and a five-car daylight *Local Express*.

The strike was a crisis of first proportion to the connecting Atlantic Coast Line, and it fell upon ACL president Rice to work something out. "Old Ed Ball was determined to run the railroad to make money," Rice later related, "and so he refused to go along with national negotiations. We felt we had to subscribe to these, but he didn't." At the time, Rice was working very closely with John Smith, the president of rival Seaboard Air Line. The two railroads had been trying to merge since 1960, and in the process their presidents had become personal friends. "He and I realized that when Ed Ball wanted to run trains with supervisors, that Jacksonville Terminal Railroad would be picketed [such boycotts of secondary targets are not forbidden by the Railway Labor Act] and shut down and tie us all up," relates Rice. "So we directed Jacksonville Terminal not to let FEC passenger trains on the property. The result was that we had to use SAL to get to Miami. All of this was worked out prior to the strike. We looked at it as a detour we had to make, and if the merger went through, we'd be in the same boat anyway."

Thus the *Florida Special, East Coast Champion, City of Miami* and *South Wind* began a rerouting used to this day by Amtrak: from Jacksonville south on Atlantic Coast Line through Orlando to Auburndale, where this line to Tampa crosses SAL's route from Jacksonville and Wildwood toward West Palm Beach and Miami. At Auburndale, passenger trains went into a remote-controlled siding on one railroad and swung around to exit onto the other railroad via a connecting track. Rice recalls the rerouting as satisfactory, although his streamliners required an extra 40 minutes to go via Orlando and Auburndale rather than down the Florida coast.

▶ *You get the conductor's view of the northbound* Havana Special *(later renamed* Gulf Coast Special*) as it passes an Atlantic Coast Line local in Smithfield, North Carolina, in September 1961. In the far background: the southbound* Everglades. *(J. Parker Lamb)*

◄ *Seaboard Air Line always played catch-up against Southern between Washington, Atlanta, and Birmingham. Here SAL's Silver Comet begins its northward run to Atlanta in July 1956 over trackage now largely abandoned. A single E8 diesel can handle the entire train. (J. Parker Lamb)*

Atlantic Coast Line's passenger department was less pleased. "The Seaboard reroute was very costly—Seaboard didn't do this for us out of compassion," says Kenneth Howes, who was to become ACL's last passenger traffic manager. ACL paid its competitor more than $1 million a year to use SAL tracks and stations on the east coast, Howes says. Moreover, "We were at Seaboard's mercy, treated like second-class citizens at their station in Miami."

Another telling cost of the FEC strike: ACL was cut off from direct service to the populous Atlantic Ocean towns of St. Augustine, Daytona Beach, New Smyrna Beach, Titusville, Cocoa–Rockledge, Fort Pierce, Stuart and Hobe Sound. "We lost some very good markets," notes Howes. Soon enough, Atlantic Coast Line people began noticing the effect of the FEC/SAL switch. The railroad kept a running tally of passenger counts on both ACL and SAL in and out of Richmond on the Richmond, Fredericksburg & Potomac. Traditionally, ACL had been the dominant railroad, accounting for some 60 percent of the total count. "After the FEC was struck," says Howes, "at times Seaboard handled more people than we."

The Florida East Coast strike would be the defining labor-relations event of that decade. Tough as nails, Ed Ball and his lieutenant, Winford Thornton (later to be chairman of Florida East Coast Industries), essentially broke the strike and proceeded to demonstrate, without any visible support whatever from the rest of the railroad industry, what a modern railroad could look like: two-person crews running on eight-hour crew districts with superbly maintained track and with a signal system so modern that even the drawbridges rose and fell by remote control.

There remained the question, unions or no unions, of the rerouted Atlantic Coast Line trains. Florida East Coast decided it could do without them, and never asked for them back. Neither was Atlantic Coast Line anxious to invite secondary picketing on its property by returning to FEC. The FEC's ramshackle station in Miami was demolished in November 1963. But that wasn't the end of it. The Miami city attorney's office burrowed through old files and discovered that the original charter of Florida East Coast required it run a daily except Sunday passenger train between Jacksonville and Miami. Florida's Railroad & Public Utilities Commission ordered service restored, and the Florida Supreme Court, while holding that FEC was required only to provide service required by "public necessity," upheld the commission.

Florida East Coast reentered the passenger train business more than two and a half years after leaving it, on August 2, 1965, using as its southern terminal the 1955-era depot at North Miami. The standard consist soon became an E9 locomotive, a lightweight coach and a tavern-lounge-observation that served as a parlor car. So as to make everyone feel perfectly unwelcome, the railroad posted conspicuous signs under the heading "Notice to the Public," that "Florida East Coast Railway Company Is Operated Under Strike Conditions/Use Premises and Ride Trains at Own Risk." Understandably, ridership was sparse on trains 1 and 2, which lasted not quite three years, until July 28, 1968.

Atlantic coast competition

When FEC's pocket-sized streamliner began in mid 1965, the railroad felt comfortable in disposing of 55 lightweight cars that it no longer needed. Both ACL and Seaboard were interested in buying a group of 36 cars—23 coaches, six diners, two each of tavern lounge observations and baggage dormitory cars, and one each of baggage, dormitory-coach and diner-lounge cars. Atlantic Coast Line, as befit its superior financial position, already owned more lightweight cars than Seaboard Air Line—by my count, 187 to SAL's 153. Moreover, the FEC fleet had been built to Atlantic Coast Line specs, to run in its feature trains. But then ACL management decided that the cars in its lightweight fleet were sufficient, and didn't bid on the FEC cars. The whole set was bought by Seaboard in November 1965, giving its passenger service a lot of flexibility.

Atlantic Coast Line probably acted wisely in avoided a bidding war, inasmuch a merger between ACL and Seaboard was thought to be imminent. What's more, ACL was spending a lot of money to rebuild the lightweight cars it owned (not to mention some heavyweights). Howes says that virtually all the cars not originally built by Budd Co. were rebuilt from the trucks up, beginning early in the 1960s. Cars from Pullman in particular were prone to interior rusting, so entire sides of cars were replaced when necessary, and trucks were replaced by ones that someone within ACL had designed.

It's hard to remember that ACL and SAL were in fact spirited rivals in the passenger train business. A lot of the differences were little things. "I always used to say," remarks Howes, "that the Atlantic Coast Line was run for its shareholders, and Seaboard Air Line for its employees. It seemed as if the Seaboard wasn't as interested in profits as Coast Line. We knew never to throw money away. For instance, in my entire career with ACL, even as passenger traffic manager, when I ate in a dining car I paid my bill.

Most Seaboard people riding their trains didn't pay a dime." The railroads even braked their trains differently. "We could make a round trip from Miami to New York on a set of brake shoes," says Howes, "whereas Seaboard had to replace them at the turn-around. I know this: ACL braking was smoother than Seaboard's. After the merger, ACL folks taught the Seaboard engineers how to do it—put the brakes on early, let the train coast a bit and then make a final application."

Competition between these roads was such that they even quarreled over dead people. Explains Ralph Progner, who was Seaboard's assistant general passenger traffic manager: "A lot of our business out of Tampa when I worked there was shipment of remains. On occasion funeral directors were short of funds for shipments, so I gave them latitude. The ACL guy in Tampa found out, complained to his treasurer, who complained to mine and I had to stop. We went after each other, all right—the Coast Line fellow even blackballed me from Rotary Club."

In the opinion of Tom Rice, his ACL and the Seaboard were "almost a standoff. We had the *Florida Special*, which was a super train, but so was Seaboard's *Silver Meteor*. We had more business to the west coast of Florida, perhaps, and Seaboard to the east coast, but I wouldn't say either of us had a clutch on the other." Luckily there was business aplenty for two railroads along the Atlantic coast, and the competition undoubtedly benefited everyone by keeping both railroads on their toes.

Aftermath of a merger

When these two railroads merged, on July 1, 1967, this much is for sure: The new Seaboard Coast Line was a passenger-train railroad like no other. By about that day, Santa Fe, Burlington and Union Pacific were admitting defeat, and Santa Fe in particular would announce by autumn a drastic slimming-down of its passenger service. And in all of the Northeast by then, there weren't but a handful of passenger trains worthy of a name. But just look at what was coming south out of Richmond every day that summer:

❐ On the old ACL side via Rocky Mount, separate *East Coast* and *West Coast Champion* sections on 35-minute headways, plus the *Gulf Coast Special*, *Palmetto* and *Everglades*. That winter the *Florida Special* would make its seasonal appearance.

❐ On the old SAL side via Raleigh, the *Silver Meteor*, *Silver Star* and *Palmland*—all for Florida—plus the *Silver Comet* and two locals for Atlanta and Birmingham. At Hamlet, N.C., the *Comet* begat a coach-only train for Miami, the *Sunland*.

There were still trains between Wilmington, N.C., and Rocky Mount, Atlanta and Jacksonville, Jacksonville and Chattahoochee (en route to New Orleans), Florence and Augusta, Montgomery and Jacksonville, Albany, Ga., and Jacksonville, and depending upon how you counted them, three to five routes to southern Florida from Jacksonville. The pages of this chapter show consist schematics of most SCL Florida trains that first winter of 1967–1968, and it's amazing almost three decades later to see so many trains by this late date.

On merger day, SCL operated more intercity passenger trains, 54 a day, or 27 each way, than any railroad but Pennsylvania. By comparison, Santa Fe that summer ran 44 a day. By virtue of its longer routes, Santa Fe ran approximately 50 percent more train miles in 1967 than Seaboard Coast Line. Still, the railroads were roughly equivalent in passenger train densities over main routes, and each still had a surprising number of short-haul trains. The principal similarity between Seaboard Coast Line and Santa Fe was that neither knew how to run a poor train. "I didn't have a favorite," insists Rice. "I rode 'em all." One suspects he rode 'em on his business car, and it's true that many years after the fact he fondly remembers being able to "eat dinner at home in Richmond, take the night train and be at work in Jacksonville at 9 the next morning."

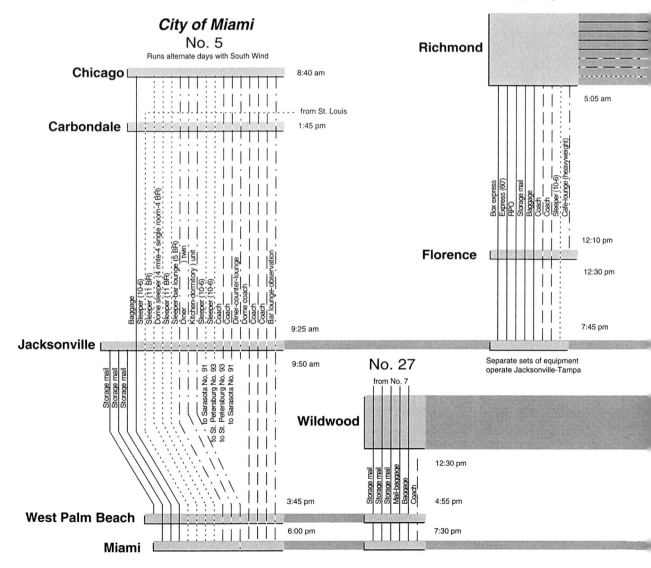

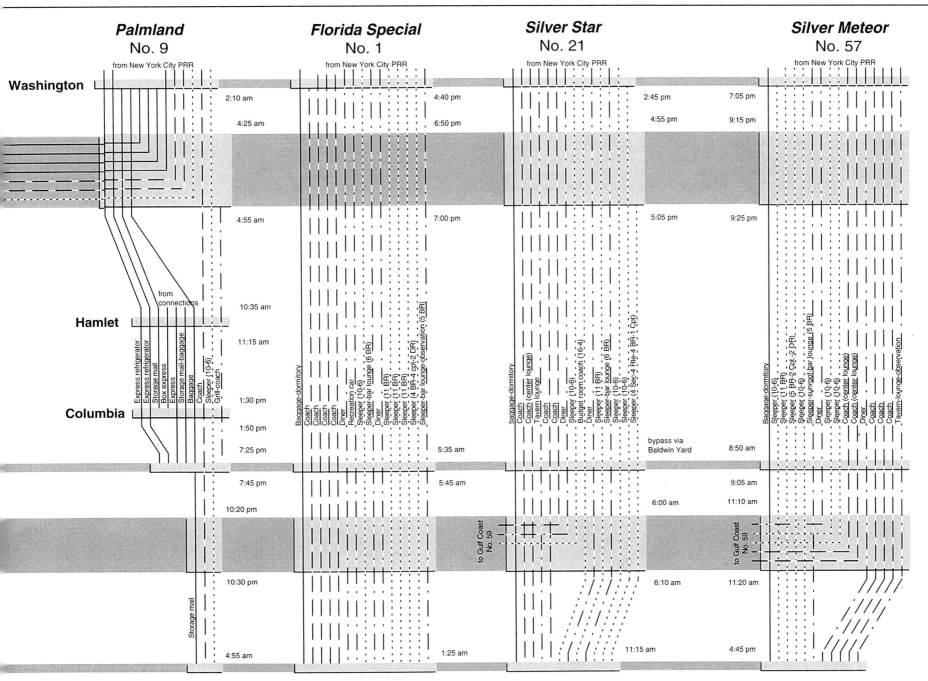

Palmland
No. 9

from New York City PRR

Washington

2:10 am

4:25 am

4:55 am

from
connections

10:35 am

Hamlet

11:15 am

Columbia

1:30 pm

1:50 pm

7:25 pm

7:45 pm

10:20 pm

10:30 pm

4:55 am

Express refrigerator
Express refrigerator
Storage mail
Box express
Express
Storage mail-baggage
Baggage
Coach
Sleeper (10-6)
Grill-coach

Storage mail

Florida Special
No. 1

from New York City PRR

4:40 pm

6:50 pm

7:00 pm

1:30 pm

5:35 am

5:45 am

1:25 am

Baggage-dormitory
Coach
Coach
Coach
Coach
Diner
Recreation car
Sleeper (10-6)
Sleeper-bar lounge (6 BR)
Diner
Sleeper (11 BR)
Sleeper (11 BR)
Sleeper (11 BR)
Sleeper (4 BR-4 cpt-2 DR)
Sleeper-bar lounge-observation (5 BR)

Silver Star
No. 21

from New York City PRR

2:45 pm

4:55 pm

5:05 pm

bypass via
Baldwin Yard

6:00 am

to Gulf Coast
No. 59

6:10 am

11:15 am

baggage-dormitory
Coach
Coach (center lounge)
Tavern lounge
Coach
Coach
Diner
Sleeper (10-6)
Budget room coach (16-4)
Diner
Sleeper (11 BR)
Sleeper-bar lounge (6 BR)
Sleeper (10-6)
Sleeper (10-6)
Sleeper (4 Sec-4 Rte-4 BR-1 Cpt)

Silver Meteor
No. 57

from New York City PRR

7:05 pm

9:15 pm

9:25 pm

8:50 am

9:05 am

11:10 am

to Gulf Coast
No. 59

11:20 am

4:45 pm

Baggage-dormitory
Sleeper (10-6)
Sleeper (11 BR)
Sleeper (5 BR-2 Cpt -2 DR)
Sleeper (10-6)
Sleeper-sunroof-bar lounge (5 BR)
Diner
Sleeper (10-6)
Sleeper (10-6)
Coach (center lounge)
Coach (center lounge)
Diner
Coach
Coach
Coach
Coach
Tavern-lounge-observation

141

▲ *The* Silver Star *has a full complement of 18 cars passing Gill, North Carolina, in August of 1969. Four cars behind the three E units is one of the last Railway Post Office cars in America, which operated then between Washington and Jacksonville. The three Railway Express cars hold storage mail. (Curt Tillotson, Jr.)*

Of course, by itself Seaboard Coast Line could no more stop the forces that were wrecking the passenger train than you or I could stand in front of a speeding truck and expect not to be rolled over. Within months of merger, the pruning began. Two items of business were especially important: tailoring the main New York–Florida trains to the demand, and rationalizing the crazy-quilt train network on Florida's Gulf coast. That first winter, so deftly that few people realized it was happening, the *East Coast Champion* simply failed to appear. Atlantic

Coast Line had gotten regulatory approval at the state level in 1963 to merge the *East Coast Champion* into the *West Coast Champion* north of Jacksonville in the spring and fall. But when the winter 1967–1968 timetable appeared, there was no *East Coast Champion*. Nor was there any formal proceeding before the Interstate Commerce Commission or the state regulators.

Only a lawyer could have thought up the disingenuous ploy that permitted the new SCL to kill its *East Coast Champion* without a shot being fired, and I suspect the "villain" was Richard Sanborn of the SCL Law Department. In this endeavor, Sanborn displayed a brilliant tactical mind that would serve him well—he became chief executive of Seaboard System Railroad (a component of CSX) and chairman of Conrail before his death from a heart attack in 1989, at the young age of 52.

The task at hand: rationalize overlapping schedules on the ex-ACL and ex-SAL lines. Excess capacity existed on the line to Miami; during the winter season of 1966–1967, the two *Champions* and the *Florida Special, Silver Meteor* and *Silver Star* carried an average of 1,072 passengers in both directions per day, but had capacity for 3,248 persons. Of course, such a statistic hides the fact that travel is predominately southward early in the winter and northward late in the season and that half of a round trip is essentially to reposition equipment. Still, SCL felt that five big trains a day from New York (six if you count the *Palmland*) was one too many.

So Sanborn, the Law Department's 30-year-old point man on passenger train litigation, wrote nearly identical letters to the each of the state railroad regulators from Florida to Virginia. In these letters, he recounted the pre-merger competition and said it had resulted in "a wasteful duplication" of service— five southbound streamliners, for instance, passing Savannah between 1:10 a.m. and 6:40 a.m. "Based upon our analysis of the efficiencies which the merger will make possible in our passenger service," Sanborn continued, "we have come to the conclusion that the merged company can provide essentially the same service this winter that was provided last winter between New York and Florida with one less train."

Now Sanborn got to his point, beginning with an implied threat: "From a strictly regulatory standpoint, the simplest approach would be to not operate the seasonal service represented by the *Florida Special*, since most State Commissions decline to exercise jurisdiction over seasonal service." But gosh, he went on, this would be the end of a train of historic importance that is "one of the most widely acclaimed passenger trains in the United States." Luckily, our SCL man had a solution: "We can enjoy the more efficient operation which our merger has made possible while retaining the seasonal *Florida Special* service, if the Commissions of the states through which we operate will permit us to reschedule the *East Coast Champion* service and operate it as the *Florida Special*."

Operate the *East Coast Champion* as the *Florida Special*? What does that mean? In a literal sense, Sanborn was proposing to take the numbers used by the *East Coast Champion*—1 and 2—and assign them to the *Florida Special*. What he was really proposing was to axe the *East Coast Champion* without actually asking to! Sanborn sought the regulators' "informal approval," and by golly, he got it. Virginia's State Corporation Commission, for example, checked off in a one-sentence letter three weeks after being asked. Sanborn went through this same song and dance with the state regulators each year until Amtrak, but although the *East Coast Champion* continued to exist in theory, in fact it was done for. A *Weekend Champion* ran three days a week during the summer of 1968 between New York City and Jacksonville, but New York–Miami service never reappeared under the *Champion* name.

Seaboard Coast Line's biggest opportunity for merger-related efficiencies existed in Florida, and

the *East Coast Champion*'s discontinuance was just one part of a larger plan. Other elements:

❐ Rename the *West Coast Champion* simply the *Champion* and make it a dedicated train for the west coast of the state. This started December 15, 1967.

❐ Turn the *Silver Meteor* into a New York–Miami train. Traditionally, it had carried two coaches and two sleepers for Tampa–St. Petersburg (on trains 59-60) and Venice (trains 61-62). The two pairs of west coast trains were eliminated, although the Venice trains remained under new numbers, 81-82

▲ *ACL's agent in Callahan, Florida, steps outside to inspect No. 5, the* City of Miami, *as it rushes by on March 23, 1965, just minutes from Jacksonville, with a train that stretches almost to infinity. More than likely there's a light load today, but going north tomorrow, these cars will be full.* (David W. Salter)

◀ *Crusing at 75 miles per hour the* Sunland *passes Maxwell, Florida, just south of Jacksonville, in March of 1968. Today's train is typically short, and one month from now the train will be discontinuerd from Jacksonville to both Tampa and Miami. (David W. Salter)*

Leesburg, but as of April 28 its only through cars from the north were off the Chicago–Florida *City of Miami* or *South Wind*, which ran on alternate days. A passenger on the *Champion* from New York who was in a hurry could make a cross-platform switch in Jacksonville and arrive in St. Pete 10 minutes ahead of the through train. If this seems confusing, it was.

❏ Discontinue the little-used *Sunland* south of Jacksonville. This ex-Seaboard Air Line local between Washington and Florida (it ran southbound as part of the *Silver Comet* as far as Hamlet, N.C.) split into Tampa and Miami sections at Wildwood; south of there each section was usually a two-car or three-car train. This change occurred April 28 as well. In September the train was removed altogether.

❏ Shorten the Washington–Miami *Palmland* to a Columbia, S.C., terminus. The train's only regular passenger-carrying cars were a New York–Miami coach and sleeping car, and a Richmond–Jacksonville coach-grill, and it ran in the dead of night through Florida. The shortened *Palmland* saw its last Florida palms on May 30, 1968.

❏ Amputate the Washington–Tampa *Gulf Coast Special*, trains 75-76, south of Jacksonville. This old Atlantic Coast Line train (once the *Havana Special*) was primarily a Miami operation prior to the Florida East Coast strike in 1963, and the overnight Jack-

(see next column). This took effect April 28, 1968.

❏ Return the *Silver Star* to bi-coastal operation. It had carried west coast cars in SAL days, but effective with the merger on July 1, 1967, became a solid New York–Miami operation. As of December 15, 1967, newly created trains 23-24 operated between Wildwood and St. Petersburg at first on the ex-SAL line, but effective April 28, 1968, their northern terminal became Jacksonville and they ran on the more populous ex-ACL line via Sanford and Orlando. This ended through service to the west coast via Wildwood.

❏ Reroute the New York–Sarasota *Champion*,

trains 91-92, beyond Tampa, by running it around Tampa Bay on the former Seaboard to St. Petersburg. The Tampa–Sarasota leg, 68 miles, was covered by newly created trains 81-82, which were extended another 20 miles, to Venice. The effect of this April 28, 1968, change was to put all the Sarasota and Venice traffic, which had operated on two pairs of trains—91-92 to Sarasota on the old ACL line and 61-62 to Sarasota and Venice via the parallel ex-SAL line—onto one pair of trains using the former SAL line. You could still make connections at Jacksonville for *another* St. Petersburg leg of the *Champion*, operating on ex-ACL lines through Gainesville and

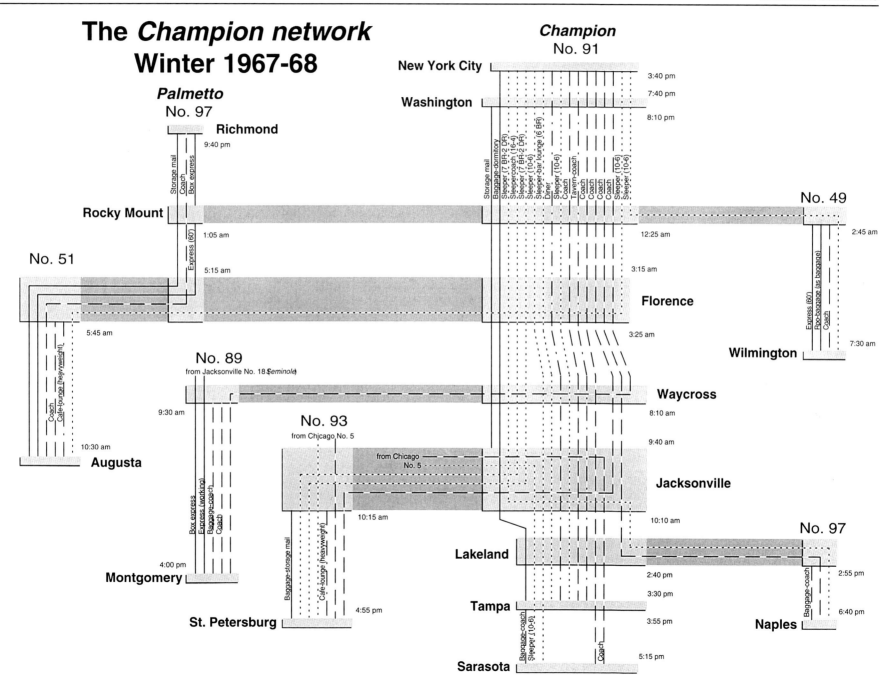

The *Champion network* Winter 1967-68

Champion No. 91

Palmetto No. 97

sonville–Tampa section via Orlando had been a three-car train (with a single coach for passengers) for several years. The train began terminating in Jacksonville in 1968.

The wonder of it all was that this ambitious restructuring took place and not a single town lost all service from a major, streamlined Seaboard Coast Line train. You could compare it to the pruning of a tree; little branches and dying limbs were removed, but the trunk remained.

The last passenger train optimist

Having accomplished this, Seaboard Coast Line left its Florida passenger service alone for the three remaining years until Amtrak. All around it on other railroads, passenger trains were bleeding to death for lack of business. Not so these trains. They remained vibrant right to the end. Is it any wonder that Tom Rice would later say of joining Amtrak, "It broke my heart"?

Seaboard Coast Line's love of its Florida streamliners did not extend to its entire passenger fleet. It tried without success to rid itself of the *Everglades*, trains 85-86, and was turned down in 1970 even though the railroad could demonstrate a loss of $255,831 for the first nine months of 1969. Thanks largely to mail and express, the Washington–Jacksonville *Everglades* had earned out-of-pocket profits of $254,000 in 1967 and $370,000 in 1968. But New York and Washington mail destined for Florida was put on piggyback freight trains in late 1968 and

◄ *A 15-car* Florida Special, *led by three of Atlantic Coast Line's E6 units, is only one curve away from the colonial depot in Alexandria, Virginia, in early 1964. (Jim Shaw)*

early 1969, and express shipments ended in February 1969.

The ICC's *Everglades* decision, rendered in April of 1970, was bizarre. On the one hand, it said a nine-month loss was not long enough to be telling. On the other hand, it said that even if the loss were real and irreversible, that SCL retained most of the revenue on mail it now carried on freight trains rather than the *Everglades*, and that in any event, the railroad was financially sound enough to bear the burden. And for good measure, the commission said that a passenger count of 75 to 80 people (total, not per mile) was proof of "public convenience and necessity." This line of reasoning moved commissioner Kenneth Tuggle to dissent: "We know that the lifeblood of these trains no longer flows through their veins." The *Everglades* lasted until Amtrak, lifeblood or not.

Truly disheartening was the dissolution of SCL's passenger service to Atlanta and Birmingham—a core Seaboard Air Line route. At the time of merger, SAL ran three round trips to and from Atlanta from the north, two of which went on to Birmingham. Two of those three trains were predominantly mail and express haulers, pulling a single coach for whoever showed up. When the post office diverted mail elsewhere in 1967 in 1968, nothing remained to support these trains. Trains 3 and 4 to Atlanta left the schedule on April 17, 1968, and nameless trains 15 and 16, which ran to Birmingham, followed three months later.

That left the *Silver Comet*, trains 33 and 34, new in 1947. In late 1967, leaving Hamlet going south, the *Comet* was four baggage and mail cars, two coaches, a coach-lounge, a diner and a sleeping car. In every respect it was outclassed by Southern Railway's *Southerner*, which had a shorter schedule over a shorter (by 60 miles) route and better equipment. The train cost SCL almost half a million dollars in avoidable losses in 1967. In 1968 it began terminating in Atlanta, and light meals from the

tavern car replaced the full diner. Northward, train 34 pulled seven or eight piggyback cars on its rear—sort of like a penniless dowager taking in laundry.

All this did no good. The avoidable loss in 1968 ballooned to more than $750,000, and was projected to reach $1 million in 1969. The train was down to two mail cars, a coach, sleeper and coach-tavern. Then came an amputation: SCL partner RF&P persuaded Virginia to let it quit running the *Comet* between Washington and Richmond as of May 9, orphaning the Seaboard portion. The *Silver Comet*, the weakest of Seaboard Air Line's three *Silver* streamliners, ran its last in October 1969.

Still, chairman Rice didn't give up. Appearing before a congressional committee the month after the *Silver Comet*'s removal, he said: "There are a few of us in the railroad business who like certain passenger trains." Speaking extemporaneously, he continued: "We have a unique situation, admittedly. A lot of old folks—let's call them senior citizens—like to go to Florida in the wintertime. They like to ride the train. I would not be remiss in saying I think some of them are afraid they might have to go by way of Havana and don't like that and they ride the train. [This was the era of planes being hijacked to and from Cuba.] . . .We have some fine trains that we operate in through service which we think are just the finest in the land. And we like them. We don't get rich on them but we get by."

We don't get rich on them but we get by. That was the voice, in late 1969, of the last passenger train optimist holding a position of responsibility in North American railroading. Many years later, Tom Rice would say of the late 1960s: "Those western boys didn't have passenger trains as popular as ours. Florida was growing. There was so much for people to travel to and see. Highways in the East were bad then. Old U.S. Highway 1, before Interstate 95, was impossible to drive. We had people standing in line to get on our trains. It was amazing to see the demise of it."

CHESSIE'S LAST STAND

For sick trains, a doctor. But was there a cure? Paul Reistrup tried to find one, and therein lies a bittersweet tale.

◀ *Before there was a Holiday Inn or a Hilton Hotel, the Pullman Co. set the standard, providing a place to sleep that was as good in Maine as it was in California. Here, in 1965, a porter prepares a roomette on Baltimore & Ohio's* National Limited *for its occupant. The* National *would cease to exist as a through Baltimore–St. Louis train within months, and four years later the company that George Pullman began in 1859 quit the business. What was civilized travel coming to? (William Howes collection)*

In January of 1964, Paul Reistrup was already a man on his way up at Baltimore & Ohio. A straight arrow, Iowa-raised, West Point-educated Reistrup had experience as a trainmaster in Ohio and Pennsylvania, and now directed car utilization from headquarters at 2 North Charles in Baltimore. Jervis Langdon Jr., B&O's 58-year-old president, had assembled a circle of such people—"my young fellas," he called them. But it was Reistrup who Langdon phoned one Saturday morning. Come in and chat, he said. Reistrup did, and his life was forever altered. "I want your ideas," Langdon began, "on how to straighten out our passenger business."

Reistrup's introduction to B&O's Passenger Services Department had been as Langdon's special deputy the previous year. His task then was to sort out a scandal involving kickbacks to railroad employees from travel agents selling school tours. Reistrup dealt with offenders quickly, decisively, quietly. Now the words "straighten out" had a different meaning. What Langdon wanted was for passenger trains to succeed on the most lenient of terms—that is, for revenues to cover direct costs. "Otherwise," Langdon

added, "we'll get rid of 'em." The boss suggested that Reistrup outline a two-year plan by Monday morning. "Needless to say," says Reistrup, "I worked all weekend." Impressed by what he heard the next week, Langdon made Reistrup director of passenger services, effective February 1, 1964. He was 31 years old.

Thus began the most-publicized bootstrap effort of the 1960s on behalf of the American passenger train. North of the border, Canadian National's Garth Campbell had already begun seeding the air with new ideas on how to increase passenger train revenues, with some initial success. Pennsylvania Railroad and its successor Penn Central would later spawn the *Metroliner*. At the midpoint of the century's seventh decade, the time was ripe for experimentation. The public harbored a perception that nothing was wrong with passenger trains that couldn't be cured by a positive attitude and lots of elbow grease. Baltimore & Ohio would supply both, in great abundance. "Frankly," confessed Langdon 28 years later, "I never thought it would work. But I wanted to make a last stand."

149

Trains in genteel poverty

Paul Reistrup's empire as B&O's new passenger czar seemed respectable indeed. A Baltimore & Ohio agent sold the first passenger-train ticket in America, in 1831, and 125 years later Langdon's predecessor, Howard Simpson, vowed that, by God, his railroad stood ready to sell the last ticket, too. And it seemed altogether possible (if you hadn't heard Langdon's fix-this-or-else injunction to Reistrup) that B&O streamliners might last as long as the rights of way over which they ran.

From an eastern hub of Baltimore and Washington, B&O passenger trains radiated west like a spider's web. Three trains ran the corridor to Chicago—the flagship *Capitol Limited* (with a connecting train from Willard, Ohio, to Detroit called the *Ambassador*), the second-tier *Shenandoah* and the *Washington–Chicago Express*. From Cumberland in western Maryland, three other trains out of Baltimore–Washington veered southwest toward St. Louis—the regally named *National Limited*, the secondary *Metropolitan Special* and an unnamed pair of locals (which went only as far west as Cincinnati and was consolidated with the *Shenandoah* east of Cumberland). Connecting the web were two Cincinnati–Detroit trains, the daylight *Cincinnatian* and the *Night Express*. All but the *Cincinnatian* carried Pullman-run sleeping cars, and all offered sit-down meals. There were also commuter-train services to Baltimore, Washington and Pittsburgh, handled mostly by 15 Budd-built Rail Diesel Cars.

These were, in short, full-service trains, but not so many that they formed a fiscal noose around the railroad's neck. The trains handled scads of Railway Post Office, storage mail and express cars to buttress ticket receipts. And competition didn't seem formidable. The Chicago–Baltimore–Washington service on Pennsy's *General* was no match for that of the *Capitol*. In the air, such carriers as American, Northwest and United were only beginning to appeal to mass markets with their 707s and 727s.

On the debit side, B&O's passenger-car fleet looked long of tooth. Baltimore & Ohio owned exactly seven regular lightweight coaches. Sixty other lightweight cars—dome coaches, twin-unit diners, diners, lounges, sleepers, dome sleepers and sleeper-lounges—augmented these cars. The rest of the fleet of 500-plus cars was either heavyweight equipment given an exterior streamlining by B&O decades earlier, or unrebuilt heavyweights of equally ancient vintage. Practically speaking, the lightweight cars could equip the *Capitol Limited* and cover all of the railroad's other sleeping car lines. Other than that, the show belonged to pre-1930 hardware, much of it in mediocre shape.

Financially, the passenger business was sick but not DOA. From 1958 to 1963, B&O's revenue passenger miles fell at a 6 percent annual rate. But it had controlled costs remarkably well. The railroad's solely related passenger deficit (as defined by the Interstate Commerce Commission) had declined every year recently, from almost $12 million in 1958 to $5 million in 1961 and a mere $260,000 in 1962. Then in 1963 that out-of-pocket loss mushroomed to almost $2.4 million. Hence, Langdon's command to bring it back down.

Overhead costs of the Passenger Services Department amounted then to some $500,000 a month—such expenses as advertising, administration, commissaries, equipment depreciation and other costs of a similar sort. Washington–Chicago trains all covered their direct costs, and were contributing, in roughly equal measure, more than $1 million annually toward those overhead expenses. On the St. Louis side, the *Metropolitan* was solidly profitable, too, thanks to its head-end revenues. But the *National Limited* barely recovered its direct costs, and the Cumberland–Cincinnati local lost money at a $400,000-a-year clip. The Pittsburgh, Baltimore and Washington commuter trains lost $25,000 per month on a direct-cost basis. So did the two Cincinnati–Detroit trains.

Cut-rate Pullmans, salty snacks

What set young Reistrup apart from most other U.S. passenger traffic managers of his era was his unabashed enthusiasm and relentless optimism. And why not? Reistrup, answerable only to the railroad's president, enjoyed extraordinary freedom. His job was to do whatever was necessary to make the trains profitable on a cash-flow basis, or to report with a clear conscience that the goal was unachievable. He couldn't lose. The harder Reistrup tried, the more credit he would get in the executive suite; the railroad would either make money or possess air-tight cases for dropping trains. Only by being half-hearted would Reistrup fail to serve the best interests of his employer. Just one impediment stood in the way: Reistrup couldn't spend his railroad's scarce capital dollars.

The first order of business was to create a structure. "I wanted a bright guy to assist me," says Reistrup. He found such a person in David Watts, then attached to B&O's Industrial Engineering Department. Watts and Reistrup were about the same age, and made a great pair—Reistrup the detail-oriented operating man, Watts the idea-generating marketing fellow. (Reistrup once said of Watts that he had 1,000 ideas a day. "One of them was good," said Reistrup, "and my job was to figure out which one it was.") James Sell, a B&O veteran possessing encyclopedic knowledge of costs and terminals, was made manager of day-to-day operations.

During nearly three years at this job, Reistrup sought to kill almost no B&O trains. An exception: the Cumberland–Cincinnati local, trains 23 and 30. Judged as hopeless, they bit the dust on Independence Day, 1964. Mainly, Reistrup worked at making the most of trains already in the timetable. Some of those trains got new names. The *Capitol Limited* and *National Limited* became simply *Capitol* and *National*, the Detroit section of the *Capitol* went from *Ambassador* to *Capitol-Detroit*, the *Metropolitan Special* was deemed no longer special

▶ *The* Capitol *was a magnificent train in July 1965, stretching out of sight as it left Baltimore. But soon, in Washington Union Station, it would add eight more cars—a tour de force behind four E units. (Herbert H. Harwood Jr.)*

and was abbreviated to *Metropolitan,* and the *Shenandoah* between Washington and Chicago took the name *Diplomat.*

Reistrup's more urgent task was to raise revenues and cut costs. Priority one: sleepers. Coach travel held up nicely, but not so business aboard the Pullmans. "We might as well have not run sleepers on Monday, Tuesday and Wednesday," says Reistrup. Rather than cut cars from the trains—the standard solution on railroads then—Reistrup sought to fill them, starting April 13, 1964, by slashing fares on midweek first-class travel by 31 percent. Reistrup wanted to call these Red, White & Blue fares. But that term was used first by Canadian National, which declined to lend the name to B&O. So Red Circle Day fares they became. Alas, Red Circle fares did little more than arrest the decline in Pullman travel, and even that effect was temporary.

Undeterred, in October 1964 Reistrup extended Red Circle Day discounts to coach travelers. This time it worked—to a degree. Coach ridership tended to rise during weekdays, as hoped. But total ridership increased only slightly. In other words, even fares competitive with Greyhound didn't lure many new customers.

There wasn't a lot of money to spend on advertisements, and incentive fares did little good if nobody knew about them. Reistrup's people did compose inexpensive classified ads for the "Personals" column of on-line newspapers. Examples:

TIGER, MEET ME AT THE ZOO IN BALTIMORE. We'll

split the money you save by taking B&O on Red Circle Fare days. It costs only $12.25 Call Mr. Thrift on 535-9141 for details.

MARCIA, I'LL FOLLOW YOU ANYWHERE. Taking B&O to Washington and saving 31% on Red Circle Fare. Enough to pay for the license and the preacher. Thanks to Mr. Thrift on 535-9141.

At the same time, Reistrup put some glitz in his premier runs, trains 5 and 6. The *Capitol* was a streamlined, usually all-lightweight train. Behind the standard quartet of E units and the RPO car in mid 1964 rolled a baggage-dormitory-coffee shop; three coaches to Chicago (one a dome car with a beneath-the-dome lounge); a coach, Pullman and sleeper-

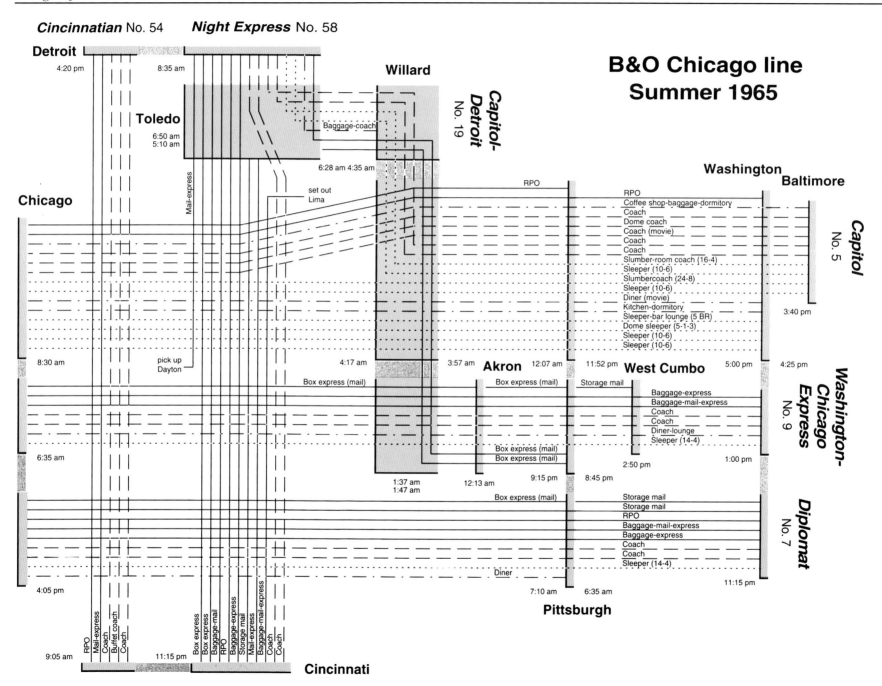

Cincinnatian No. 54   **Night Express** No. 58

B&O Chicago line
Summer 1965

Detroit
4:20 pm   8:35 am

Willard

Toledo
6:50 am
5:10 am

Capitol-Detroit No. 19

Baggage-coach

Mail-express

6:28 am 4:35 am

Washington
Baltimore

Chicago

set out
Lima

RPO
RPO
Coffee shop-baggage-dormitory
Coach
Dome coach
Coach (movie)
Coach
Coach
Slumber-room coach (16-4)
Sleeper (10-6)
Slumbercoach (24-8)
Sleeper (10-6)
Diner (movie)
Kitchen-dormitory
Sleeper-bar lounge (5 BR)
Dome sleeper (5-1-3)
Sleeper (10-6)
Sleeper (10-6)

Capitol No. 5

3:40 pm

8:30 am   pick up Dayton

4:17 am   3:57 am **Akron** 12:07 am   11:52 pm **West Cumbo**   5:00 pm   4:25 pm

Box express (mail)   Box express (mail)   Storage mail

Baggage-express
Baggage-mail-express
Coach
Coach
Diner-lounge
Sleeper (14-4)

Washington-Chicago Express No. 9

6:35 am

Box express (mail)
Box express (mail)

2:50 pm   1:00 pm

1:37 am   12:13 am   9:15 pm   8:45 pm
1:47 am

Box express (mail)

Storage mail
Storage mail
RPO
Baggage-mail-express
Baggage-express
Coach
Coach
Sleeper (14-4)

Diplomat No. 7

4:05 pm

Diner

7:10 am   6:35 am

11:15 pm

Pittsburgh

9:05 am   11:15 pm

RPO
Mail-express
Coach
Buffet coach
Coach

Box express
Box express
Baggage-mail
RPO
Baggage-express
Storage mail
Mail-express
Baggage-mail-express
Coach
Coach

Cincinnati

▶ *B&O's Lincoln Street coach yard in Chicago gives you an appreciation of the infrastructure that supported passenger service. In this 1966 scene a switcher assembles the eastbound Capitol. After backing its six-car cut onto the baggage-dormitory-coffee shop car on the track at right, it will grab the twin-unit diner and two sleepers on the adjacent track. (William Howes collection)*

lounge to Detroit; a Slumbercoach and Pullman; twin-unit 64-seat diner and kitchen-dormitory; dome sleeper; two additional Pullmans and a sleeper-lounge-observation. Few trains anywhere had so much dining and recreational space. Trains 1 and 2, the *National* on the St. Louis route, were a miniature of the *Capitol* but with no dome car and a single-unit diner.

What did premier trains lack? Why, movies, of course. So Reistrup introduced first-run movies. He leased projectors from In-Flight Motion Pictures to mount in the ceilings of the *Capitol*'s diner and in coaches assigned to both that train and the *National*. "Anybody riding first class or Slumbercoach could come to the diner after dinner for the movie," says Reistrup. "The coach was reserved seating, and we sold those seats on a first-come basis."

The movie era on B&O got off to a disastrous start. Reistrup sent Watts to Washington to supervise a non-public test run. At that time, the *Capitol* out of Baltimore backed into Washington Union Station and coupled to the diners, three sleepers and an observation car that already sat at the bumping post. Then the locomotives cut off to add the RPO on the head end. On this day the non-revenue coach with an In-Flight projectionist aboard was attached to the

RPO car on a pocket track. "The engineer knew he always backed to a certain spot with the RPO to recouple to his train," says Reistrup. "But he forgot that he had the movie coach behind the RPO, didn't pay attention to signals and was still going full tilt when he slammed into the body of the train." A minor derailment ensued.

Watts witnessed the collision and ran to a trackside

phone to call Reistrup in Baltimore. "This is Dave Watts!" he announced. Interrupted the boss: "Let me guess: You derailed the movie car." It turned out that the stationmaster in Washington got word of the derailment and phoned Reistrup the bad news an instant before the dumbfounded Watts.

The movies, by all accounts, proved quite popular with passengers. An informal survey of coach

▶ *The* National *leaving Baltimore two months before its September 1965 demotion and 11 months after the fact. But even the shortened version retains the sleeper-observation. (Herbert H. Harwood Jr.)*

passengers showed 99 percent acceptance of the idea. It didn't hurt, of course, that Reistrup featured them on the cover of B&O passenger timetables of that era. They lasted almost three years. (Footnote: Moviegoers in the diner got free munchies—the saltier the better, as an inducement to order drinks from the bar.)

Autos and food bars

Another Reistrup touch: Take your car along. This helped inspire Eugene Garfield's *AutoTrain* of the 1970s, which flourishes today under Amtrak ownership between the Washington, D.C., area and cen-

◀ *B&O commissioned these photographs aboard the* National *in 1965, shortly before it became a Baltimore–Cincinnati local. The effect is like stepping into a time warp. Clockwise from upper left: a modernized heavyweight dining car, heavyweight coach, baggage-dorm-lounge (comfortably occupied by a deadheading crew) and lightweight River-series sleeper-lounge-obs. (William Howes collection)*

tral Florida. B&O's modest effort, however, was limited to a single bilevel autorack car attached to the rear of the *Washington–Chicago Express*, which left its namesake cities several hours ahead of the *Capitol Limited*. For a $60 surcharge, passengers could drop their cars in late morning, board the *Capitol* in late afternoon and pick up their waiting and freshly washed autos upon arrival.

The experiment generated more news media attention than anything else Reistrip did. Response, however, was underwhelming—less than one auto a day in each direction, on average. Watts figured that the $12,500 revenue more than covered costs. But the auto-ferry idea lasted only a single season, the summer of 1965. "The big problem," says William Howes Jr., who was to become B&O/C&O's last director of passenger service, "was a significant amount of damage to the autos. Things got shaken loose—bumpers and fenders, for instance. Because of that, the experiment was never repeated."

As for equipment, Reistrup, Watts and Sell sought to make the most of what they had—those seven lightweight coaches, for instance. Previously, four had run each day on the *Capitol* and *Capitol-Detroit* (two in each direction), with the others kept as spares in Chicago, Washington and Detroit. Watts said to run them all every day. The executives graded their fleet for passenger comfort, too. Henceforth, A cars were to be used before B cars, B cars before C cars and so on. With both yardmasters and the Passenger Services Department staff thus on notice, fewer unrebuilt heavyweight cars found their way onto premier trains.

And speaking of heavyweights, many were simply scrapped. In 1963, B&O needed 43 coaches a day to cover its basic service. Requirements averaged 60–85 cars a day during summer, and as many as 117 coaches around Easter, Fourth of July, Labor Day and Christmas. So dozens of coaches stood by for only occasional use. Reistrup reckoned that B&O required one Mechanical Department employee per

The auto-ferry service for Capitol *riders was seldom as popular as this publicity photo suggests. But it foretold the* AutoTrain. *(William Howes collection)*

passenger car, no matter how often the equipment went into service. By simply getting rid of older, seldom-used cars, maintenance expenses fell with little loss of revenue. And what wasn't scrapped started getting cosmetic surgery and rebuilding of the truck assemblies below the floors. This yielded a more attractive appearance from bright-colored interiors, and smoother rides.

Other cost-cutting measures went into effect. B&O's loss ratio on dining cars was one of the worst in the industry. For every $1 coming in during 1964, $1.54 went out in over-the-road costs (95 cents of it in crew wages), and total deficits amounted to $75,000 a month. Watts says the railroad had "a

very conscious policy" of not gouging passengers on dining car prices. Yet surely food-service expenses could be cut. Reistrup asked the Cornell University School of Hotel Administration for ideas, and got plenty. But he had trouble convincing his uncompromising superintendent of dining cars, James Martin, to adopt them. Finally, Reistrup took Martin to Cornell. The two sat down to eat—and grade—meals prepared by the school. The food got terrific marks. What Martin didn't know was that it was all assembled from frozen, precooked portions in plastic pouches. "Jim was a hard sell," says Reistrup, "but that meal converted him."

Precooked meals fit perfectly into yet another Reistrup-Watts innovation, the food bar-coach. Dining cars, B&O people noticed, were patronized primarily by sleeping car passengers. Ninety percent of the *Capitol*'s Pullman passengers ate dinner in the diner, versus just 31 percent of coach riders, and coach riders tended to select the cheapest dining car meals. So the railroad converted five streamlined heavyweight cars into 38-seat coaches with a food-preparation area and service counter at one end, staffed by one employee rather than the four to six required by a diner (or the nine to 13 employed on the *Capitol*'s twin-unit set). When the *Cincinnatian*'s cafe-lounge in mid 1964 was replaced by prototype food bar cars 3067 and 3068, offering mainly hamburgers and sandwiches, revenues shot up 30 percent and a $3,200-a-month deficit immediately dissolved. By 1968 only the *Capitol Limited* among B&O trains retained a regular diner.

"There really weren't a lot of brand-new ideas," Reistrup later remarked of the 1964–1966 period. "The first guy to try something new is going to have trouble. What we tried to do was put it all together." Reistrup's talent was to remain alert to any idea, no matter where it came from, that might bring passenger service closer to that break-even goal. B&O and its parent C&O, for instance, became among the few railroads in the mid 1960s to accept the

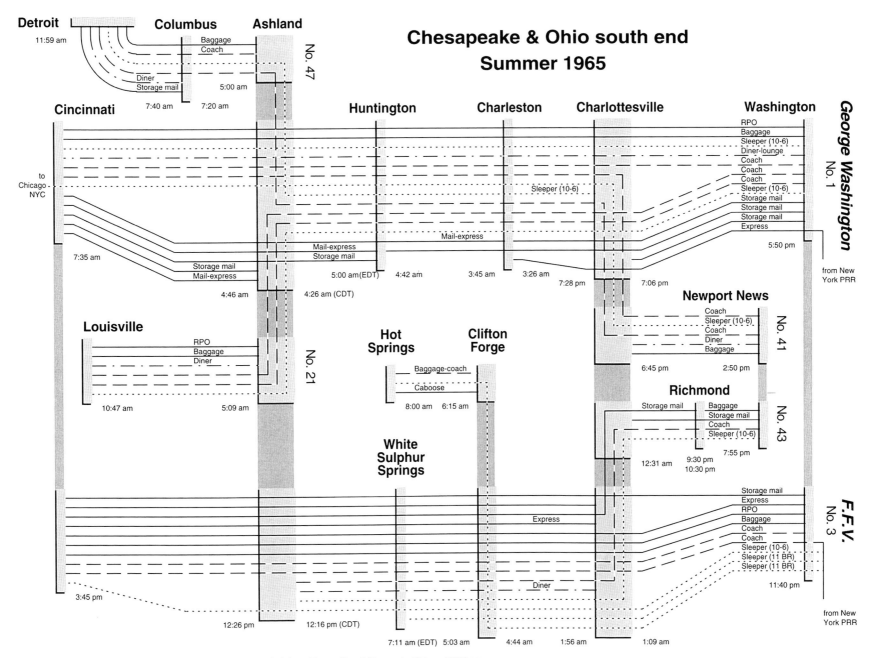

Chesapeake & Ohio south end
Summer 1965

Detroit
11:59 am

Columbus
Baggage
Coach
Diner
Storage mail
5:00 am
7:40 am   7:20 am

Ashland
No. 47

Cincinnati
to Chicago NYC
7:35 am
Storage mail
Mail-express
4:46 am

Louisville
RPO
Baggage
Diner
10:47 am   5:09 am

No. 21

Huntington
Mail-express
Storage mail
5:00 am(EDT)   4:42 am
4:26 am (CDT)

Charleston
Sleeper (10-6)
3:45 am

Charlottesville
Mail-express
3:26 am
7:28 pm   7:06 pm

Washington
RPO
Baggage
Sleeper (10-6)
Diner-lounge
Coach
Coach
Coach
Sleeper (10-6)
Storage mail
Storage mail
Storage mail
Express
5:50 pm
from New York PRR

George Washington
No. 1

Hot Springs

Clifton Forge

Newport News
Coach
Sleeper (10-6)
Coach
Diner
Baggage
6:45 pm   2:50 pm

No. 41

Baggage-coach
Caboose
8:00 am   6:15 am

Richmond
Storage mail   Baggage
Storage mail
Coach
Sleeper (10-6)
12:31 am   9:30 pm   7:55 pm
10:30 pm

No. 43

White Sulphur Springs

Storage mail
Express
Express
RPO
Baggage
Coach
Coach
Sleeper (10-6)
Sleeper (11 BR)
Sleeper (11 BR)
11:40 pm
from New York PRR

F.F.V.
No. 3

Diner

3:45 pm
12:26 pm   12:16 pm (CDT)
7:11 am (EDT)   5:03 am   4:44 am   1:56 am   1:09 am

Not shown: No. 47 (RDC coach, baggage trailer); Leave Newport News 8:30 am, arrive Richmond 10:00 am

157

◄ *The Washington and Newport News sections of the eastbound George Washington have separated at Charlottesville, Virginia, in this 1969 scene, and now the capital-bound portion, right, is leaving town. (William E. Warden)*

mous amount of C&O's prestige and pride lay in the Greenbrier, a magnificent facility nestled in the Alleghenies just west of the Virginia border and so close to the tracks that from your $300-a-night suite you can hear the eastbound coal trains struggling toward the summit. White Sulphur Springs remained largely inaccessible then by air, and highway distances to urban areas were considerable. Rail service to the Greenbrier was deemed vital.

Chessie was losing buckets of money on passenger trains, too—by 1964, almost $7.5 million, according to the ICC's formula on solely rated costs, or more than three times as much as B&O. Deficits pegged solely to the Pullmans reached $1.1 million. But losses didn't seem terribly important to C&O's toothpick-thin chief executive, Walter J. Tuohy. Chessie's coal business made it one of railroading's few no-lose bets. In 1964, operating income of $51 million equalled an incredible 14 percent of revenues. By comparison, B&O's net that year of $21 million was a mere 5 percent of revenues. "A dime a share—that's what Tuohy used to call the impact of passenger losses on shareholders," says Reistrup. "C&O's $4-per-share dividend was practically guaranteed." Never mind that Tuohy underestimated by a factor of eight the drain of passenger trains on C&O's profitability. He simply wasn't game to get rid of them.

But it made little sense for the two railroads, now jointly owned if separately operated, to go their separate ways with passengers, since some of their

popular American Express and Diners Club cards as payment for fares. The cut-rate fares originated with Canadian National, the movies and general-use credit cards with airlines, the auto ferry with the Department of Commerce, the food-service changes with Southern Pacific.

Meows of the Chessie cat

A year into Reistrup's two-year mission, at the beginning of 1965, he took custody of Chesapeake & Ohio passenger trains, too. B&O had come under control of Chessie in 1963. But initially passenger

services of the two railroads shared nothing but a common public timetable. C&O passenger trains remained under the supervision of its Public Relations Department—a legacy of former Chairman Robert R. Young, who believed that passenger trains were part of his railroad's public image and recast the line of authority accordingly.

And the whole Chessie setup revolved around needs of the Greenbrier, C&O's five-star resort hotel in White Sulphur Springs, W.Va., and its equally famous (but independently owned) competitor in nearby Hot Springs, Va., the Homestead. An enor-

▶ *Minutes after sunset on a July 1969 evening, the westbound* George Washington *hustles through Waynesboro, Virginia, on the aptly named Mountain Subdivision, with three locomotives and 14 cars.* (William E. Warden)

trains served common points and even common routes. A lot of money could be saved, for example, by moving B&O out of Detroit's massive Michigan Central Station (owned by New York Central) and into more-modest (and Chessie-run) Fort Street Union Depot. This was quickly accomplished.

Reistrup had a more-pressing concern in 1965: the *National*. This Baltimore–Washington–Cincinnati–St. Louis train wasn't responding to revenue-producing ideas. Two years earlier, the *National* was detoured over branch lines for five months (at the cost of a three-hour delay) while tunnels were enlarged between Clarksburg and Parkersburg, W.Va. Afterward, patronage never really bounced back. Slumber-room economy sleepers, movies and even the return of its classic ex-New York Central sleeper-lounge-observation cars (the *River*-series round-end affairs) for 14 months didn't make a difference. In 1964, the train failed by some $150,000 to cover its direct costs.

Chessie's flagship passenger train, the *George Washington*, also ran between Washington and Cincinnati on an elapsed time only 40 minutes longer. It also served a much larger population. Unlike the *National*, the *George Washington* earned its out-of-pocket costs and a bit more. So Reistrup in early 1965 began to study a semi-consolidation of the two trains—the guts of the *National* (its two Baltimore–St. Louis coaches, a sleeper and Slumber-room sleeper) to go to the *George Washington* east of Cincinnati. B&O's 1 and 2 would continue as before,

but as three-car locals 31 and 32 between Baltimore and Cincinnati. West of Cincinnati, B&O 1 and 2 would assume the *George Washington* name and haul the through St. Louis cars.

Cost analysis indicated a savings of $500,000 a year, including elimination of helper engines on the West End grades between Keyser and Grafton, W.Va. Reistrup canvassed his department, asking people to "uncover all possible 'ringers' so that we can overcome them." The most heartfelt response came from H. H. Lehkamp, sales manager in Cincinnati. "I realize it seems foolish to operate two trains from the

same city, on practically the same schedule, with the same ultimate destination," Lehkamp wrote Reistrup. "Yet I hate to see such a fine train as the *National,* in my opinion the only really first-class passenger train operating in and out of Cincinnati Union Terminal, discontinued."

The change went into effect on September 5, 1965, anyway. What remained of the *National* was a vest-pocket streamliner for local Baltimore–Cincinnati business. But the *River* sleeper-lounge-observations made a reappearance, to provide both limited Pullman and dining service.

Surrender, then abject defeat

In early 1966, his two years up, Reistrup faced facts. His medicine wasn't curing the patient. Yes, this tonic or that worked. And yes, some vital signs looked good. The decline in B&O ridership had been arrested. Measured by both passengers carried and revenue passenger miles, business held rock-steady in both 1964 and 1965 (versus those 6 percent annual declines in prior years).

But so what? Dr. Reistrup's mission was to make the trains financially healthy. On that score he was losing ground. B&O's out-of-pocket deficit actually rose in 1965 by 67 percent, to almost $4 million. (These are ICC figures, not those kept internally by the railroad, but they correspond roughly with Reistrup's recollections.) "I thought we could pull it off—we really tried," Reistrup would later say. Adds Watts: "Paul and I saw eye to eye. We finally concluded there was nothing within reason we could do that would turn things around."

More than anything else, Reistrup couldn't make enough headway against high fixed costs. In a July 1965 memo to the staff, operations manager Sell outlined the problem:

❐ Joint costs with other railroads at terminals were exorbitant. B&O paid $45 per car just to pass through Washington Union Station. The straight-through-town charge was $24 per car at Cincinnati Union Terminal, $59 at St. Louis Union Station (going in, then out the other way), $10 at Pittsburgh and $33 at Detroit's Fort Street Union Depot. To actually switch a passenger car in or out at these stations could more than double the charge.

❐ Based on an average direct expense of 15 cents a car mile, it cost B&O almost $800 per day to add a car between Baltimore and St. Louis. Installing new brakeshoes on a six-axle coach cost $126 in parts and labor. A new set of wheels represented a $700 expense, and a new window pane $130.

❐ How about extra business—say, a special excursion? B&O promoted these vigorously under Re-istrup. But even they may have lost the railroad money. Sell analyzed one hypothetical excursion—a Cincinnati–Washington round trip involving 500 passengers using 10 coaches, two diners, a crew dormitory and a diner-observation. Fares would total almost $10,000, and revenue from set-menu meals another $3,825. In more than six pages of single-spaced analysis, Sell ticked off the costs: $3,520 to assemble equipment in Cincinnati and return it later; $4,053 in dining car costs; $5,634 in terminal and car and locomotive expenses; $1,982 in crew costs and $288 to lease a Pullman and porter for the dormitory. Result: a $1,722 loss. Take away the dining car and coach attendants, and the trip would have produced a 10 percent profit—still far short of the 25 percent margin that Sell set as a goal. You could almost conclude that the more people you carried, the more you lost.

Jervis Langdon, the inspiration of Reistrup's efforts, had left B&O in late 1964 to run Rock Island Lines. On March 15, 1966, Reistrup wrote Gregory DeVine, a C&O Coal Department alumnus who was then president of both railroads, recommending that passenger trains be phased out. DeVine, however, acted deaf. For nearly a year no wheels were set in motion to carry out that recommendation. Partly, Howes said later, DeVine feared political upheavals and community and shipper ill will that seemed inevitable from a raft of train-off cases. Then Tuohy, Chessie CEO since 1948, collapsed of a heart attack on the eve of C&O's annual meeting in May 1966 and died that night. As his successor, DeVine had a full plate of problems, including an approaching merger (which never occurred) of his railroads with Norfolk & Western. Profits from C&O's coal afforded him the luxury of indecision.

And for 43 mad, glorious days in the summer of 1966 it seemed as if the terminally ill patient might undergo a miracle cure after all. The catalyst for hope: a strike against several trunk airlines that effectively shut down air service between Washington and the Midwest. This was the break Reistrup wanted—a chance for his trains to strut their stuff to new customers.

To its everlasting credit, Baltimore & Ohio rose to the occasion. "We were aware this was a chance to make new friends," says Watts, "and performance was remarkably good—trains were pretty much on time throughout." Every piece of equipment Reistrup and Watts could lay hands on they threw into the pot. "The only thing we didn't do," says Reistrup, "was put seats in baggage cars." The Chicago and Detroit sections of the *Capitol*, instead of combining east of Willard, ran separately. And had you watched No. 5 making its 2.5-mile backup move into Chicago's Grand Central Station from Western Avenue Junction during that period, your jaw would have dropped: Five cars . . . 10 . . . 15 . . . 20! Here's 19-car No. 5 entering Chicago on July 22, 1966, behind three B&O E units:

RPO
RPO
Baggage-dorm-coffee shop *Harpers Ferry*
Coach (HW)* 3574
Coach (HW)* 3568
Coach C&O 1653
Dome coach-lounge 5551
Coach (movie) *LaPaz*
Sleeper (10-6) *Allegheny*
Sleeper-lounge (5 BR) *Wawasee*
Slumber-room coach (16-4)* *Swan*
Slumbercoach (24-8) *Dreamland*
Diner (movie) 1092
Kitchen-dormitory 1093
Sleeper (10-6) *Muscatatuck*
Sleeper (14-4)* *Monocacy*
Sleeper (10-6)* *Opeguon*
Sleeper (10-6)* *Shenango*
Sleeper (10-6)* *Youghiogheny*
　　*extra car

"We cleaned up," says Reistrup, referring not

only to revenue but to good comments on service that flowed his way. "We figured that if in those 43 days we couldn't break even, we never would. And for the fleet as a whole we may have even gotten to break even in that brief period—I don't remember." What he does remember is how fast the bubble burst after the airlines got back in business. The hope was that B&O's new customers would tend to stick around—that patronage would, at worst, gradually taper off to pre-strike levels. But the strike bonanza ended as quickly as a candle is extinguished in the wind. In a day's time, the trains were as empty as before. It meant, in a sense, abject defeat.

Orderly withdrawal

Reistrup left the Passenger Services Department early in 1967 to run B&O's Coal Traffic Department. "I had a young family, and I wanted to have a future on the railroad," he says. "I could tell there was no future in passenger trains." (Ironically, within six months Reistrup was lured by Illinois Central to run—what else?—its passenger service.) Watts moved up to replace him, and 27-year-old William Howes Jr. came in, like Watts before him, from the Industrial Engineering Department as deputy.

It was a bleak period, Howes concedes. The out-of-pocket loss on B&O passenger trains had fallen in 1966, thanks perhaps to that airline strike, to $2.7 million—just above the 1964 level. Mail revenues rose in '66, too. But ridership resumed its interrupted decline late in 1966, and this trend accelerated going into 1967. "The mail business—particularly the Railway Post Office cars—sustained everything," says Howes. "There were trips when the mail cars generated more revenue for the *Capitol* than all of its passenger cars combined."

Results on B&O for the first quarter of 1967 were sobering. The non-commuter trains fell $16,000 short of covering their basic over-the-road costs. Worst performer was the Baltimore–Cincinnati remnant of the *National* (a three-month loss of $104,000) and

the best was the coach-only *Metropolitan* between Washington and St. Louis, which netted almost $200,000, thanks to its mail contracts. The *Capitol* still cleared its direct costs—barely—but revenue fell $90,000 from the same three-month period of 1966.

Throw in commuter runs and other passenger-related expenses—headquarters costs and costs of locomotive and car repairs, for instance—and B&O's three-month result was a loss of almost $1.9 million—a 41 percent jump from a year earlier. More and more, mail revenue held everything together, accounting for 55 percent of revenue. So the deci-

▲ *If ever there were an image to remember C&O's George Washington by, it's this scene of a magnificent streamliner pausing in Alexandria, Virginia, on its last stop into Washington, D.C., in April 1968. The tracks and the station remain heavily used, but no train like this comes calling today. (Herbert H. Harwood)*

◀ *The combined B&O*
Ambassador (the Capitol's Detroit
section) and C&O's Sportsman
leave Detroit in late 1966. The
trains will separate in Toledo; the
B&O train running on to Willard,
Ohio, and the C&O train to its
connection in Ashland, Kentucky.
(J. David Ingles)

Specials to the resorts

And on May 11, 1968, C&O succeeded—finally—in discontinuing No. 3 (*F.F.V.*) and No. 4 (*Sportsman*) between Washington and Cincinnati, plus their connecting trains between Newport News and Charlottesville, Va. An earlier attempt in 1967 had failed disastrously.

Sensitivity toward the *F.F.V.–Sportsman* was acute because they affected the Greenbrier in White Sulphur Springs and the Homestead in Hot Springs. In those days, first-class rail travel to these spas mattered a lot to Chesapeake & Ohio. Chessie's industrial customers held business meetings at the Greenbrier, which was so often used by the railroad to entertain customers that it constituted a thinly veiled means of traffic solicitation. "C&O kept extra sleeping car capacity on hand just to serve the Greenbrier," says Watts. "Whenever there was a special movement to the hotel, no expense was spared."

No expense spared? The same could be said of *regular* service to the two hotels. Westbound in those days, Pennsy's No. 175 out of New York City would leave Penn Station at 5:45 p.m. for Washington with an 11-bedroom sleeper for both the Greenbrier and Homestead. Chessie's No. 3, the *F.F.V.*, departed Washington with the two sleepers at 10:40 p.m., and set out the Homestead sleeper at Clifton Forge, Va., at 5 o'clock the next morning. From Clifton Forge, after a 75-minute layover to insure an on-

sion by the U.S. Postal Service to abolish RPO runs on B&O/C&O trains that autumn, as part of its shift to regional distribution centers for sorting of mail, struck the railroad with the force of a dagger to the heart. Of 17 Railway Post Office assignments on Baltimore & Ohio, only those on the *Metropolitan* and *Cincinnatian* lasted into 1968. Chesapeake & Ohio's only RPO runs to survive were on trains between Chicago and Grand Rapids and Detroit and Grand Rapids. The last of these were removed in 1969. Storage mail was cut significantly. In one swoop, B&O lost $1.9 million a year in mail revenues, and C&O $900,000.

Watts, estimating that the combined direct-cost deficit of B&O and C&O trains would soar from $9 million in 1966 to $12 million in 1967, launched a get-rid-of-'em campaign to balance service and costs against vastly decreased revenue. Right after Labor Day 1967 the *Night Express*—one half of the Cincinnati–Detroit service—quit running. The westbound *Chicago–Washington Express* and eastbound *Diplomat* ceased to operate west of Pittsburgh that November. In the first days of 1968 the old *National* was abolished west of Parkersburg. That May, Washington–Detroit sleepers left the *Capitol*, and St. Louis sleepers quit the *George Washington*.

the-minute departure, mixed train No. 303 ran west 12 miles to Covington and trundled up the 25-mile Hot Springs Branch with the sleeper, a baggage-coach, caboose and perhaps a coal car or two, reaching the picture-book depot at the foot of the sprawling Homestead complex at the civilized hour of 8 a.m. Then the mixed returned with the combine, empty sleeper and caboose to Clifton Forge for servicing and layover. Meanwhile, No. 3 continued up and over the Allegheny summit, depositing the Greenbrier sleeper on the pocket track at White Sulphur Springs. Passengers could occupy their rooms until 7:30, when a limousine took them across the street to the Greenbrier.

Eastbound movements were even more complex. From Clifton Forge early each evening, a passenger extra—roadswitcher, combine and sleeping car—ran back up the mountain to Hot Springs, loaded passengers and returned down the branch to the main line at Covington. From there, the two-car train headed west 22 miles to White Sulphur Springs. Again, the locomotive ran around its little train, coupled on to the 11-bedroom sleeper that No. 3 had deposited at daybreak and brought the combine and two sleepers back east to Clifton Forge. There the sleepers sat until after 3 the next morning, when No. 2, the eastbound *George Washington,* paused to pick them up. From Washington the two cars rode another Pennsy express to New York City, arriving at 1:50 p.m. In addition, a Newport News–Chicago sleeper ran daily, and a Charlottesville–Chicago sleeper seasonally, on the westbound *George Washington* and eastbound *Sportsman*—both primarily to serve the two resorts from the west; beyond Cincinnati, the cars were attached to New York Central's *James Whitcomb Riley.*

Even this incredible level of service simply wouldn't do on Sunday and Wednesday nights, when the Greenbrier's VIP clientele tended to leave for home. For these people, a 1:50 p.m. arrival in the

Big Apple meant a working day wasted. On such evenings ran the *Resort Special,* a train simply without parallel anywhere in the Americas. A passenger extra, as usual in late evening, made the Clifton Forge–Hot Springs–Covington–White Sulphur Springs–Clifton Forge circuit. Meanwhile, hours earlier, *another* locomotive and rider coach left Clifton Forge for White Sulphur Springs. There it reversed direction, becoming the *Resort Special.* Departing White Sulphur at 7:25 p.m., engine, rider coach and 11-bedroom sleeper (plus additional sleepers as necessary) ran passenger extra straight to Washington, where the sleeper was attached to a Pennsy express at 2 a.m., arriving in New York City Mondays and Thursdays at 6:50 a.m. The *Special* paused at Covington for folks, brought from Hot Springs via limousine, who couldn't wait for the later connection at Clifton Forge with No. 2.

Special moves associated with conventions could swell the *Resort Special* to impressive lengths. Such was the case September 18, 1967, when nine sleepers chartered by Arthur Young & Co. came down the mountain from Hot Springs to Clifton Forge, where they were attached to the *Resort Special* from White Sulphur Springs. "C&O was deadheading sleepers and other equipment all over the place, to line things up for special moves," says Howes. "Plus, there were an incredible number of office car trips. We decided there must be some edict that no C&O car could stand still overnight."

Specials to end all specials
So it's no wonder that tradition, pride, local politics and, no doubt, pressure from the resorts made tinkering with trains 3 and 4 touchy. As part of the deal with regulators for dropping the *F.F.V.* and *Sportsman,* Watts and Howes agreed to run, for seven weeks of high season in late spring of 1968 and for two months that fall, the *Resort Specials* to end all resort specials—not one schedule or two, three or even four, but five.

❒ From the west each Tuesday and Saturday came the *Western Resort Special.* The eastbound *Capitol* from Chicago on those afternoons included an extra 11-bedroom sleeper, which it set out at Fostoria, Ohio. Through Fostoria soon came C&O's No. 46 from Detroit with another special 11-bedroom sleeper. It picked up the Chicago car and continued on. A third extra sleeper left Cincinnati aboard No. 2, the *George Washington.* From Ashland, Kentucky, where No. 46 terminated, the *Western Resort Special* departed in the pit of the night, at 2:05 a.m., with a rider coach and the Chicago and Detroit sleepers. At Hinton, W.Va., the Cincinnati sleeper that No. 2 had left was added. The four-car train paused at 7 a.m. at White Sulphur Springs to let off the Greenbrier folks. Then it ambled across the Virginia border to Covington, where the Chicago and Detroit sleepers were deposited to await the regular Hot Springs mixed train from Clifton Forge. The *Western Resort Special* tied up at Clifton Forge with its rider car and the sleeper from Cincinnati, whose inclusion on the mixed would have overtaxed the GP7 going up the grade to Hot Springs. Headed back, the sleepers operated on the westbound *George Washington* and its connections Wednesday and Sunday evenings; the only change was that the Chicago car went to Cincinnati to connect with Penn Central's *James Whitcomb Riley.*

❒ Special number two operated the five days of the week not taken by the *Western Resort Special,* with only the sleeper from Cincinnati and a rider coach, and tied up at Clifton Forge, where remaining passengers boarded the Hot Springs mixed train.

❒ Special number three began as one 11-bedroom sleeper each for White Sulphur Springs and Hot Springs, attached to Penn Central's No. 175 from New York City at 5:45 p.m. on Tuesdays and Saturdays. In Washington, a rider coach for the crew joined the sleepers to form the westbound *Eastern Resort Special,* leaving at 11 p.m. on roughly the schedule of now-discontinued No. 3 and running passenger extra. At Clifton Forge the Hot Springs sleeper was left for the branch mixed train. The *Special* terminated at White Sulphur Springs with the other sleeper, then deadheaded back to Clifton Forge. From Clifton Forge, meanwhile, mixed train No. 303 took the New York City–Hot Springs sleeper, picked up those from Chicago and Detroit at Covington and proceeded up the Hot Springs Branch, bringing the unloaded cars back to Clifton Forge for layover.

❒ Next, the eastbound *Eastern Resort Special* deadheaded Wednesday and Sunday from Clifton Forge to White Sulphur Springs, loaded two 11-bedroom sleepers, reversed direction and headed east with those cars and a rider coach. It stopped in Covington to load people brought by limousine from the Homestead at Hot Springs and continued on to Washington and a PC connection for a breakfast arrival in New York City.

❒ The final special schedule ran the five nights per week that the eastbound *Eastern Resort Special* was idle. It left Clifton Forge at 8:30 p.m., going to White Sulphur Springs to collect the daily 11-bedroom sleeper and returned to Clifton Forge, where the New York City sleeper was picked up by No. 2.

C&O literally went the extra mile for the resorts. But the *Eastern Resort Special*, at least, was sparsely used. The all-first class train carried, on average, just a dozen people in its two sleepers during its spring incarnation in 1968, and only 18 that fall. Howes treated his parents to a trip on one occasion, and the three of them were the only people aboard their car. Thereafter, Greenbrier visitors had to detrain and board regular cars of the *George Washington* at decidedly unluxurious hours—10:38 p.m. westbound and 2:40 a.m. eastbound.

The downward spiral

From mid 1968 on, the name of the game was steady contraction—a job given to Bill Howes when Watts got a new assignment in May of 1969. The *Metro-*

◀ No. 303, the morning Hot Springs local, veers off the C&O main stem in Covington, Virginia, with a train perhaps unmatched anywhere in the U.S. in mid 1964: combine, lightweight sleeper, caboose and a car of coal, consigned to the Homestead resort in Hot Springs. Once in the tiny resort village, passengers will be dispatched to the hotel across the street, the hopper will be spotted for unloading and the rest of the train will return to Clifton Forge, on the main line, for servicing and layover. This evening, the whole drill will occur in reverse. In the 1990s folks would cross the globe to ride this train, which died in obscurity in 1968. (Michael J. Dunn III)

politan ceased operating west of Cincinnati in September of 1968, the *Capitol*'s Detroit section from Willard fell the next March (replaced by a rather successful and economical bus connection at Fostoria) and the old *National*, running as trains 31 and 32 under the name *West Virginian*, was truncated to a Washington–Cumberland local that August. Missing by early 1969 were several Baltimore–Washington shuttle trains. Through car service to Baltimore had ended in 1966 for the *Capitol* and in late 1967 for the *National*, when both were cut back

to Washington. By 1969, in fact, the Chicago line saw just the *Capitol* and trains 7 and 8, which ran only between Akron, Ohio, and Washington. The *Capitol*'s dome sleepers departed after 1965 to Canadian National and later Seaboard Coast Line, and the twin-unit diners were replaced by a single car in October 1967. But some earlier name changing had been undone: Long before, the *Capitol* again became the *Capitol Limited*, the name it should have retained all along. Now trains 7 and 8 regained the name *Shenandoah*.

For ridding themselves of trains, the railroads adopted with great success what Howes calls "Ohio strategy." In Ohio, as long as another train remained on a route, a railroad could dump other passenger trains by simply giving 30 days' notice; public hearings, if held at all, came after the fact. So by first ending service on a train in Ohio, and then posting the remnants for discontinuance in neighboring states, opposition seldom materialized. Watts first used this tactic to drop the *Night Express* between Cincinnati and Toledo in September 1967, and subsequently to thin out service on the Chicago line from three trains each way to two, and from Cumberland to Cincinnati, from two trains to one. It turned out to be a low-cost solution for B&O's Law Department, which didn't have to prepare for tedious proceedings before the ICC.

With resources left to them, Watts and Howes fashioned a level of service that brought their employer no shame. Howes in particular mastered the art of making less seem like more:

❏ The *Capitol Limited* as late as the summer of 1968 offered three distinct amenities to its passengers—the "Chessie Tavern" in its 38-seat diner, the "Iron Horse Tavern" at the snack bar of the dome coach and the "Capitol Club" in the blunt-end sleeper-bar lounge-observation car. By December of that year, in a masterful stroke of economy, Howes had squeezed all three services into a single car, the 1920-series lunch counter-diner-lounge-observations built for C&O in 1950 for the never-run *Chessie* streamliner. The first 26 feet of these cars held the kitchen and pantry, the next 16 feet a take-out counter and wet bar ("Iron Horse Tavern"), the following 28 feet dining space for 32 ("Chessie Tavern") and the final 15 or so feet abutting the observation windows, lounge space for 10 passengers ("Capitol Club").

❏ Later, because of demand for bedrooms, Howes reinstated the *Capitol*'s sleeper-bar lounge-observation (the cars *Dana*, *Metcalf* and *Wawasee*), thus

adding bragging rights for a "Starlight Sleeper, lounge and magazine library." In the autumn before Amtrak, the *Capitol Limited* might have been the coziest li'l train in the nation. Leaving Washington, its eight cars included three mail and baggage cars, two coaches, the sleeper-bar lounge (two rooms used as a dorm for the diner crew), a full sleeper and the diner-takeout counter-lounge-observation.

❏ The dome coaches removed from the *Capitol* late in 1968 worked briefly on the *Cincinnatian*, returned to the *Capitol* one final time for the summer of 1969 and then went to trains 7 and 8, the Washington–Akron *Shenandoah*. No. 7 was combined with No. 11, the *Metropolitan*, out of Wash-

▲ *Beneath the landmark train shed of Chicago's Grand Central Station, the conductor and trainmen confer beside a glistening Strata-Dome coach minutes before the* Capitol Limited *will depart for Washington, D.C. The date is November 11, 1967. Two years later, this classic depot on the edge of downtown would close, as B&O and C&O trains moved to North Western Station a mile to the northeast. (William D. Middleton)*

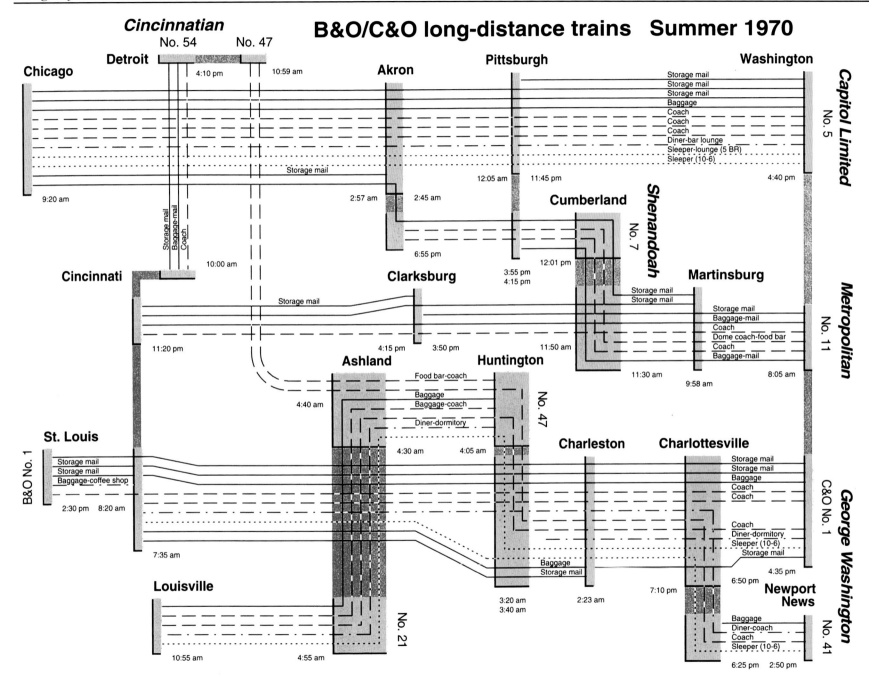

B&O/C&O long-distance trains   Summer 1970

Cincinnatian
No. 54   No. 47

Detroit   **Akron**   **Pittsburgh**   **Washington**

4:10 pm   10:59 am

Chicago

Storage mail
Storage mail
Storage mail
Baggage
Coach
Coach
Coach
Diner-bar lounge
Sleeper-lounge (5 BR)
Sleeper (10-6)

Capitol Limited No. 5

Storage mail

12:05 am   11:45 pm   4:40 pm

9:20 am   2:57 am   2:45 am   **Cumberland**

Shenandoah No. 7

Cincinnati   **Clarksburg**   6:55 pm   12:01 pm   **Martinsburg**

Storage mail   3:55 pm
                               4:15 pm
Storage mail
Baggage-mail
Storage mail   Storage mail
10:00 am   Storage mail
                                                Coach
                                                Dome coach-food bar
                                                Coach
                                                Baggage-mail

Metropolitan No. 11

11:20 pm   4:15 pm   3:50 pm   11:50 am   8:05 am

Ashland   **Huntington**   11:30 am
                                       9:58 am
Food bar-coach

Baggage
Baggage-coach   No. 47

4:40 am   Diner-dormitory

St. Louis   **Charleston**   **Charlottesville**

4:30 am   4:05 am

Storage mail   Storage mail
Storage mail   Storage mail
Baggage-coffee shop   Baggage
                                                               Coach
                                                               Coach

B&O No. 1

2:30 pm   8:20 am   Coach
                                                               Diner-dormitory
                                                               Sleeper (10-6)
                                                               Storage mail

C&O No. 1   *George Washington*

7:35 am   Baggage   4.35 pm
                                               Storage mail
                                                              6:50 pm
Louisville   3:20 am   2:23 am   7:10 pm   **Newport
                                   3:40 am   News**

Baggage
Diner-coach
Coach
Sleeper (10-6)

No. 21   No. 41

10:55 am   4:55 am   6:25 pm   2:50 pm

166

▶ *On manicured station property a stone's throw from the exclusive Greenbrier hotel, the most unremarked all-Pullman train in America, the* Resort Special, *prepares to leave White Sulphur Springs, West Virginia, for New York City on a June 1964 evening. The usual locomotive for this train was a boiler-equipped Geep. But this evening there's a formidable line of cars to move, and two E units come to the rescue. The resort remains in 1998, but not so the* Resort Special. *(Michael J. Dunn III)*

ington. But after the summer of 1970, when the last of the storage mail cars left, it was quite a sight west of Cumberland—just an E8 diesel and dome coach. The train tied up in Akron each evening and returned the next morning as No. 8.

❏ In July 1968 Watts replaced the *George Washington*'s Washington–Cincinnati Slumbercoach and bedroom-roomette Pullman with a single car containing four double bedrooms, six roomettes and six sections—the sections to be sold in lieu of rooms in a Slumbercoach, then only 40 percent utilized. This was sacrilege to C&O's oldtimers, who well remembered Robert R. Young's highly publicized campaign to rid Chessie of such open sleeping space in the late 1940s. Watts figured C&O would save $100,000 in this manner, and kept the 6-6-4 Pullmans running until that December. At the same time, the diner-lounge was replaced by a diner-dormitory to provide sleeping space for the car's crew, who had used spare Pullman rooms.

❏ In the best Paul Reistrup tradition, Howes made a virtue of the political impossibility of cutting train frequencies east of Cumberland by promoting it as B&O's "Potomac Valley Service." In reality, the service by 1970 consisted of the *Capitol*, the *Metropolitan* and two pairs of one- or two-car scoots between Washington and Cumberland; the once-upon-a-time *National Limited*'s ghost between Washington and Martinsburg, W.Va., and two Washington commuter trains to Brunswick, Md. If not substantial, the Potomac Valley Service at least gave the appearance of being so.

❏ Likewise, the Pere Marquette network in Michigan—two trains each way between Grand Rapids and Detroit, and one between Grand Rapids and Chicago and between Holland and Muskegon—all reached irreducible lengths of a single coach apiece by the autumn of 1970.

"After 1967," says Howes, "what really went on was a plan for total withdrawal. Dave and I couldn't envision the day when the *Capitol Limited* and *George Washington* would be gone. But it was all a matter of timing." Amtrak beat them to the punch.

TWILIGHT LIMITEDS

The railroad alliance that gave us the *Twentieth Century Limited, Broadway Limited* and *Merchants Limited* ultimately gave us heartburn.

The top executives of New York Central, Pennsylvania, New Haven and the railroad they all became, Penn Central, didn't seem to lose a moment's sleep, from the mid 1960s on, worrying whether you or I had a satisfactory trip on their passenger trains. The question that has hung in the air all these years since is simply this: Did those railroads' executives murder their passenger trains? Or did it matter what they did or didn't do to build or destroy their passenger businesses—would the result have been the same? I now think there is reason to reach either conclusion.

At the end of World War II, all three of the railroads which would comprise Penn Central spent huge amounts of money to reequip their passenger services. Between them, the Penn Central's future components put into service between 1946 and 1954 more than 1,400 lightweight cars, virtually all of them passenger-carrying cars, and almost all earmarked for intercity as opposed to commuter service. Their commitment at the dawn of the 1950s seemed beyond question. But having made this financial commitment, the railroads could not sustain

what they had created, especially in the face of the new jetliners and limited-access highways and the private automobiles bought by newly affluent Americans. Overwhelmed, they gave up.

New York Central and New Haven had little choice. The option was to invest for long-haul and short-haul service, respectively. Pennsy's choice was broader. It could invest in Northeast Corridor trains between New York City and Washington, or the long-haul business connecting New York with Chicago and St. Louis. Mistakenly, it chose the latter.

The Penn Central railroads wasted their money. Their hundreds of millions invested in passenger service brought them nothing. In addition, all were inexorably involved in the commuter-train business. Their bread-and-butter freight trains depended upon smokestack industries that were dispersing across the country.

I should hasten to say that these railroads displayed a lack of management skills. As service descended to abysmal levels by the mid 1960s onward, those responsible for these trains hadn't a clue how to sell passenger train transportation to the public.

The disappearing steel fleet

New York Central was by far the most enthusiastic booster of passenger trains after World War II. It put into service 742 new lightweight intercity cars—as many as Pennsy and New Haven combined. But what payback it ever got is hard to discern.

The backbone of the NYC passenger structure was its service across the state of New York. As of mid 1951, 33 first-class trains operated in each direction west of Albany—19 through or express trains, nine mail, express and milk trains and five locals. Imagine that: 66 trains a day is more than you will see, passenger and freight, on almost any rail segment today. Other parts of New York Central were heavily trafficked, too—between Buffalo and Cleveland, 23 first-class trains in each direction in 1951, and between Elkhart and Chicago, 18 round trips. All of this was on four-track and three-track main lines looked after by 152 interlocking towers between Grand Central and LaSalle Street stations that passed trains from one to another much as railroads in England had done since the last half of the nineteenth century.

For better and for worse, New York Central came under the control in 1954 of Robert R. Young (1897–1958), a Wall Street multimillionaire who ousted the NYC's existing management in a bitter proxy fight that hinged in part upon Young's assertion that Central could profitably operate *more* passenger trains rather than fewer. The man he recruited to run the Central, Alfred Perlman (1902–1983), had absolutely no attachment to passenger service. Perlman, a civil engineer by training, had been general manager of Denver & Rio Grande Western. At NYC, he quickly and no doubt correctly grasped that the railroad would go broke unless bold steps were taken, and those bold steps obviously included fewer passenger trains. Perlman then proceeded to pull off one of the boldest railroad turnarounds ever. In just a few years, the four tracks and three tracks became two, and the towers and their battalions of

levermen all but vanished, replaced by centralized traffic control that permits bidirectional operation on both tracks or through sidings. Modern retarder yards were built in the gateway cities—Albany (New York City and New England), Elkhart (Chicago connections) and Indianapolis (the St. Louis gateway). Layer upon layer of costs were shed.

And all the while passenger trains were cut off like limbs on a maturing tree. By 1956, before Perlman had even gotten a good start, the 33 round trips between Albany and Utica had become 26, the 23 trains between Buffalo and Cleveland were 19, and the 18 pairs of trains between Elkhart and Chicago shrank to 14. Buffalo-born John Kenefick had been brought to the NYC by Perlman in 1954 from Rio Grande, and was assistant general manager in Syracuse in 1956. "My mother lived in Buffalo," says Kenefick. "She invited us to Thanksgiving dinner. The New York Thruway had just opened. I had my own private business car, but what did we do? We plopped the baby in the back seat and took the Thruway. I remember thinking, 'With a convenience like this, who would want to ride a train?' "

New York Central in the 1950s may have been an exception to the rule that the Interstate Commerce Commission's formula for calculating fully allocated passenger train costs greatly overstated the actual costs. NYC, in company with Pennsylvania and New Haven, was so heavily laden with passenger trains that had you taken them *all* away overnight, truly huge savings might have resulted. In his autobiography *Keeping the Railroads Running: Fifty Years on the New York Central* (Hastings House, 1974), Karl Borntrager, NYC's senior vice president, recounts a cost study based on 1955 operations that assumed cessation of all passenger trains. His methodology presumed disinvestment in all the coach yards and engine terminals associated with passenger trains, including Grand Central and LaSalle Street stations, Cleveland Union Terminal and St. Louis Union Station. Concluded Borntrager: "I also assumed

that our own line between New York and Chicago would be reduced to a two-track operation. The results of this study indicated that the economies resulting from abandonment of passenger service exceeded the revenue derived by an amount substantially equal to the passenger service loss indicated by the ICC formula for dividing freight and passenger expense."

The noose kept tightening. In 1962, but nine pairs of trains roamed west of Buffalo. In 1965, the Albany–Utica corridor saw 14 train pairs, four of them exclusively devoted to mail and express, and the Elkhart–Chicago segment only seven, two of them mail-only. "Perlman's policy," insists Kenefick, who became NYC's VP-operations and later the president and chairman of Union Pacific, "was not to get out of the passenger business because we wanted to. It was to get out of the passenger business because we were losing our shirt." By mid 1966 the New York Central could be said to have but four trains worthy of note:

❏ *Twentieth Century Limited* (New York City–Chicago), a 14-car streamliner that still called forth the red carpet at Grand Central Station each afternoon. But famous feet weren't stepping on that carpet. It was not a "smart" train to take anymore. This is not to say that Central quit trying. To the contrary, internal memos as late as the summer of 1967 set down rigid rules on just what equipment could be assigned to the premiere train. The problem was, nobody noticed. Some nights the *Century* was almost uninhabited. On May 20, 1967, the westbound *Century* carried but 18 people in coach, 34 in the sleepercoach (budget sleeper) and 40 in sleeping cars; its eastbound counterpart had 31 in coach, 42 in sleepercoach and 20 in the sleepers. In other words, you could have seated almost everyone in one seating in the twin-unit dining car.

❏ *New England States* (Boston–Chicago), by then an abbreviated train that nonetheless merited a twin-unit diner, too. Interestingly, NYC still ran five trains each way between Boston and Albany, but three were mail and express trains that carried no passengers and the fourth a Budd Rail Diesel Car.

❒ *Ohio State Limited* (New York City–Cincinnati), which going west fed cars to the Central's last passenger-carrying train to St. Louis, and going east handled sleepers and coaches from the Toronto connection at Buffalo.

❒ *Wolverine* (New York–Chicago), routed via Canada and Detroit and including four sleepers.

I never rode the *Twentieth Century,* although from trackside in 1966 it struck me as a handsome train. Many years later I discovered that a friend of mine, James McClellan, later to become Norfolk Southern's strategic planner, had started work that year for New York Central's Marketing Department. He too was impressed by the *Century* from afar, but upon riding it in 1966 reached a different conclusion: "It was a piece of junk." The train still had dedicated equipment, he said, but it was visibly undermaintained. The clientele was old—that, or railroaders riding on passes—and sleeping cars were shabby. "I knew on that first trip," says McClellan, "that the *Twentieth Century* was dying, that it wasn't going to last much longer. The corporation didn't care—certainly Al Perlman didn't. He called his passenger trains 'a stupid waste of money.' "

McClellan was right—the *Century* lived on borrowed time. The next summer a memo from the Passenger Transportation Department chided the terminals for substituting other cars for the assigned

▶ *Manhattan bound on a beautiful April morning in 1965, the* Twentieth Century Limited *(top) exits Breakneck Ridge Tunnel in Cold Spring, New York. Just ahead of it that morning was No. 16, the* Ohio State Limited. *(Victor Hand)*

equipment. But abruptly, on Saturday, December 2, 1967, with virtually no advance word, New York Central called a halt to its traditional way of running passenger trains. Effective November 5, it had combined the *Century* and *New England States* west of Buffalo. Late that same month the New York Public Service Commission gave its cautious assent to a wholesale restructuring of service within that state. Henceforth, eight trains would leave New York City at roughly two-hour intervals starting at 8:30 a.m., five of the eight departures continuing on from Albany to Buffalo. A similar pattern was begun between Buffalo and Grand Central.

More about the new Empire Service in a moment. What knowledgable rail travelers noticed first was what did *not* run. Gone in both name and amenities were the *Twentieth Century Limited*, *Empire State Express* and *Ohio State Limited*, not to mention the *Wolverine*, Chicago–Detroit *Twilight Limited* and every other name train except the Chicago–Cincinnati *James Whitcomb Riley*. The account of the *Century*'s last westbound trip was perhaps best told by Rogers E. M. Whitaker, a *New Yorker* staff member who described his railroad exploits under the name "E. M. Frimbo." Whitaker had ridden the *Century* probably 50 times over his long life. Fortunately, a collection of his stories, *All Aboard With E. M. Frimbo*, was republished in 1997 in expanded form, with Anthony Hiss as coauthor.

Whitaker went to bed in the sleeping car *Missouri Valley* while the *Century* waited in Buffalo for

◄ Flagships: Central's Twentieth Century Limited (top), at South Bend, Indiana, in 1965, and Pennsy's Broadway Limited, arriving Chicago in 1964, represented the best their railroads could offer. (Louis A. Marre, top, and John Gruber)

a late *New England States* out of Boston. When he got up late the next morning, his train hadn't even reached Cleveland, because of a derailment ahead of it that eventually led to a detour on the parallel rails of Norfolk & Western. "She sure is dying hard, isn't she?" said the conductor. Caught behind a slow N&W freight, the Central's finest train made 60 miles in seven hours.

The sentimental journey was turning to farce.

▲ The bane of New York Central was the bitter, snow-strewn winter its people and trains endured. In January 1963, train 90, the eastbound Chicagoan, slogs through Batavia, New York, near Buffalo, with an icicled 12-car train. (Victor Hand)

◀ *Passing in style, the* Twentieth Century Limited *going east meets the* Iroquis *on double track in South Bend, Indiana, on April 8, 1961. (Louis A. Marre)*

Relates Whitaker in his account of the last trip:

Lunch, after Cleveland, was a quiet meal. The steward was cheerful, and said, "Want to sit down? Here's a seat right here. Things aren't so bad." The passengers were glum. We had some more asparagus soup and a mushroom omelet. There was no liquor, because there are laws in Ohio and Indiana about Sunday drinking. Afterward, we went back to the observation car [*Wingate Brook*], along with a number of other people, to look at Ohio, and by and by everyone cheered up. Four sailors sat down with a pack of cards and started to play poker.

The sun came out. A woman who told us she was from Milwaukee said, "When we were stopped in those fields in the middle of the night, I felt just like Dr. Zhivago." And a woman wearing a mink hat said, "Everyone seems placid, and I'm glad. I guess maybe it's because it's the last run there will ever be of the *Twentieth Century Limited*."

The train reached LaSalle Street just before 7 o'clock that Sunday evening—"late for its own funeral," I wrote in the next morning's *Chicago Sun-Times*. Thereafter you could still travel between New York City or Boston and Chicago, on roughly the same schedules as those of the old *Twentieth Century Limited* and *New England States*, on a nameless train created as their substitute. But it was an altogether different experience. "For those who rode the *Century*," wrote Richard J. Cook Sr. in *The Twentieth Century Limited 1938–1967* (TLC Publishing, 1993), "it was not the train's luxury appointments they remembered, but the aura of smartness that notables created for it." Well put, and the aura of smartness was gone at the end of 1967, as were the red carpet at Grand Central, the observation car and (for a while) the twin-unit diners.

You must concede this about the Empire Service, which began the next day, December 3: It showed that New York Central briefly tried to come to grips with its passenger service constructively. People simply weren't riding New York Central trains across its entire distance. So NYC sought to make the best of its core business within New York State. Forty coaches or snack bar-coaches were overhauled. Eleven westbound trains (10 eastbound) became eight each way—shorter, faster and cleaner than before. The man who undertook this project, Robert Timpany, an assistant vice president of operating administration, had Central's management trainees under his wing, and used them during the first few months to monitor the service, distribute timetables and generally make sure that the concept of short trains on brisk schedules did not die of corporate neglect. For a brief period, the plan appeared to be succeeding.

Central's steel fleet of 1966

A mere 18 months after this snapshot of New York Central streamliners, all had essentially been crammed into one basic train—see the diagram on page 184 of trains 27/61.

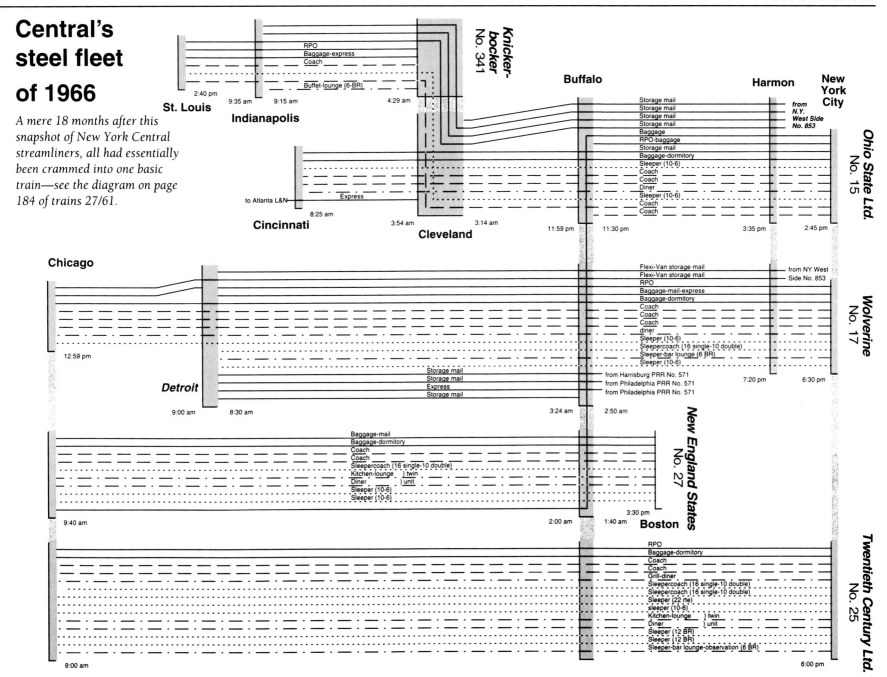

St. Louis
2:40 pm

Indianapolis
9:35 am   9:15 am   4:29 am

RPO
Baggage-express
Coach
Buffet-lounge (6-BR)

Knicker-bocker No. 341

to Atlanta L&N
8:25 am
Cincinnati
Express

3:54 am   3:14 am
Cleveland

Buffalo
11:59 pm

Harmon

New York City
11:30 pm   3:35 pm   2:45 pm

Storage mail
Storage mail
Storage mail
Storage mail
Baggage
RPO-baggage
Storage mail
Baggage-dormitory
Sleeper (10-6)
Coach
Coach
Diner
Sleeper (10-6)
Coach
Coach

from N.Y. West Side No. 853

Ohio State Ltd. No. 15

Chicago

12:59 pm

Detroit
9:00 am   8:30 am

Flexi-Van storage mail
Flexi-Van storage mail
RPO
Baggage-mail-express
Baggage-dormitory
Coach
Coach
Coach
diner
Sleeper (10-6)
Sleepercoach (16 single-10 double)
Sleeper-bar lounge (6 BR)
Sleeper (10-6)
Storage mail
Storage mail
Express
Storage mail

from NY West Side No. 853

from Harrisburg PRR No. 571
from Philadelphia PRR No. 571
from Philadelphia PRR No. 571

3:24 am   2:50 am   7:20 pm   6:30 pm

Wolverine No. 17

9:40 am

Baggage-mail
Baggage-dormitory
Coach
Coach
Sleepercoach (16 single-10 double)
Kitchen-lounge   } twin
Diner   } unit
Sleeper (10-6)
Sleeper (10-6)

2:00 am   1:40 am   **Boston**
3:30 pm

New England States No. 27

9:00 am

RPO
Baggage-dormitory
Coach
Coach
Grill-diner
Sleepercoach (16 single-10 double)
Sleepercoach (16 single-10 double)
Sleeper (22 rte)
sleeper (10-6)
Kitchen-lounge   } twin
Diner   } unit
Sleeper (12 BR)
Sleeper (12 BR)
Sleeper-bar lounge-observation (6 BR)

6:00 pm

Twentieth Century Ltd. No. 25

175

◀ *Streamlined cars on the Corridor were apt to be those of other railroads. A GG1 leading an RF&P coach speeds the* Edison *through New Brunswick, New Jersey, toward Washington in 1963. (Victor Hand)*

Pennsylvania Railroad

Pennsy's *Broadway Limited* outlived its old New York Central rival in name by almost three decades, until Amtrak let it die in 1995. The *Broadway Limited* was, in fact, the next-to-last daily train in America to be totally composed of only first-class cars, giving up this distinction in 1967 just a few months before Illinois Central's *Panama Limited* added coaches, too. But that's Pennsy for you. Love it, hate it, the Pennsylvania Railroad stood in a class by itself. New York Central in 1966 chalked up 1.1 billion passenger miles (one passenger carried one mile). Pennsy left it in the dust: 1.9 billion passenger miles. There was scarcely a passenger-train market in the eastern half of the country that the Mighty Penn did not figure in.

As an east-west passenger hauler, Pennsy stood on a par with New York Central through the 1960s, dominating the southern portion of the Northeast and upper Midwest while Central ruled the northern part. New York Central, for instance, had pretty much vacated St. Louis by 1960. It scheduled just one round trip for passengers, the *Southwestern–Knickerbocker*, whereas the Pennsylvania had three. The one important route they held in common was New York City–Chicago.

However, the east-west lines paled beside Pennsy's north-south passenger line between New York City and Washington—what we know today as the Northeast Corridor. These 226.6 high speed,

electrified miles were unique to American railroading, combining a high volume of freight trains with an even higher volume of suburban, corridor and long-distance passenger trains in not just the colors of Pennsylvania Railroad but also those of New Haven, Southern, Chesapeake & Ohio, Atlantic Coast Line, Seaboard Air Line and Richmond, Fredericksburg & Potomac.

The Corridor could have been Pennsy's meal ticket. Internal studies concluded that it was operated profitably, thanks to high train loads. But hav-

▲ *By September of 1963, the Pennsy had but one rural branch line passenger train remaining, the* Delmarva Express, *which ambled 97 miles south of Wilmington to Delmar, on the Maryland border. Here the trainset rests, behind an RS3, awaiting its late afternoon departure for Wilmington. (Jim Shaw)*

▲ *The flagman of train 571, the* Buffalo Day Express, *awaits a highball at Emporium, Pennsylvania, on March 13, 1965. The pastoral scene is a collage of Pennsycana: P70 coaches, keystone herald, position light signals and Victorian-era interlocking tower guarding the junction with the Erie branch. (Victor Hand)*

and 25 lounge and observation cars bought for long-distance east-west service after World War II, Pennsylvania ordered but 64 Northeast Corridor cars—the *Congressional* and *Senator* trainsets of 1952. This was a misallocation of resources—an error in corporate judgment—of monumental proportions.

In view of all this, the words of chairman Martin Clement, written in 1951 to vice president of operations James Symes, stand out as a prophecy that his own railroad did not heed:

Methods of transportation come and go, and it is clearly indicated that rail passenger transportation as a general mode of transportation is passing out. . . . I do not desire to prejudge or to influence, but I have watched road after road go out of the passenger business, into the freight business, and become prosperous. . . . The Pennsylvania Railroad must face the issue, and it's a paradoxical one. In the heavy concentration of population between Washington and Boston there is bound to continue for a long time to come sufficient volume of passenger transportation, on account of the convenience of terminals, the speed of operation, and the supportable frequency of service, to indicate a profitable passenger operation; but not on the rest of the system. And, it would seem that with proper mail and express rates and sufficient volume, there is warranted an overnight service between some of the principal key points—Buffalo, Cincinnati, Cleveland, Chicago, Detroit—with the big eastern cities. . . . But, outside of that, the service would seem to be done.

The decline in ridership was ultimately hastened by the Pennsylvania's edict during the recession of 1957 to forgo heavy maintenance of its passenger cars. The following year, when rival New York Central added coaches to its *Twentieth Century Limited*,

ing sunk a quarter of a billion dollars into the electrification of its New York–Washington and Philadelphia–Harrisburg routes in the 1930s, Pennsy thereafter spent very little for new passenger cars to run over them. Instead, it lavished its capital after World War II on its east-west "blue ribbon" trains, particularly the long-haul runs dominated by sleeping cars. And it was these trains, rather than the short-distance Corridor trains, that lost ridership quickly as the 1960s progressed. In contrast to the 212 sleeping cars, 144 overnight coaches, 40 diners

Pennsy relaxed the maintenance ban on *Broadway Limited* equipment for what vice president-operations J. P. Newell called "sprucing up" of the all-Pullman train. That summer Newell instructed his regional managers to have officers ride the trains—in short, to "fly the flag"—in order to improve morale, which was reported to be low. The most minor repairs were authorized and a four-page pamphlet explaining the need for better service was distributed to rank and file. This was a sort of bootstrap program on the cheap for the cash-short railroad. Yet in 1961 the general ban on passenger car repair remained in effect! By then, reported Gregory L. Thompson of Florida State University in *The Journal of Transport History*, 621 of 793 coaches, 140 of 169 diners and 34 of 88 parlor cars were past due for repairs and making their infirmities known to passengers.

Even knowing all this, you cannot help but be drawn to that era. If you close your eyes, you can almost imagine the summer of 1960. It's 1:45 a.m. On one of the through tracks beneath cavernous Washington Union Station, RF&P has brought the *Havana Special* in from Miami, and Southern Railway its *Piedmont Limited* from New Orleans. From these trains and other equipment, a Washington Terminal RS1 switcher concocts a remarkable train, in this order: an Atlantic Coast Line baggage car, a Pennsy P70 heavyweight and three ACL lightweight coaches, trailed by ten New York City-bound sleepers—two out of Florida on the *Havana Special*, one from Richmond, three off the *Piedmont* from New Orleans and points south of Washington and four of Pennsy's sleepers added at Washington. A car inspector hands the airbrake clearance to the engineer on the forward of two GG1 electric locomotives. Presently train 108 will head north.

A mile away Dwight Eisenhower sleeps in the White House. But here off North Capitol Street, the half-century-old station never rests. The combined southbound *Havana Special–Piedmont* is being separated on adjacent tracks. C&O's northbound *F.F.V.* is due at 3 o'clock and Southern's *Crescent Limited* at 3:10, to be combined and leave town with 15 sleepers, a Southern diner and two coaches. Then will come the first of three southbound mail trains and before long, the dawn of another day. That day would later see leaving for New York the *Afternoon Congressional*, still the finest day train in America. Its eight-year-old equipment will include six coach-lounges, a twin-unit diner and kitchen-bar lounge and six parlor cars, one of them a blunt-end observation car.

The Pennsylvania Railroad of 1960 looks quaint to our eyes because it was not changing, adapting, renewing and downsizing as were New York Central and the newly merged Erie and Lackawanna. Perhaps this comforted people at the time, but it fore-

At Pana, Illinois, a one-car remnant of Central's last St. Louis run, the Southwestern–Knickerbocker, *about 1967. (Walter A. Peters; Herbert H. Harwood collection)*

told troubles later on. As the sixties wore on, the Pennsy wore out. There was too much fixed plant to maintain and more services to deliver than Pennsylvania could afford. But the railroad chose not to face up to this. The Pennsylvania of 1960 still bore witness to the great Standard Railroad of the World of its past. Soon enough it would evolve into the sad mess we remember today as Penn Central.

Pain Central

Railroads weren't my beat at the *Chicago Sun-Times*, but I kept inventing reasons to write about them. On Tuesday, March 3, 1970, my sources came in handy. That morning, I got off the overnight *Capitol Limited* from an assignment in Pittsburgh and went straight to work. Never before or after was I greeted at the door of the city room. But today Mac, the assistant city editor, leapt to his feet. "Fred!" he said, and led me to his desk. "Bill Granger was at an ICC hearing yesterday and overheard two Penn Central people talking to one another. From what he could infer, the railroad is going to dump all of its passenger trains except those on the East Coast. I want you to help Bill confirm this." William Granger, later to become a columnist for the rival *Chicago Tribune* and a novelist of some note, was a superb reporter whose intuitions proved absolutely right. By that evening we'd nailed down the story, which went to the top of page one in the next morning's late editions. And later that next day, after initial denials by PC, it became official, weeks before Penn Central intended: The mother of all railroads, reeling from two years of reversals and less than four months from its own bankruptcy, wanted to dump every passenger train west of Harrisburg and Buffalo. But I didn't know the half of it.

Everything that could spoil the Pennsylvania–New York Central merger of February 1, 1968, did. The executives of the two railroads had vastly different philosophies of how a railroad should be run,

and they would compromise neither individually nor collectively, resulting in checkmate at the top. Divided authority meant that no hand was on the tiller. The merger should have had the top people doing what they did best: chairman Stuart Saunders handling the politicians, president Alfred Perlman doing a bench-press on PC's inflated costs and VP-finance David Bevan providing the financial controls as well as the capital. But the three men seemed to have a mutual disregard for one another, and none did his job well. Even the Pennsy and NYC computers spoke in incompatible tongues.

Ten months into the merger, on January 1, 1969, the already unwieldy Penn Central was saddled with the New York, New Haven & Hartford—an adoption it had agreed to as a condition for its own wedding. The New Haven last made money in 1956 and entered bankruptcy in 1961. By its own estimation, 44 percent of New Haven's workers and $11 million of its $17 million operating loss in 1964 were attributable to passenger trains, both suburban and intercity. The next year it tried to rid itself of all its passenger trains, to no avail—the ICC said the New Haven could limp and wheeze along until Penn Central absorbed it and remedied its losses! Of course, nothing of the sort occurred within Penn Central. Rather, the decay just got worse, hurried along by cancellation of Railway Post Office and storage mail contracts in late 1967.

The attitude of the top executives of Penn Central toward passenger trains deserves special note.

◀ *The trains on this and the opposite page couldn't have done the solvency of Penn Central any good. At left, a New London, Connecticut-to-Boston local stops at Kingston, Rhode Island, in October 1969. (William D. Middleton)*

Chairman Saunders lived in Ardmore, Pa., nine miles west of Suburban Station in Philadelphia. But did he ever ride Pennsy's own trains to work? No. Explained Saunders in an interview, after his sacking, with *Philadelphia Bulletin* reporters Joseph R. Daughen and Peter Binzen in *The Wreck of the Penn Central* (Little Brown, 1971): "At least a third of the days I wouldn't even go to the office. I was going to New York. Or I was going to Chicago or Detroit. I had suitcases, briefcases—I always had four or five briefcases. How the hell could I get on a Paoli Local with all that?" When one of Perlman's sons, who lived in Bucks County, Pa., west of Trenton, complained about Penn Central's dirty, late, hot and cold trains to Manhattan, all his father could think to say was, "If you don't like it, walk!"

Outside the New York City–Washington corridor, the only train of any flair that remained after the merger was the *Broadway Limited,* and even the *Broadway* had been shorn of glory. Just prior to the merger, the Pennsy, quietly working its way from one state railroad regulator to another, achieved every railroad attorney's sweetest dream. With no fanfare whatever, it got rid of its premier passenger train even though that train was clearing its direct costs! This takes some explaining. The all-sleeping-car *Broadway*, trains 28 and 29, was the train that state regulators allowed to be dropped. Few but regular riders noticed, because the Pennsylvania transferred the *Broadway*'s name to trains 48 and 49, the *General*. According to figures compiled by the railroad, both trains more than covered their above-the-rail costs during the 12 months through August of 1967—the *Broadway* by $145,000 on revenue of $3.1 million and the *General* by $205,000 on revenue of $3.7 million. But the railroad made its case that it could save $1.4 million per year by merging these two trains, which arrived Chicago and New York City within 35 minutes of each other—the difference being that the *General* had a Washington-Harrisburg section and coaches whereas the *Broadway*

◀ *This branch line run between New London and Worcester lasted in bucolic splendor until Amtrak. Train 572 in 1970 leaves the Shore Line route at Groton, Connecticut, and later ambles past woodland near Auburn, Massachusetts. Notice at left, towering above the Thames River, the nemesis of the New Haven: Interstate 95. (William D. Middleton)*

had neither. The last "old" *Broadway Limited* ran December 12, 1967, 10 days after the *Twentieth Century*'s demise. The "new" *Broadway*, now numbered 48 and 49, had five coaches along with six sleepers and the twin-unit diner, but no longer the *View*-series observation car.

In the Northeast Corridor, as the Boston–New York City–Washington line was now called, the *Afternoon Congressional* of 1960 had pretty much been impeached by 1969, reduced to three coaches, a coach-snack bar, a parlor and a parlor-lounge. By then, aside from Florida trains and the *Broadway*, only the Boston–Washington *Senator* carried a dining car in the corridor.

Something good had happened, however: the *Metroliners*, the first of which began running between New York and Washington on January 16, 1969. The Pennsylvania Railroad was a supporter of legislation in 1965 that committed the government to spending $12 million, and the railroad $45 million, toward instituting high-speed service. The suspicion—vigorously denied by Pennsy then—was that this burden was assumed by the railroad as a way to lubricate the regulatory gears then grinding their way toward approving its merger with New York Central. (The government did not oppose the merger.) At any rate, the railroad's commitment eventually rose to $70 million, of which $21 million went toward an order for 61 Budd Co. electric mul-

◄ *Soon before New Haven's merger into Penn Central, EP-5 motor 373 leads the Bay State out of New York City for Boston. The 1955-era locomotive and its Pullman-built lightweight cars have obviously seen better days. (Victor Hand)*

tiple-unit cars—a mixture of 76-seat coaches, 60-seat coach-snack bar cars and 34-chair parlor cars. (Less than 50 of the cars had been accepted before formation of Amtrak in 1971.)

By October of 1969 six round trips per day were established. The one-way coach fare was $17, versus $15 for a conventional train. All trainsets were identical: two coaches, two coach-snack bars and two parlor cars. One of the round trips was a nonstop run of 150 minutes; the others took two hours. On a bitterly cold Monday morning in February of 1970 I rode No. 100, the 7:30 a.m. nonstop train from Washington, and was very impressed, up to a point. That point was somewhere east of Princeton Junction, N.J., when my speedliner ground to a halt and stood still for an hour while the crew bustled around outside, muttering something about a fire beneath the floor of my parlor car. Finally the northbound *Silver Meteor* stopped alongside our train and we all abandoned ship. I rode into Pennsylvania Station in a sleepercoach room.

This was typical of the original *Metroliner* cars through their entire lives. The bad-order ratio for these cars early on was as high as 30 percent. Even a rebuilding by Amtrak in the 1970s didn't really debug them. They were grossly overweight and rode like Sherman tanks. Ultimately Amtrak gave up and demoted the equipment. In their place, Amtrak ran *Metroliners* during the 1980s and 1990s with Budd-built cars of the same design but hauled by locomotives. In an interview with the authors of *Wreck of the Penn Central*, Saunders said: "Well, they operated test cars for six or eight months up here on the test track before the cars were actually built—to get experience. And as the cars were being built. Beyond that, we had such pressure on us from the government to put these damn things in operation. And we put them in operation before we should have. Because the politicians were hollering so and then [Transportation Secretary] Alan Boyd was putting the pressure on us."

The downward spiral

But the *Metroliners* back then were a sideshow to the main event, which was the steady deterioration of all other passenger trains PC ran. Perlman hated the damn things but was preoccupied. Saunders, more politically attuned, had other things on his mind, too. Even so, efforts were made at lower levels within the company to confront the cash losses in a positive way. One important catalyst was Carl R. Englund Jr., a New York Central alumnus from the 1940s and 1950s and then a consultant with a keen view of what made the former NYC and Pennsy tick. At the behest of H. C. Kohout, Penn Central's vice president of passenger service, Englund studied traffic flows not only of Penn Central, but of competing plane and bus carriers, on every route but the Northeast Corridor and New Haven lines.

His conclusions, delivered in mid 1969 from data collected late in 1968, were devastating. Almost nobody rode the trains, nor should they, given the time the trains took, the low standard of service and the ticket costs. "A high proportion" of trains operating west of Albany and Harrisburg carried fewer than a busload of passengers most days. Whatever lift had been given patronage by the introduction of Empire Service between New York City and Buffalo a year earlier had dissipated, and then some. Fewer than a dozen people per day were ticketed from New York City all the way to Buffalo. Excluding train 61-27, the successor to the *Twentieth Century*, the other four westbound trains left Albany with an average of 40 passengers each. By Rochester, the typical headcount was down to 25. The Water Level Route delivered, via Cleveland, an average of just 113 people per day to Chicago, and all but 35 were aboard train 61-27. East of Albany, the train that replaced the *New England States* typically hauled just two dozen people in its sleeping car and coach.

On the former Pennsylvania Railroad side, the news was equally bad. True, going west an average of 382 people a day passed through Pittsburgh on

Penn Central's steel fleet

February 1969

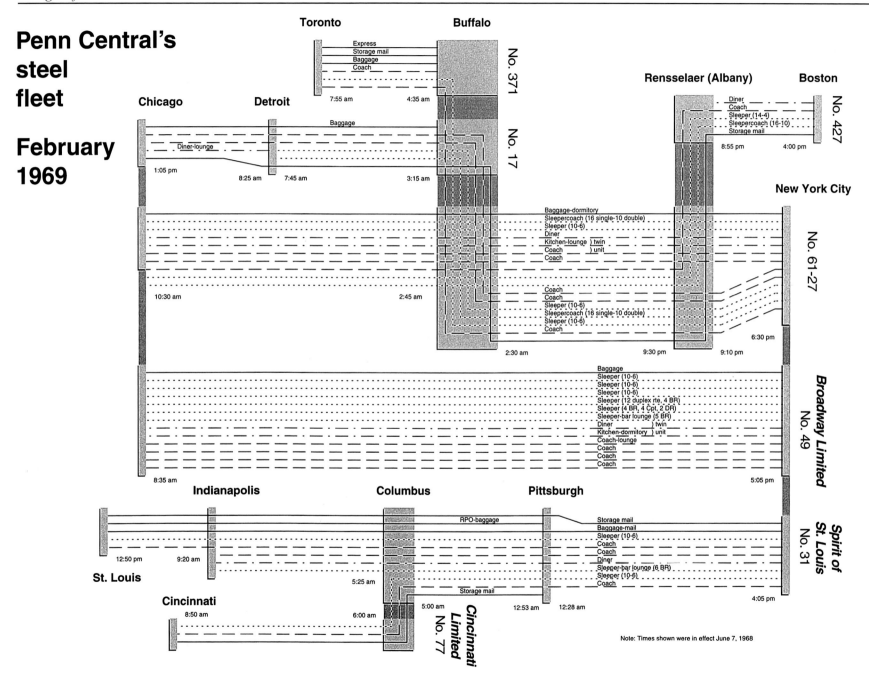

Toronto

Buffalo

Express
Storage mail
Baggage
Coach

7:55 am   4:35 am

No. 371

No. 17

Rensselaer (Albany)   **Boston**

Diner
Coach
Sleeper (14-4)
Sleepercoach (16-10)
Storage mail

8:55 pm   4:00 pm

No. 427

Chicago   **Detroit**

Baggage

Diner-lounge

1:05 pm

8:25 am   7:45 am   3:15 am

New York City

Baggage-dormitory
Sleepercoach (16 single-10 double)
Sleeper (10-6)
Diner
Kitchen-lounge) twin
Coach   ) unit
Coach

Coach
Coach
Sleeper (10-6)
Sleepercoach (16 single-10 double)
Sleeper (10-6)
Coach

10:30 am   2:45 am

2:30 am   9:30 pm   9:10 pm

6:30 pm

No. 61-27

Baggage
Sleeper (10-6)
Sleeper (10-6)
Sleeper (10-6)
Sleeper (12 duplex rte, 4 BR)
Sleeper (4 BR, 4 Cpt, 2 DR)
Sleeper-bar lounge (5 BR)
Diner   ) twin
Kitchen-dormitory) unit
Coach-lounge
Coach
Coach
Coach

8:35 am

5:05 pm

Broadway Limited
No. 49

Indianapolis   **Columbus**   **Pittsburgh**

RPO-baggage

Storage mail
Baggage-mail
Sleeper (10-6)
Coach
Coach
Diner
Sleeper-bar lounge (6 BR)
Sleeper (10-6)
Coach

12:50 pm   9:20 am

5:25 am

Storage mail

5:00 am   12:53 am   12:28 am

4:05 pm

Spirit of St. Louis
No. 31

St. Louis

Cincinnati

8:50 am   6:00 am

Cincinnati Limited
No. 77

Note: Times shown were in effect June 7, 1968

Penn Central trains. But more than 100 of those were on the *Broadway Limited*, and the other six westbound trains delivered, on average, 40 passengers apiece.

Patronage of PC's Chicago–Cincinnati trains, via either Lafayette (ex-NYC) or Logansport, Ind., (ex-Pennsy), was but a trickle. And talk about trickles: On the route of the *Ohio State Limited*, between Cleveland and Cincinnati, less than a dozen people per day rode its coach-only successor. Outside the Northeast Corridor, Englund said, Penn Central was losing $57 every minute on passenger trains—$30 million per year.

Having delivered his bitter diagnosis of PC's passenger service, Englund proposed a solution of sorts: Do for the Pennsy side of Penn Central what the Empire Service had done for the Central side—pare down, simplify, shorten. By late 1968 40 cars had undergone rehabilitation for the Empire Service. Englund figured that fixing 40 more would permit Penn Central to conduct almost all off-Corridor passenger business with 34 two-car, one-diesel trainsets. There would be but one overnight train, between New York City and Pittsburgh, almost no arrivals after 8 p.m. and few departures before 8 a.m. Englund estimated the first-year losses of such service at $8.5 million (including $2.8 million to rehab coaches) and the second-year loss at $5.1 million—a tremendous reduction from the $30 million drubbing then being incurred.

A briefing was arranged for Englund to present his plan to chairman Saunders. According to accounts, it never began. Arriving at the briefing room after lunch, Saunders took one look at the assembled faces and the row of flipcharts, burped, said, "Kill the [expletive] trains!" and strode away. Thus began months of preparatory work that Bill Granger and I so rudely interrupted with our *Chicago Sun-Times* story.

The train-off hearings conducted by the ICC in the late spring and early summer of 1970 give us a graphic picture of the service Penn Central provided. Combined ridership of the two round trips in and out of St. Louis in 1969 was less than 100 people a day—and just half that number by the end of the year, which comes to about a dozen people per train. Cleveland–Indianapolis Trains 315-316 on the old NYC carried a combined 16 people a day west of Crestline, Ohio, or about the number who rode the Harrisburg–Buffalo trains. The Chicago–Florida *South Wind*, run in conjunction with Louisville & Nashville and Seaboard Coast Line south of Louisville, had been preemptively reduced by Penn Central to a coach and lounge car. Frequency east of New Haven on the Shore Line was down to eight trains each way, and they carried an average of 80 people per train, or about what would fit into one densely packed car.

Were passengers the problem?

Yet in reading the ICC's documentation of these trains, I was struck by something else: So far as the railroad could ever show, they had about as much to do with Penn Central's failure as the cycles of the moon. Penn Central had a railroad operating loss of $193 million in 1969 and $102 million in the first three months of 1970. The railroad claimed that the 34 trains it wanted to shed had incurred a combined deficit of $8.9 million in 1969, on revenue of almost $22 million. The ICC figured the loss was really $5.7 million. On top of that, the commission noted that PC on March 3, 1968, had begun to divert bulk mail from its passenger trains onto solid mail trains, and this decreased the revenues of the 34 passenger trains at an annual rate of almost $5 million, or about what their proven losses were. In 1969, in fact, Penn Central grossed almost $23 million from six pairs of mail trains operating between New York City and Chicago, New York City and St. Louis, New York City and Buffalo, Chicago and Cincinnati, Philadelphia and Indianapolis and Boston and Albany. In times past, this would have been consid-

ered revenue in the passenger department's domain. Something besides intercity passenger trains was killing Penn Central.

I found particularly interesting the economics of operating the *Broadway Limited*. Of all the trains under the gun just then, it had (by PC's reckoning) the most labor-intensive operation but also the lowest annual deficit—$103,000. How could this be? Each day's *Broadway* in each direction required 48 employees: six engineers, firemen and conductors, eight brakemen, five ticket collectors, eight porters and attendants and nine dining-car employees. Yet it was carrying about 120 people a day the entire way between New York City and Chicago—about one third of them in sleeping cars—and paltry as these numbers may seem, they were a lot better than almost any other train could muster. The *Broadway*'s revenues, almost totally from passengers, were roughly twice those of any other train on the block, and its terminal costs were relatively minor compared to those of trains entering and leaving St. Louis. (Trains 27-28, the former *Twentieth Century Limited*, were claimed by PC to have lost $870,000 between Buffalo and Chicago; that portion east of Buffalo wasn't involved.)

The ICC concluded that Penn Central could take off seven of the 17 round trips. But events had overtaken the commission. While hearings on this huge case were underway, Penn Central declared itself bankrupt. And by the time the commission's decision was rendered, President Nixon and Congress had reached consensus: The federal government would step in to preserve what was left of the intercity passenger train, and the status quo would prevail until a national system could be put in place. Unquestionably, Penn Central's dramatic train-off case, followed by its bankruptcy, jolted the government to quit wringing its hands and actually do something. From that came Amtrak.

AMERICA'S MAIN STREET

Illinois Central cut passenger costs drastically, but not its train frequency heading south from Chicago. Mr. Johnston would be proud.

◄ How many million miles had engine 4001 covered in the 19 years prior to this scene, captured in 1960? The E6 unit is nearing Tolono, Illinois, with the Creole, *and the engineer has every intention of getting this train to Chicago on time. (J. Parker Lamb)*

Wayne A. Johnston was old school—*real* old school. From his office on the northeast corner of the sixth floor of venerable Central Station in Chicago, he could gaze directly down at the passenger trains of his beloved Illinois Central. He had the habit of doing so at precisely 9 o'clock each morning, after pulling a pocket watch from the vest wrapped around his ample midsection. If the Illinois Central president could see the brown-and-orange locomotives of his beloved No. 6 poking from the train shed, all was well, and he sat down satisfied. Otherwise, he'd punch the intercom on his desk and bellow to Otto Zimmerman, his vice president of operations, "*Zim, where's the Panama?*" Says someone who witnessed this scene: "Zim would do anything not to get that call."

Johnston cherished his passenger trains so much that from 1959 until 1967, after he relinquished the IC presidency to become chairman, the railroad shed only one branch line passenger train—that's all. That IC stood pat for so long is amazing, more so because Johnston's background was as an accountant. Told that coaches needed to be added to the all-sleeping-car *Panama Limited* because it was hemorrhaging millions of dollars a year, Johnston replied that he liked it just fine as it was, adding that the negative

numbers were surely overstated. He was among his railroad's biggest shareholders, and in the scheme of things, the *Panama* was small potatoes to him.

His successor as president come 1966, William Johnson, had some affection for passenger trains, too. He came to IC from Railway Express Agency, having brought it out of bankruptcy and back to profitability. But Johnson soon recognized that he needed help with the passenger service. In mid-1967, he lured Paul Reistrup to Illinois Central from the Baltimore & Ohio and Chesapeake & Ohio, on the basis of Reistrup's reputation for aggressively shedding some passenger trains while maintaining high standards of service on those that remained. Reistrup resisted the lucrative offer, knowing that the passenger side of railroading was a career-killer. Only when he and Johnson agreed on an 18-month assignment as VP of passenger services did Reistrup relent.

So the scene was set for big changes. Wayne Johnston did not live to see them. On Thursday, November 30, 1967, hundreds of civic leaders honored him at a dinner in the Palmer House. The next day was his last as chairman. Late the following Monday afternoon, he sat down in his home to read the *Wall Street Journal.* That's how his housekeeper found him the next morning.

The Franchise from Heaven

But just a minute. We've made Wayne Johnston look like an idiot. The son of a Philo, Ill., farmer, he was anything but. Johnston became president of a Class 1 railroad in his 40s and remained top dog for 22 years while his railroad prospered mightily. So obviously he did a lot of things right. One of them was to notice that IC during the first half of the 1950s more than covered its out-of-pocket costs of running passenger trains. As happened with other railroads, the 1957–58 period saw a sharp, painful recession, and passenger results swung to huge losses. But the railroad cut some of its biggest money losers (including two of its three Chicago–St. Louis streamliners and one of its Iowa trains) and emerged in 1960 making money again, on an out-of-pocket basis. Call the man complacent, but he had reason to be.

The fact of the matter is that Illinois Central was the "Main Street of Mid-America" for good reasons. The railroad cut a swath from Chicago to the South, over double track that was signaled across much of Illinois for 100 mph (and often run somewhat faster). Its passenger service possessed trump cards besides speed. Most important, there was no competition until the late 1960s—none at all within most of Illinois. Most rail corridors ran east–west, giving IC a sort of rail monopoly all the way south. Entire generations of African Americans rode Illinois Central trains north to make new starts and to return to visit their families (a subtheme of Steve Goodman's classic song "City of New Orleans," made famous by Arlo Guthrie).

Interstate highways—what are they? None existed in the late 1960s up and down the IC franchise. The IC linked Chicago to two huge sources of traffic—the University of Illinois at Champaign-Urbana and Southern Illinois University at Carbondale—and party-happy students from either school filled entire trains during weekends and holidays. And to serve these constituencies, Illinois Central possessed a surge fleet of heavyweight coaches—close to 90 going into the late 1960s—that it could press into service on short notice. Some, of course, were in daily service on scheduled trains. But the rest were available when called upon, which they frequently were.

More vulnerable were the trains over secondary routes, such as the ones connecting Chicago and St. Louis, St. Louis and the north–south line at Carbondale (three trains each way per day), two trains each way between Chicago and Iowa, and finally an east–west train between Meridian, Mississippi, and Shreveport, Louisiana. They faced competition, high costs, interstate highways, low population density or any or all of those.

The first round of service reductions occurred in March of 1967, months before Reistrup arrived. They raised so much dust on line that it's no wonder Bill Johnson reached out to Reistrup for help. Three sets of trains were involved. The Chicago–New Orleans trains 25 and 28, called *Southern Express* southbound and *Creole* northbound, were dropped south of Carbondale, and the stubs renamed the *Campus*. At the same time, trains 15 and 16, the *Chickasaw*, between St. Louis and Memphis, were dropped south of Carbondale, too. And the Chicago–St. Louis *Green Diamond* became a Chicago–Springfield train called *Governor's Special*. This last change recognized two facts: Gulf Mobile & Ohio controlled the Chicago–St. Louis corridor in terms of people and mail, and the cost of getting in and out of St. Louis over the Terminal Railroad Association pretty much ate all of a train's revenue. As a three-car train with a cafe-lounge, hauled by a steam-boiler-equipped Geep roadswitcher, the *Governor's Special* would last as a short, swift daytime turnaround between Chicago and Springfield until Amtrak. I rode it myself numerous times and enjoyed it hugely.

Makeover for the Panama

Reistrup's mandate from Johnson: Reduce intercity passenger train miles by half. It's a bit odd, therefore, that the first project he undertook, in the second half of 1967, was to add a new passenger train—sort of.

Panama Limited Summer 1967

Baggage-mail-express
Sleeper (10-6)
Sleeper (11 BR)
Lounge
Diner
Kitchen-dormitory
Sleeper (10-6)
Sleeper (10-6)
Parlor   (Chicago-Jackson)
Sleeper (10-6)**
Parlor-observation

** St. Louis-New Orleans; pick up at Carbondale

He recollects that the *Panama Limited* was then losing, on the basis of fully allocated costs, $5 million per year. Even if the above-the-rails loss was only $1 million, it was intolerable for a railroad that earned only $18 million in 1966. There's no denying the beauty of this all-lightweight streamliner (see above).

The problem was that with a capacity of just 110 or so people in the sleepers, occupancy averaged only 40 percent, and there was no head-end revenue to speak of, either. Meanwhile, Reistrup discovered that Illinois Central often had trouble accommodating the demand for coach travel south of Illinois. The all-coach *City of New Orleans*, trains 1 and 2, started from Chicago and New Orleans at 8 a.m. and reached the other end about midnight, running nowhere near the *Panama*'s schedule. The *Louisiane* was the only other option for coach passengers, and using heavyweight coaches, it took 21 hours to make the Chicago–New Orleans run, almost four more than the *Panama* and *City*.

But remember, Wayne Johnston remained the railroad's chairman in 1967, and he opposed anything that would cheapen the *Panama Limited*. What to

▶ *Wonder no more why the* City of Miami *remained popular right up until Amtrak. Illinois winters were brutal, as witness this December 1960 morning in Champaign, Illinois. The flagman is preparing for departure, and every mile hereafter will bring those aboard No. 53 closer to a warm climate.* (J. Parker Lamb)

do? Reistrup's solution—in hindsight, a brilliant one because it skirted Johnston's objection to change—was to leave the *Panama* pretty much as it was, an all-Pullman sleeper train. He created a new name train, the all-coach *Magnolia Star* (only two cars at first), between the same two cities that *just happened* to have the same schedule as the *Panama Limited.* At the time, I was outraged by what I considered Reistrup's subterfuge. I was a *Chicago Sun-Times* reporter, and telephoned Reistrup to get the story. Paul just laughed. "There will be a gate," he explained, trying to control his mirth. "You can't wander between the two trains—I promise."

Today, the *Magnolia Star* strikes me as marketing genius—Paul Reistrup at his very best. It infused some badly needed revenue into the *Panama* (which subsequently lost "six figures per year instead of seven," recollects Reistrup), lessened the pressure on the railroad to take more-drastic measures and by 1969 came as four or more cars. At the end of 1968, IC ended the charade of calling the coach portion of the *Panama* by another name.

The Shining Cities

Reistrup recollects that both the daily *City of New Orleans* and every-other-day *City of Miami* covered their direct operating costs at the time he arrived at IC, or close to it. (Decades later he is vague on profit and loss numbers, but says in his defense: "I wasn't hired to reduce the passenger deficit. I was hired to get rid of half the train miles. It's a subtle difference.")

City of Miami Winter 1961–62

Baggage-dormitory	Miami	IC 1906	IC 1905
Sleeper (11 BR)	Miami	Benton	Baton Rouge
Sleeper (10-6)	Miami	Centralia	Calvert
Sleeper (4-4-2)	Miami	Imperial Drive	Imperial Ranch
Sleeper (4-4-2)	Miami	Imperial Mark	Imperial Leaf
Sleeper (4-4-2)	Miami	G Wash Bdge	Grenada
Sleeper-bar lounge	Miami	Gen. Jackson	Gen. Beauregard
Diner	Miami	IC 4128	IC 4127
Kitchen-dormitory	Miami	IC 4128A	IC 4127A
Sleeper (11 BR)	Miami	Brookhaven	Belleville
Sleeper (10-6)	Sarasota	Lackawana	Kittatinny
Sleeper (10-6)	St. Petersburg	Coles County	Buchanan County
Coach	St. Petersburg	CGA 672	CGA 670
Coach	Sarasota	CGA 671	ACL 248
Diner-counter-lounge	Jacksonville	IC 4201	IC 4200
Coach	Miami	FEC Canal Pt.	ACL 247
Coach	Miami	FEC Lantana	FEC Sebastian
Coach	Miami	IC 2629	IC 2630
Observation-lounge	Miami	IC 3320	IC 3300

Anyway, these two trains were pretty much left alone by Reistrup and those who followed, because there was nothing that needed fixing.

To my mind, the star of Illinois Central during the 1960s was the *City of Miami,* trains 52 and 53, which ran every other day to and from its namesake city, with connections between Jacksonville and Florida's west coast as well. Southeast of Birmingham, IC's partners were Central of Georgia to Albany, Georgia, and (after 1967) Seaboard Coast Line from Albany to Florida. Close your eyes and imagine this train behind three big IC E units during the winter of 1961–62, handling 19 perfectly matched cars (see above).

I rode the *City of Miami* to Florida in February of 1968. Picture the day: bitterly cold in Chicago, with leaden skies leaking tendrils of snowflakes that be-

come sleet by the time train 53 reaches Champaign. The gloom never lets up, but as you enter Kentucky and then Alabama, the temperature rises and you're in a rainstorm. You see all this from the dome sleeping car. Then you wake up the next morning approaching Waycross under a brilliant blue sky in 60-degree weather. It's hard to describe the pleasure of going to sleep in one season and awakening in another, then enjoying eggs, bacon, and toast served over a white tablecloth by an attentive waiter. And your entire trip is blessed by the *City of Miami's* signature car—that dome sleeper leased from Northern Pacific and seasonally painted by Pullman to match the IC livery. Even in 1968, the *City of Miami* remained a world-class train. If I could have, I wouldn't have changed a thing.

Future Amtrak engineer Phil Gosney wouldn't have altered the *City of New Orleans,* which is the one he considered to be IC's best. In the summer of 1966, with money from his newspaper route, the Memphis boy persuaded his parents to let him and a friend ride train 1 from Memphis to Durant, Mississippi, returning on the first-class parlor car of the northbound *Panama Limited.* The *City's* consist then was infinitely expandable, up to about 18 cars. If demand exceeded that, a second section ran as far south as Memphis. The basic train then was seven coaches (one running St. Louis–New Orleans via Carbondale and three between Chicago and Jackson, Miss.), a diner-counter lounge (called a Palm Grove Cafe) and a round-end observation bar and lounge, plus several head-end cars, including a Chicago–Memphis Railway Post Office car and (southbound only) a Flexi-Van container car with U.S. mail.

July 31 is Phil's big day. In comes No. 1 to Central Station with 16 cars. The four E units cut off to be watered while a black GP7 switcher plucks the RPO. The *City* leaves on time. Decades later, Phil remembers his dinner in the Palm Grove Cafe, served on china: sirloin steak, a baked potato, three-bean salad, and bread. Back in the obs car, he and his buddy secure the two rear-facing seats and sit transfixed for at least 50 miles as the train barrels through north Mississippi at 79 mph. Getting off at Durant, the boys inform the ticket agent they want parlor car tickets back to Memphis. The agent says fine, he'll flag the *Panama.*

It's now dark and very humid. Phil and his friends put on ties—after all, they are riding Mr. Johnston's *Panama Limited.* When an approach bell sounds in the ticket office, the agent lights two kerosene lanterns, one with a clear globe and the other green. As train 6 approaches, its chime whistle disturbing the evening peace, the agent swings his lanterns in big arcs. As the three E units and baggage car roar past, Phil is certain the train can't possibly stop. But then brake-shoe smoke and swirling dust erupt, and the *Panama's* last car, a parlor-observation, stops right in

▶ *IC streamliners were a joy to watch and ride, but heavy-weight trains like this brought in loads of revenue, too. Here is the northbound* Creole *racing through Arcola, Illinois, and a crossing of Pennsy's branch to Decatur, in January of 1960. (J. Parker Lamb)*

front of them. The train, 12 minutes late from meeting the southbound *City of New Orleans,* is moving by the time the boys enter their car.

They don't stay long in the parlor-obs, because it's already past 9, and they're hungry again. So off they go to the almost-empty twin-unit diner for dessert and milk. The steward, in formal wear, kids them about the milk, but Phil reports the service as excellent. Refilling their water glasses, the waiter leaves some room for splashing, "as the man up front is trying to make up time." Sure enough, when the *Panama* reaches Central Station, train 6 is again on time.

The point of all this: Late in the passenger train era, Illinois Central maintained standards worthy of a Santa Fe or Atlantic Coast Line. Mr. Johnston would have it no other way. Within 18 months, the challenge confronting Wayne Johnston's successors, including Paul Reistrup, was to dampen the threat of ballooning deficit caused by the loss of most mail business and declining ridership, while at the same time giving the public its money's worth. Reistrup had an idea how to do that.

Birth of the Mini-Corridor

Sometimes it doesn't matter so much what you do, but how you spin it. Or to state it Reistrup's way, don't be too proud to borrow someone else's good idea. He needed to cut passenger-train miles. You can do it the lawyerly way, by marching to the regulators and enduring the hearings and political pressures. Or you can present your rationalization as an improve-

ment. Reistrup admired how Al Perlman restructured New York Central service over the 635 miles east of Buffalo as the Empire Service, with every-other-hour departures from New York City to Albany and points west. So starting in June 1968, IC's passenger chief concentrated his efforts on the 307 miles between Chicago, Champaign, and Carbondale, dubbing it the Mini-Corridor.

"The idea was to improve service where we could," Reistrup later said, "and get rid of the rest—both goals pursued in tandem, together." The Chicago–New Orleans *Creole,* shortened in 1967 to run only between Chicago and Carbondale and renamed the *Campus,* was the first step in the direction of fashioning bobtailed trains, and predated Reistrup. By mid-1969, the process was complete. You had

only the *City of New Orleans* and *Panama Limited* as the Chicago–New Orleans trains. The *City of Miami* continued every other day to and from Florida. The former Chicago–New Orleans *Louisiane* became the Chicago–Memphis *Mid-American,* running overnight southbound and in daytime northbound. The *Seminole,* the secondary Florida train, evolved into the Chicago–Carbondale *Shawnee,* leaving Chicago an hour behind the *Panama,* at 6 p.m., and returning north 12 hours later. And the *Campus* was radically rescheduled southbound to leave Chicago at 3 p.m. instead of 11 p.m., and Carbondale at 1 p.m. instead of 11:50 a.m., renumbered as trains 7 and 8 and renamed *Illini.*

That's it—six trains each way a day between Chicago and Carbondale on those days that the *City of*

◀ *Illinois Central trains wasted no time entering and leaving Chicago. Tracks 5 and 6 were reserved for through passenger trains, and south of 28th Street, they could do 75 mph. No. 1, the southbound* City of New Orleans, *looks to be doing every bit of 75 as it hustles past 115th Street with three locomotives and an endless train, on July 15, 1964. (William D. Middleton)*

◀ *Its long train stretching out of sight behind the E8s, the northbound* City of New Orleans *snakes its way into Central Station in Memphis on a June afternoon in 1963. Few U.S. streamliners could match the passenger count of trains No. 1 and No. 2. (Steve Patterson)*

trains each way to four. South of Memphis, the train count fell from four to two. The east–west Meridian–Shreveport train? Poof! The same could be said of two of the three connecting trains between St. Louis and Carbondale. Now all trains except the *City of Miami* left Chicago and Carbondale on the hour. In place of two Iowa trains from Chicago, there was now one. But still, the center held.

And as it always had, Illinois Central catered to its natural constituency in the Mini-Corridor—college students. Future Amtrak marketing whiz Ira Silverman remembers the elongated weekend trains of that era for the easy-to-clean, plastic-upholstered seats in

Miami operated (plus the Chicago–Springfield *Governor's Special* as far south as Gilman). Remarkably, this was the same train frequency in 1969 as at the start of the 1960s. I cannot think of another rail corridor where the same could be said, including Boston–New York and New York–Washington. In that respect, it's as if Wayne Johnston were still pulling his pocket watch from his vest at 9 every morning.

What changed, of course, was service south of Carbondale, where frequency shrank from seven

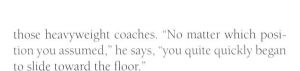

▶ *For Illini football games, IC could really put on a show. On October 3, 1959, three specials from Chicago, two from St. Louis and one from Springfield, descend on Champaign for the U. of Illinois–Army game, which starts in just over an hour. The E6 in the foreground brought a special from Chicago. In the background is one of the St. Louis trains. (J. Parker Lamb)*

those heavyweight coaches. "No matter which position you assumed," he says, "you quite quickly began to slide toward the floor."

Illinois Central had never owned dome cars, preferring to lease them for the *City of Miami* in winter months, when owner Northern Pacific had extras to spare. But Wayne Johnston Jr., son of the late chairman and an AVP in the Passenger Department, in mid 1967 found for sale six Missouri Pacific dome coaches—three built by Budd for the *Colorado Eagle* and three by Pullman-Standard for the *Texas Eagle.* "It's hard to believe," says Reistrup, "that we had all those heavyweight coaches but were still short of capacity. Wayne Jr. stumbled upon these, and they were really cheap but in great shape." Kids used the dome section on Chicago–Carbondale bobtail trains as a study hall. They were also assigned at various times to the *City of New Orleans* and *City of Miami.*

The difficulty of serving college markets is that—not a surprise to parents of an 18-year-old—the clientele are fickle, unpredictable. I remember being shown in 1966 a book in which the railroad kept meticulous records over the years of passenger counts on individual trains on important weekends and holidays to and from the college towns. The idea,

to anticipate future demand, was folly to even try. Reistrup says the railroad never succeeded in knowing when people would descend on its stations to ride particular trains. "In the Mini-Corridor, we'd ask them on the train at the start of a break when they'd be going back. They'd all say earlier, but they really went later. So we'd run all the cars south from Chicago empty when they said they'd return, and here came 1,000 school kids for the last train."

The solution, born of necessity, was to size each southbound train from Chicago to the crowd that

appeared to ride it. And it was remarkably easy to do, once people figured out how. "Eddie Smith, who was manager of intercity passenger services, would go trackside and load each train from the front back," says Reistrup. "As he filled the first car, the lights were turned on in the second car and it began loading, and so on down the line of empty coaches. When time came to leave, you just uncoupled the last full car and left the others for the next train. This way we didn't have to figure those people out—at least, heading back at the end of a break. Coming

▲ *Cooling off an iron horse? Actually, on an August evening in 1959, train No. 2 is getting a bath in Champaign to rid its headlight and windshields of bug carcasses. (J. Parker Lamb)*

from the schools, it was harder, because kids cut classes and left early. I tried surveys and all that, but they never worked."

The Fadeout

On pages 201–202 you'll find the basic consists of every Illinois Central train as of the autumn of 1969. This is pretty much how the service looked right up to the start of Amtrak almost two years later. Remember, these were the minimum trainsets, and they could swell to just about any size during weekends and holidays or for college sports events. This was Illinois Central's last stand, but it didn't hold. Paul Reistrup in early 1969 went on to head the railroad's young intermodal service, and eventually its entire marketing department. Later still, he became Amtrak's second president. In 1970, the railroad sought to discontinue the *Panama,* the *Governor's Special,* the last St. Louis–Carbondale train and the *Mid-American* between Carbondale and Memphis. By then, however, the Interstate Commerce Commission could sense that Congress was about to pass legislation creating Amtrak, and pretty much suspended all train-off cases before it.

"There is no problem in passenger service that money won't cure," Bill Johnson told a U.S. Senate hearing in late 1969. "If the public, through the government, will tell us what they want us to do and pay for it, I will do whatever they want to do." In response to criticism of rail passenger service, he replied: "I don't think I have ever met a railroad man that really wanted to louse up his business and do a bad job. . . . We are one of those railroads which have hung on and cherished the notion longer than some others that we should continue to operate passenger trains to the best of our ability." He said there appeared to be a real public benefit in providing train service for the students in Champaign and Carbondale. Beyond that, Johnson said, "We should probably file right now" to get rid of every other passenger train. Again, the fact remains that at the end of the

▶ *Illinois Central and New York Central were partners in running the Chicago–Cincinnati* James Whitcomb Riley, *and every couple of days IC ponied up a couple of passenger-ready GP9s to front the train. Today's edition, seen in Kankakee, Illinois, also has an IC Railway Post Office car.* (Louis A. Marre)

▶ *Two dome coaches once belonging to Missouri Pacific and one of IC's flat-end tavern-observation cars are on No. 1 in May of 1969 as the* City of New Orleans *passes through Memphis at Central Station.* (Phil Gosney)

game, on April 30, 1971, you could ride as many Illinois Central trains south from Chicago as you could have a dozen years earlier, threadbare as those trains may have become.

On the last weekend before Amtrak took over, the Illinois Central family paid a sort of tribute to its passenger trains. Bill Johnson, now chairman, attached his private car to the rear of the southbound *Panama* that Friday, and invited friends to share a last round trip to New Orleans. So did Alan Boyd, the railroad's president since 1969, whose business car was on the front. (Boyd would follow Reistrup as a president of Amtrak.) Extra sleeping cars were attached, and they quickly filled with IC officials and their families—all riding on passes, of course.

Douglas Hagestrom, hired by Reistrup in 1969 in the Marketing Department, was one of those aboard, with his wife. "We had a *huge* train," he recalled shortly before his death in 2007. "I don't recall much about the trip going down, but coming back Monday morning we were blocked at Champaign because there had been a derailment north of Gilman. So a decision was made to detour the train west over a branch line to Clinton on the St. Louis line, and then back north to Chicago. I'm sure the Illinois Division superintendent had a lump in his throat for this unplanned inspection of a lightly used line at 10 miles per hour. On the other hand, it was sort of like the *Panama*'s 'farewell tour' to some central Illinois communities. We finally got to Chicago about 1 p.m. But it was truly a great ride." Five days later, the Illinois Central passenger tradition that had been nourished and protected all those years by Wayne Johnston became but a pleasant memory.

◀ *Two GP9s equipped with steam boilers lead the seldom-photographed* Land O' Corn *through Rockford, Illinois, in March of 1967, five months before the Chicago-to-Waterloo, Iowa, train was discontinued. Note the four Flexi-Van containers on the front. (Mike Schafer)*

17 Trains, 352 Cars, 24 Hours

The Saturday before Christmas—December 21, 1963—dawned dry but cold in Carbondale, Illinois, the thermometer reading a bitter 0 degrees Fahrenheit, and it would get no warmer than 18 that day. The nation was still emotionally raw from a president's assassination less than a month earlier, but Illinois Central did its part to bring families together for the holidays. All six main line passenger trains visited Carbondale, as did the three pairs of connecting trains that operated between Carbondale and St. Louis. From records in the old Carbondale train dispatcher's office, Steve Parsons of Sparta, Illinois, reconstructed this remarkable day in the life of an Illinois Central hub city. Origin and destination stations for individual cars are shown when known. Descriptions of head-end cars is by type, not contents. Scheduled arrival and departure times are shown.

First No. 1
(Advance Section)
City of New Orleans
(Chicago–Memphis)
12:45–1:00 pm
(all lightweight)

4018	E8 locomotive
4012	E7 locomotive
2699	Coach 48 seats
2634	Coach 56 seats
2899	Coach 72 seats
2850	Coach 64 seats
2805	Coach 64 seats
2803	Coach 64 seats
4110	Diner
2725	Coach 52 seats
2827	Coach 64 seats
2730	Coach 44 seats
2717	Coach 52 seats
2628	Coach 56 seats
2682	Coach 52 seats
2694	Coach 38 seats
2684	Coach 52 seats

15 cars

Second No. 1
(Regular Section)
City of New Orleans
(Chicago–New Orleans)
12:45–1:00 pm
(all lightweight)

4024	E8 locomotive
4106	E9B locomotive
4031	E8 locomotive
405	Mail & express

402	Mail & express
1902	Baggage-dormitory
2630	Coach 56 seats
2601	Coach 60 seats
2623	Coach 56 seats
3335	Coach-club lounge 24 seats
2614	Coach 56 seats
2610	Coach 48 seats
2637	Coach 56 seats
2681	Coach 52 seats
4106	Diner
2627	Coach 56 seats (pick up Carbondale; from St. Louis No. 101)
2629	Coach 56 seats
2632	Coach 56 seats
2612	Coach 48 seats
3305	Club lounge-observation

17 cars

First No. 2
(Advance Section)
City of New Orleans
(Memphis–Chicago)
6:22–6:35 pm
(all lightweight unless noted)

4033	E8 locomotive
674	Baggage
2710	Coach 56 seats
2755	Coach 52 seats
2718	Coach 52 seats
2733	Coach 44 seats
3854	Club lounge (HW)
4110	Diner

2735	Coach 56 seats
2734	Coach 44 seats
2762	Coach 48 seats

10 cars

Second No. 2
(Regular Section)
City of New Orleans
(New Orleans–Chicago)
6:22–6:35 pm
(all lightweight)

4020	E8 locomotive
4042	E9 locomotive
403	Mail & express
404	Mail & express
1906	Baggage-dormitory
2695	Coach 48 seats
2635	Coach 56 seats
2633	Coach 56 seats
3336	Coach-club lounge 24 seats
2616	Coach 56 seats
2613	Coach 48 seats
4107	Diner
2625	Coach 56 seats (set out Carbondale; to St. Louis No. 102)
2615	Coach 56 seats
2611	Coach 48 seats
3304	Club lounge-observation

14 cars

First No. 3
(Advance Section)
Louisiane
(Chicago–Memphis)
2:20–2:45 am
(all heavyweight)

9219	GP9 locomotive
9207	GP9 locomotive
7914	Box express
7924	Box express
2840	Coach 64 seats
2852	Coach 64 seats
2701	Coach 44 seats
2762	Coach 48 seats
2734	Coach 44 seats
2735	Coach 56 seats
3854	Club lounge
2733	Coach 44 seats
2718	Coach 52 seats
2755	Coach 52 seats
2710	Coach 56 seats

13 cars

Second No. 3
(Regular Section)
Louisiane
(Chicago–New Orleans)
2:20–2:45 am
(all heavyweight unless noted)

4026	E8 locomotive
4027	E8 locomotive
4033	E8 locomotive
514	Storage mail
679	Baggage & express
1804	Baggage & express (LW)
GTW 5311	Coach 62 seats
GTW 5312	Coach 62 seats

GTW 5319	Coach 62 seats
2704	Coach 56 seats
2738	Coach 56 seats
2809	Coach 64 seats
2815	Coach 64 seats
2855	Coach 64 seats
3307	Club lounge (to Memphis) (LW)
N&W Sussex County	Sleeper 10 roomettes 6 bedrooms (N&W) (to Memphis) (LW)
King Cotton	Sleeper 6 sections 6 roomettes 4 bedrooms (to Memphis) (LW)
UP American Insignia	Sleeper 6 sections 6 roomettes 4 bedrooms (to Memphis) (LW)

15 cars

No. 4
Louisiane
(Memphis–Chicago)
12:25–12:45 am
(all heavyweight unless noted)

4022	E8 locomotive
4032	E8 locomotive
EL Lackawanna	

	Sleeper
	10 roomettes
	6 bedrooms
	(deadhead) (LW)
501	Storage mail
101	Railway post office
695	Baggage & express
1805	Baggage & express
2859	Coach 48 seats
2813	Coach 64 seats
2814	Coach 64 seats
2854	Coach 64 seats
2803	Coach 58 seats
2805	Coach 64 seats
2950	Coach 64 seats
2899	Coach 72 seats
3309	Club lounge
King Cotton	
	Sleeper 6 sections
	6 roomettes
	4 bedrooms (LW)
15 cars	

No. 5
Panama Limited
(Chicago–New Orleans)
9:06–9:21 pm (all lightweight)

4036	E9 locomotive
4021	E8 locomotive
1820	Baggage & express
Floosmoor	Sleeper 22 roomettes
Crystal Spgs	Sleeper 10 roomettes 6 bedrooms
NP 310	Dome sleeper 4 roomettes 4 bedrooms 4 single rooms
Clifton	Sleeper 10 roomettes 6 bedrooms

3314	Club lounge
4125	Diner
4125A	Kitchen-dormitory
Benton	Sleeper 11 bedrooms
Carbondale	Sleeper 10 roomettes 6 bedrooms (to Memphis)
Centralia	* Sleeper 10 roomettes 6 bedrooms (from St. Louis; added Carbondale)
Memphis	Sleeper-lounge-observation 2 compartments 1 drawing room (12 from Carbondale)
11 cars	

* From St. Louis No. 105; added at Centralia

No. 6
Panama Limited
(New Orleans–Chicago)
3:48–4:00 am (all lightweight)

4004	E7 locomotive
4003	E6 locomotive
1821	Baggage & express
Fort Dodge	Sleeper 22 roomettes
Calvert	Sleeper 10 roomettes 6 bedrooms
NP 310	Dome sleeper 4 roomettes 4 bedrooms 4 single rooms
Coles County	Sleeper 10 roomettes

	6 bedrooms
3309	Club lounge
4126	Diner
4126A	Kitchen-dormitory
Baton Rouge	Sleeper 11 bedrooms
Champaign	Sleeper 10 roomettes 6 bedrooms
N&W Sussex County	Sleeper 10 roomettes 6 bedrooms (from Memphis)
Clarksville	Sleeper 10 roomettes 6 bedrooms (to St. Louis; set out Carbondale)
Gulfport	Sleeper-lounge-observation 2 compartments 1 drawing room (12 from Carbondale)
13 cars	

No. 8
Creole
(New Orleans–Chicago)
11:33–11:59 am
(all heavyweight)

4028	E8 locomotive
4029	E8 locomotive
7928	Passenger box car
576	Storage mail
649	Baggage & express
732	Baggage & express
724	Baggage & express
153	Railway Post Office-storage mail
536	Storage mail
584	Sorage mail
709	Baggage & express
2826	Coach 64 seats

2833	Coach 64 seats
2810	Coach 72 seats
2701	Coach 44 seats
2852	Coach 64 seats
2840	Coach 64 seats
15 cars	

No. 9
Seminole
(Chicago–Jacksonville)
10:10–10:28 pm
(all heavyweight unless noted)

4007	E7 locomotive
4019	E8 locomotive
4017	E7 locomotive
797	Baggage & express (pick up Carbondale; from St. Louis No. 105)
786	Baggage & express (pick up Carbondale; from St. Louis No. 105)
337	Railway Post Office-storage mail
REX 7357	Express refrigerator
710	Baggage & express
756	Baggage & express
2830	Coach 64 seats
2731	Coach 48 seats
2854	Coach 64 seats
2832	Coach 64 seats
2812	Coach 68 seats
2723	Coach 44 seats
2741	Coach 50 seats
2829	Coach 64 seats
2714	Coach 56 seats
2838	Coach 64 seats
2822	Coach 64 seats
3985	Diner-lounge
Banana Road	Sleeper 6 roomettes 6 sections 4 bedrooms (LW)
Erie American Way	

	Sleeper
	6 roomettes
	6 sections
	4 bedrooms (LW)
1990	Crew dormitory
21 cars	

No. 10
Seminole
(Jacksonville–Chicago)
4:30–5:03 am
(all heavyweight unless noted)

4006	E7 locomotive
CofGa 812	E8 locomotive
CofGa 811	E8 locomotive
Sou 134	Baggage & express (set out Carbondale; to St. Louis No. 108)
REX 6945	Express refrigerator (set out Carbondale; to St. Louis No. 108)
PRR 2013	Box express (set out Carbondale; to St. Louis No. 108)
REX 6963	Express refrigerator (set out Carbondale; to St. Louis No. 108)
REX 7161	Express refrigerator (set out Carbondale; to St. Louis No. 108)
REX 6407	Express refrigerator (set out Carbondale; to St. Louis No. 108)
REX 7494	Express refrigerator
738	Baggage & express
337	Railway Post Office-storage mail
726	Baggage & express
734	Baggage & express
2711	Coach 56 seats
2851	Coach 64 seats
2839	Coach 64 seats
CofGa 531	Coach 58 seats
2853	Coach 64 seats
ACL 1039	Coach 52 seats

4111	Diner-lounge
Magnolia State	Sleeper
	6 roomettes,
	6 sections
	4 bedrooms (LW)
1990	Crew dormitory
20 cars	

No. 15
Chickasaw
(St. Louis–Memphis)
2:10–2:30 am
(all heavyweight)

8909	GP7 locomotive
9042	GP9 locomotive
REX 6833	Express refrigerator (set out Carbondale)
REX 810	Horse express
REX 7122	Express refrigerator (set out Carbondale)
578	Storage mail
673	Baggage & express
609	Baggage & express
566	Storage mail
608	Baggage & express
102	Railway Post Office
2761	Coach 48 seats
2696	Coach 48 seats
2686	Coach 48 seats
7929	Box express (pick up Carbondale)
7919	Box express (pick up Carbondale)
12 cars	

No. 16
Chickasaw
(Memphis–St. Louis)
3:30–4:50 am
(all heavyweight)

9042	GP9 locomotive
9216	GP9 locomotive
102	Railway Post Office

600	Baggage & express
719	Baggage & express
799	Baggage & express
2761	Coach 48 seats
2696	Coach 48 seats
2686	Coach 48 seats
Centralia	Sleeper
	10 roomettes
	6 bedrooms
8 cars	

No. 25
Southern Express
(Chicago–New Orleans)
7:55–8:25 am
(all heavyweight)

9045	GP9 locomotive
7927	Box express
806	Baggage & express
789	Baggage & express
755	Baggage & express
810	Baggage & express
788	Baggage & express
2817	Coach 64 seats
2860	Coach 64 seats
2707	Coach 40 seats
2691	Coach 52 seats
10 cars	

First No. 52
City of Miami
(Miami–Chicago)
12:05–12:25 pm
(all lightweight)

4041	E9 locomotive
4107	E9B locomotive
4025	E8 locomotive
1905	Baggage-dormitory
Brookhaven	Sleeper
	11 bedrooms (set out Carbondale; to St. Louis No. 108)
Corinth	Sleeper
	10 roomettes

---

	6 bedrooms
Hammond	Sleeper
	4 compartments
	2 drawing rooms
	4 bedrooms
Hattesburg	Sleeper
	4 compartments
	2 drawing rooms
	4 bedrooms
Haleyville	Sleeper
	4 compartments
	2 drawing rooms
	4 bedrooms
Gen. Jackson	Sleeper-club lounge
	1 compartment
	1 drawing room
	3 bedrooms
4127	Diner
4127A	Kitchen-dormitory
Belleville	Sleeper
	11 bedrooms
Durant	Sleeper
	10 roomettes
	5 bedrooms
N&W Buchanan County	Sleeper
	10 bedrooms
	6 bedrooms
CofG 670	Coach 52 seats
2621	Coach 56 seats
2620	Coach 56 seats
15 cars	

Second No. 52
City of Miami
(Miami–Chicago)
12:05–12:25 pm
(all lightweight)

4020	E8 locomotive
4042	E9 locomotive
4201	Diner counter lounge
ACL 247	Coach 54 seats
2640	Coach 56 seats
2626	Coach 56 seats

2603	Coach 56 seats
3320	Club lounge-observation
6 cars	

No. 101
City of New Orleans
(St. Louis–Carbondale)
12:15 pm
(all heavyweight unless noted)

9042	GP9 locomotive
9216	GP9 locomotive
366	Railway Post Office-storage mail
2800	Coach 72 seats
2627	Coach 56 seats (to New Orleans Second No. 1) (LW)
3 cars	

No. 102
City of New Orleans
(Carbondale–St. Louis)
6:50 pm
(all heavyweight unless noted)

8909	GP7 locomotive
366	Railway Post Office-storage mail
2800	Coach 72 seats
2625	Coach 56 seats (from New Orleans Second No. 2)* (LW)
3 cars	

No. 105
Panama Limited–Seminole
(St. Louis–Carbondale)
8:40 pm
(all heavyweight unless noted)

| 9216 | GP9 locomotive |
| REX 6502 | Express refrigerator (deadhead; to Atlanta) |

REX 6998	Express refrigerator (deadhead; to Jacksonville)
797	Baggage & express (to Jacksonville No. 9)
786	Baggage & express (to Birmingham No. 9)
Centralia	Sleeper
	10 roomettes
	6 bedrooms (to New Orleans No. 5) (LW)
2754	Coach 48 seats
792	Baggage & express
7 cars	

No. 108
City of Miami
(Carbondale–St. Louis)
12:30 pm

9216	GP9 locomotive
9042	GP9 locomotive
Sou 134	Baggage & express (from No. 10)
REX 6945	Express refrigerator (from No. 10)
PRR 2013	Box express (from No. 10)
REX 6963	Express refrigerator (from No. 10)
REX 7161	Express refrigerator (from No. 10)
REX 6407	Express refrigerator (from No. 10)
576	Storage mail
649	Baggage & express
781	Baggage & express
2802	Coach 64 seats
2736	Coach 56 seats
Brookhaven	Sleeper
	11 bedrooms (from Miami No. 52)
12 cars	

The Mini-Corridor in 1969

By autumn of 1969, the Chicago–Carbondale Mini-Corridor service looked pretty much as it would until the coming of Amtrak a year and half later. These were the basic consists, which were almost infinitely expandable as demand justified.

No. 1
City of New Orleans
(Chicago–New Orleans)
Chicago 8:00 am
New Orleans 12:55 am

No. 2
City of New Orleans
(New Orleans–Chicago)
New Orleans 7:00 am
Chicago 11:55 pm
(all lightweight)

Baggage   Chicago-New Orleans
Baggage-mail   " - Memphis
Coach   " -   "
Coach   " - New Orleans
Coach   " -   "   "
Dome coach   " -   "   "
Diner counter lounge
                  " - Jackson
Coach   " -   "
Dome coach   " -   "
9 cars Chicago-Memphis
7 cars Memphis-Jackson
4 cars Jackson-New Orleans

No. 3
Mid-American
(Chicago to Memphis)
Chicago 9:00 pm
Memphis 8:00 am
(all heavyweight unless noted)

Storage mail   Chicago-Memphis
Baggage   "   - "
Dormitory-coach*   "   - "
Food-bar-coach**   "   - " (LW)
Coach   "   - " (LW)

Mail & Papers   " - Champaign
(returns on No. 10)
*cars 2726-2727 assigned
**cars 3340–3342 assigned
6 cars Chicago-Champaign
5 cars Champaign-Memphis

No. 4
Mid-American
(Memphis to Chicago)
Memphis 11:15 am
Chicago 8:55 pm
(all heavyweight unless noted)

Storage mail   Memphis-Chicago
Baggage   "   - "
Dormitory-coach*   "   - "
Food-bar-coach**   "   - " (LW)
Coach   "   - " (LW)
*cars 2726–2727 assigned
**cars 3340–3342 assigned
5 cars

No. 5
Panama Limited
(Chicago to New Orleans)
Chicago 5:00 pm
Carbondale 9:55–10:10 pm
New Orleans 9:30 am

No. 6
Panama Limited
(New Orleans to Chicago)
New Orleans 4:15 pm
Carbondale 3:40–4:00 am
Chicago 8:55 am
(all lightweight)

Baggage-dormitory
             Chicago-New Orleans
Coach   " - "   "
Coach   " - "   "

Coach   " -   "   "
Coach   " - Carbondale
Sleeper (as parlor)#
               " -   "
Club lounge*
               " -   "
Sleeper 10 rte 6 BR
         Carbondale-New Orleans
         (from/to St. Louis No. 105/106)
Diner   Chicago - "   "
Sleeper 10 rte 6 BR
               " -   "   "
Sleeper 10 rte 6 BR
               " -   "   "
*car 3309 assigned
#car line discontinued 8-24-69
10 cars Chicago-Carbondale
8 cars Carbondale-New Orleans

No. 105
Panama Limited
(St. Louis to Carbondale)
St. Louis 6:30 pm
Carbondale 8:30 pm

No. 106
Panama Limited
(Carbondale to St. Louis)
Carbondale 6:00 am
St. Louis 8:15 am
(all lightweight)

Baggage
             St. Louis-Carbondale
Coach   " " - "
Coach   " " - "
             (Friday, Saturday, Sunday)
Sleeper 10 rte 6 BR
(to/from New Orleans No. 5/6)
             " " - "
3 cars (4 Friday, Saturday, Sunday)

No. 7
Illini
(Chicago to Carbondale)
Chicago 3:00 pm
Carbondale 7:55 pm

No. 8
Illini
(Carbondale to Chicago)
Carbondale 1:00 pm
Chicago 5:55 pm
(all heavyweight unless noted)

Coach   Chicago-Carbondale
Coach   "   -   "
Food-bar-coach*   "   -   " (LW)
*cars 3343–3345 assigned
3 cars

No. 9
Shawnee
(Chicago to Carbondale)
Chicago 6:00 pm
Carbondale 10:55 pm
(all heavyweight unless noted)

Baggage   Chicago-Carbondale
Coach   "   -   "
Food-bar-coach   "   -   " (LW)
Coach   "   -   "
4 cars

No. 10
Shawnee
(Carbondale to Chicago)
Carbondale 6:00 am
Chicago 10:55 am
(all heavyweight unless noted)

Baggage   Carbondale-Chicago
Coach   "   -   "

Coach   "   -   "
Food-bar-coach   "   -   " (LW)
Baggage (deadhead)   Champaign -   "
4 cars Carbondale to Champaign
5 cars Champaign to Chicago

No. 11
Hawkeye
(Chicago to Sioux City)
Chicago 7:00 pm
Sioux City 8:30 am

No. 12
Hawkeye
(Sioux City to Chicago)
Sioux City 6:10 am
Chicago 7:15 am
(all lightweight)

RPO-baggage   Chicago-Sioux City
Coach   "   -   "   "
Coach   "   -   "   "
3 cars

No. 21
Governor's Special
Chicago 8:15 am
Springfield 11:35 am

No. 22
Governor's Special
Springfield 5:15 pm
Chicago 8:45 pm
(all lightweight)

Baggage-coach   Chicago-Springfield
Diner counter lounge   "   -   "
Coach   "   -   "
3 cars

No. 52
City of Miami
(Miami to Chicago every other day)
Birmingham 3:40 am
Chicago 5:40 pm

No. 53
City of Miami
(Chicago to Miami every other day)
Chicago 8:40 am
Birmingham 10:20 pm
(all lightweight)

		Assigned cars—	
Baggage-dormitory	Chicago-Miami	1902	1905
Coach	" - "	ACL 248	ACL 247
Dome coach	" - "	2200	2200
Club lounge	" - "	3315	3314
Coach	" - Albany	SCL 5100	CofG 671
Coach	" - St. Petersburg	CofG 663	CofG 670
Sleeper 10 rte 6 BR	" - " "	Pool	
Diner	" - Miami	4110	4105
Sleeper 11 BR	" - "	Pool	
Sleeper 10 rte 6 BR)	" - "	Pool	
10 cars			

THE END (AND THE NEW BEGINNING)

The great trains—those that remained, at any rate—were dinosaurs.
Would they, too, become extinct? How a few people made a difference.

◀ It is a few minutes before 10:30 a.m., on April 30, 1971. Momentarily, Charles Dust will take the last Milwaukee Road Morning Hiawatha from the bowels of Chicago Union Station toward Minneapolis. But first he poses beside his FP7 locomotive—a proud man and a tired machine. Could there have been a more poignant reminder that an era had ended? Amtrak would begin the next day, and there would be no turning back. (Jack Dykinga—Chicago Sun-Times)

Amtrak had many midwives, but no mother. If anyone reflected its difficult birth, it would be Anthony Haswell. Born in the depth of the Great Depression to well-off parents in Dayton, Ohio, Haswell earned a law degree from the University of Michigan, worked two years for the Illinois Central Railroad and briefly as a Cook County public defender in Chicago before entering private practice. In 1963, at age 32, Haswell wrote as an individual to Wisconsin and Minnesota public officials opposing Chicago & North Western's effort to discontinue its 400 passenger train. Then in 1965 he tried, singlehandedly, to reopen the Interstate Commerce Commission's 1956–1959 investigation of the passenger-train deficit problem. Was he jousting at windmills? Yes, but Haswell saw himself not only as a visionary, but as someone who could make a difference. Thus in April of 1967, meeting in New York City's Plaza Hotel with a few friends and fellow visionaries (among them Peter Lyon, author of *To Hell in a Day Coach*), he formed the National Association of Railroad Passengers. I met Tony Haswell soon afterward, was impressed by

his intelligence and sincerity but doubted that he could ever be taken seriously. I was wrong. Haswell was like the ant who went after the rubber tree plant: He simply would not give up.

By 1968, the railroads were in a fix. The wholesale removal of first-class mail from passenger trains in 1967, coupled with a noticeable decline in ridership that year, had pretty much knocked all props from beneath passenger trains. William Howes, director of passenger service for Baltimore & Ohio and Chesapeake & Ohio, contends that the defining moment was Santa Fe's decision to get rid of a majority of its passenger trains late in 1967—if Santa Fe couldn't stay in that business, the thinking went, how could anyone? During the last half of 1967, 75 of the 725 intercity trains were discontinued, and as 1968 began, 108 others were the subjects of discontinuance proceedings.

It would fall to individuals like Haswell, to railroaders like Howes and to political figures, up to and including the President of the United States, to save something of value. I'm pleased to say that they rose to the challenge.

Solutions: The early calls

One of the early proposals to revamp passenger services—a remarkably prescient one at that—came in 1965 from Howes himself. A 25-year-old management trainee at Baltimore & Ohio, Howes wrote a paper proposing that all railroads in the East consolidate their passenger operations under a single new company, which he called Trans East Railways. It would own the locomotives and cars and run the trains, paying rental to the participating railroads. Owner railroads would reimburse TER for losses. Howes argued that TER would eliminate duplication, attract capable management, permit the trains to be actively marketed and make possible a modern reservations system.

Howes sent copies to every major railroad in the region, with mixed results. Replied Chairman William White of Erie Lackawanna: "Frankly, I do not have the time to read and analyze the report and therefore it is being returned to you." Pennsy's general manager of passenger sales called it "novel and interesting" but with "no immediate practicality." But Paul Reistrup, director of passenger service for B&O and Chesapeake & Ohio, responded enthusiastically and later asked that Howes be assigned to the passenger department. Nobody knew it then, of course, but Howes had described the structure of Amtrak—just make his regional organization national, and substitute government subsidies for railroad largess.

By 1968 momentum began building within the rail industry and government to do *something*. The Interstate Commerce Commission proposed that Congress give it one year to decide train-off cases and also impose a two-year moratorium on discontinuances involving the last passenger train on a route, while the Department of Transportation studied the future of intercity passenger trains. ICC chairman Paul Tierney testified: "This may well be our last opportunity" to stem the decline.

The Department of Transportation wasn't sure a problem even existed. Early in 1968 the Federal Railroad Administration, an arm of DOT, assembled a task force to advise it whether long-distance passenger trains then being run were really needed, and if so, how to support those that lost money. The group included Howes of B&O/C&O and Matt Paul of Illinois Central, but was composed for the most part of FRA employees. The recommendation of this task force was basically to keep hands off—to let unprofitable trains lapse and to substitute bus service for necessary trains that lost money. "I don't believe DOT ever publicly espoused this policy," says Howes. "By then the issue was, 'How much is it going to cost to keep some semblance of an intercity rail passenger network?' "

Instead DOT made public its estimates of the cost of subsidizing intercity service—or rather, a range of estimated subsidies, ranging from 50 cents per train mile for 25 percent of the trains operating as of 1967 ($13.6 million) to a $2-per-mile subsidy for all trains then in service ($217 million). But FRA's administrator, A. Scheffer Lang, did not endorse a subsidy. Lang told a congressional committee in mid 1968: "We are not ready in this period of fiscal stringency to come up here and propose that kind of a subsidy program." He favored a two-year-long study of the problem, but opposed, as confiscatory to railroads, any moratorium on discontinuances in the interim. Reminded by a congressman that in two years there might not be any passenger trains, Lang said, in effect, so be it.

Solutions: The plot thickens

The ICC's recommendations weren't adopted. But it's evident, reading the transcripts of congressional hearings then, that the passenger train had sympathizers in Congress—as time went on, more and more allies appeared. Equally evident is the lack of any convincing rationale for either spending public money or forcing railroads to sustain the burden of losses beyond a reasonable length of time. It was too bad that passenger trains were failing right and left, or so thinking went.

But accounting for their costs was such a nightmare that any talk of subsidy foundered because nobody really knew what losses were really being incurred. Do you use *solely related costs* (those identified specifically with a particular train), *fully allocated costs* (the passenger train's share of all the railroad's common expenses), *avoidable costs* (costs that would not be incurred if the train didn't run) or some other definition of cost? And in each instance, were those costs being sensibly calculated? Late in 1968, the ICC took a big step toward providing a rationale for subsidies by launching an ambitious study on the cost (and therefore the losses) of providing intercity passenger train service. The ICC research focused on avoidable costs—what would be saved if passenger trains did not operate—and was limited to the intercity trains of eight rail systems for the year 1968. The ICC concluded that the losses were real and alarmingly high:

B&O/C&O	$12.7 million
Great Northern	$11.6 million
Illinois Central	$ 7.4 million
Missouri Pacific	$ 3.5 million
Santa Fe	$26.7 million
Seaboard Coast Line	$19.3 million
Southern	$14.9 million
Union Pacific	$22.0 million

In all, these nine railroads incurred $118 million in losses they could have avoided had they not run their passenger trains. That number was remarkably similar to the $115 million these same roads lost using the ICC's formula for calculating solely related costs. So it's probably fair to say that if the ICC had calculated the avoidable losses for *all* passenger-carrying railroads, the total would approximate the $198 million in solely-related-cost deficits that the entire industry reported in 1968. (On that basis, Stuart Saunders later noted, Penn Central's portion was $63 million, or almost one third of the total.) Yes, $198 million was a *lot* of money. By then, even the Association of American Railroads was in favor of government subsidy.

Solutions: Here comes Railpax

All this time Anthony Haswell and his National Association of Railroad Passengers continued to plug away. At first, NARP's primarily testified at public hearings on train discontinuances and filed briefs. Haswell hoped to recruit 1,000 members in the first year, and got 1,900 within 12 months. But it was a struggle. You could join for as little as $1, and the dues for a "general member" were a mere $4.99 per year. Haswell wanted to limit his direct subsidy of NARP to no more than $20,000 a year—a lot of money, then as now. Instead, by the end of 1968, 19 months after founding the association, he had put in $112,000. This was due partly to the cost of litigation that NARP had become involved in on behalf of passenger trains, and partly to the fact that the association opened a Washington office and hired its own lobbyist. Haswell, too, moved to Washington in April, 1970. That January NARP's ranks had reached 4,300 and were increasing at the rate of 500 a month. Things were coming to a head.

NARP had initially asked only that the Interstate Commerce Commission be given better control over the number and quality of passenger trains. But NARP soon decided more dramatic action was needed. In August 1969, Representative Brock Adams, a House Democrat from Washington State, introduced legislation substantially drafted by Haswell to provide federal dollars to rehabilitate and replace the passenger car fleet. Another bill drafted by Haswell (and introduced by Adams with 90 co-sponsors) would have given the ICC power to set standards of service on trains. Nothing came directly of those bills, but the legislation creating Amtrak incorporated many of their provisions.

The real impact of NARP then was to lend cred-

The map outside the office of Santa Fe train order operator Jess Gomez, in Richmond, California, says it all. Amtrak is 11 days away. (Ted Benson)

ibility to the idea that there was a body of people wanting to keep the passenger train alive. NARP was their voice—an articulate, sane and responsible one, too. By and by Haswell and Price were relied upon by the staff of the Senate Commerce Committee to help it analyze proposals and draft bills. Even the railroads, which had officially ignored NARP, began consulting Haswell with their ideas before taking them to the Senate committee.

Pieces of legislation too numerous to mention bubbled up in both houses of Congress by mid 1969.

Testifying to the Senate Commerce Committee on November 4, FRA administrator Reginald Whitman (later to distinguish himself as the last chairman of the Missouri–Kansas–Texas Railroad) first outlined what would become Amtrak. He called it Railpax and said it was one of three alternatives under study at the FRA. As Whitman explained it then, Railpax would stitch together a very basic route structure to be run by railroads under contract. Ownership would be both public and private, and financing would come from railroads who would pay to be relieved of their responsibilities to subsidize the losses of these trains.

Hopes for a Department of Transportation proposal kept both houses of Congress at bay the rest of 1969 and into 1970. Then on March 5 came Penn Central's bid to end passenger service west of Harrisburg and Buffalo. One week later, tired of waiting on DOT to propose its own plan, the Senate Commerce Committee approved, by a 12–3 vote, legislation advanced by Democrat Vance Hartke of Indiana, to provide $35 million to subsidize 80 percent of the losses of trains the government deemed essential. That got DOT, which favored Railpax over direct subsidies, involved. For whatever reasons—probably resistance from the Nixon White House—DOT never formally unveiled Railpax in legislative form. But the FRA sent its people to work with the Senate staff in April, and on May 1 Hartke and Republican Winston Prouty of Vermont substituted a Railpax bill for the Hartke subsidy legislation. On May 6 the Senate voted yes, 78–3.

A lot of things then happened—the Penn Central bankruptcy, for one thing, and campaigning for the fall Congressional elections, for another—to divert the attention of the House from its own Railpax legislation. Haswell became afraid that it would fall through the cracks in the rush to final adjournment, and it almost did. But on October 14, on the last day of the 91st Congress, the House passed its Railpax legislation on a voice vote and the Senate

▶ *Watching Seaboard Coast Line's* Silver Meteor *race through south Florida toward Hialeah, you'd never guess there was a passenger train crisis. Yet on this day in 1971, the* Meteor *was only three and a half months from becoming a ward of Amtrak. (David W. Salter)*

immediately approved the House version. Sixteen days later, Richard Nixon signed it into law. Then began the wait until May 1, 1971.

Goodbye time

Who would ride the new Amtrak's trains? My journeys that winter offered proof that young people and families had deserted railroads. Even on the classy *Silver Meteor*, the clientele seemed to be a few of me—railfans—and a lot of elderly people. Seaboard Coast Line advertised in 1969: "If you want to go to Miami without a stopover in Havana, call us," read one newspaper ad in huge type. Yes, it had come to this: Seaboard Coast Line was reduced to using fear of Fidel Castro as a means of attracting riders. If the new Railpax couldn't find an audience, quickly, it would not long last.

As it turned out, Amtrak became the great leveler. On the one hand it destroyed what remained of the great trains by trampling on their little individual virtues and traditions that had survived the traumatic decade—the esprit of the *Super Chief*, the glitter of the dome-studded *Denver Zephyr*, the civility of the little *Capitol Limited* (for some years after 1971 not run by Amtrak). All trains essentially became the same. And yet Amtrak ultimately brought enormous improvement along the entire breadth of the West Coast, in the form of the *Coast Starlight*, while popularizing train travel across great parts of America that had lost the habit.

At the start of the 1960s I had not believed the doomsayers. I was stubborn enough, or blind enough, to believe there was a bedrock standing ready to support the best of the great trains we rode. And in a sense there was such a bedrock: the U.S. mail. As people deserted trains, the railroads substituted mail, often inadvertently hurrying the desertion by making schedule adjustments that favored mail over people. But it was that or perish. And when the mail was taken away in late 1967 and early 1968, the economics of passenger trains collapsed like a castle made of postcards. No passenger train operation could withstand that final blow.

The upshot: Passenger trains became a ward of government, run by Amtrak and subsidized by taxpayers instead of by railroads and the post office. As I write this, a quarter century after nationalization of passenger trains, Amtrak still tries to define its mission. There is talk in Washington of privatization—imagine that, passenger trains that make money! I hope that day comes to pass. This book was written about a transitional decade, not so long ago, when the great trains served a public purpose, sometimes making decent money, and when certain of us hoped they all would, forever after.

INDEX

BOOKS IN THE RAILROADS PAST AND PRESENT SERIES

FRED W. FRAILEY

is a columnist and special correspondent for *Trains* magazine. He worked for 21 years at *Kiplinger's Personal Finance* as deputy editor and then editor. Prior to that, he spent 16 years on the staff of *U.S. News & World Report* as Chicago bureau chief, associate editor, and assistant managing editor. Fred grew up in Kansas and Texas, graduated from the University of Kansas, and now lives in McLean, Virginia. He is author of five railroad books, including *Southern Pacific's Blue Streak Merchandise; Rolling Thunder;* and *Zephyrs, Chiefs & Other Orphans.*